MARRIAGES
of
GRAINGER COUNTY, TENNESSEE

1796-1837

Marriages

of

Grainger County, Tennessee

1796–1837

Compiled by
EDYTHE RUCKER WHITLEY

With an Index by Patti Matulonis

CLEARFIELD

Reprinted for
Clearfield Company, Inc. by
Genealogical Publishing Co., Inc.
Baltimore, Maryland
1996, 2000

Introduction

GRAINGER COUNTY was created on April 22, 1796, the second county created by the Tennessee Legislature. It was carved from Hawkins and Knox counties and named in honor of Mrs. William Blount, whose maiden name was Grainger. The county seat at Rutledge was not established until 1801 when the courthouse was erected, although the court was organized as early as June 13, 1796, less than two months after the county was created.

The Grainger County marriage bonds were recorded in a register by the Work Projects Administration. This present work is a rather free transcription of that register. So far as is known no other compiled record of the marriages was ever made, for the county clerk apparently did not record the returns of either bonds or licenses. In the time that has elapsed since the register was first compiled many original bonds and licenses have been lost. The WPA register is therefore the most complete record of Grainger County marriages we are ever likely to have.

The reader should note that the first date given in each entry is the date of issue of the marriage bond. The date following (in parentheses) is the date the marriage was performed. If no date of marriage is given, then the single date provided refers merely to the date of issue of the marriage bond and does not prove that a marriage actually took place. The reader should note further that the abbreviation *BM* signifies *bondsman*.

Edythe Rucker Whitley
Nashville, Tennessee

GRAINGER COUNTY, TENNESSEE

Marriages, 1796-1837

1796

James Short to Nancy Moses, Sept. 28, 1796.
  Ambrose Yancey, BM.

1797

Kain Acuff to Patsey Kitchen, July 29, 1797.
  James Cocke, BM.
James Allsup to Abigal Carmichal, Aug. 17, 1797.
  Martin Ashburn, BM.
Jonathan Blige to Nancey Shelton, Dec. 29, 1797.
  Wm. Kirkham, BM.
Hugh Carrigan to Elizabeth Lynhart, Aug. 17, 1797.
  Thomas Henderson, BM.
Joseph Cobb to Sarah Blair, Dec. 29, 1797.
  John Smith, BM.
John Cooper to Susanna Howell, June 5, 1797.
  Henry Howell, BM.
Phillip Counts to Rebecca T. Ore, May 19, 1797.
  Martin Ashburn, BM.
Ritchard Cristol to Elizabeth Rhea, Feb. 2, 1797.
  John Lebow, BM.
Nimrod Dodson to Elisabeth Chisum, Oct. 21, 1797.
  John Ward, BM.
Timothy Dunn to Elizabeth Eress, Nov. 7, 1797.
  Hartin Dixon, BM.
Kimbles Edyman to Polly Nicholas, Oct. 10, 1797.
  Isaiah Midkiff, BM.
Benjamin Ferguson to Franky Holt, May 8, 1797.
  Bartin Scrogins, BM.
Jno. Gilmore to Anny Mitchel, Jan. 13, 1797.
  Aaron Smith, BM.
Joseph Guest to Fellis McVay, Jan. 12, 1797.
  John Guest, BM.
William Guynn to Rana Neal, July 18, 1797.
  James Moore, BM.
Matthew Hipshur to Sarah Pastle, Dec. 27, 1797.
  Wm. Henderson, BM.
Phillip Hodge to Candis Howell, Jan. 18, 1797.
Moses Hodges to Delila Ivey, Aug. 11, 1797.
  Welcome Hodges, BM.
Jacob Humbard to Martha Gains, Dec. 13, 1797.
  Joseph Rhea, BM.

Vardaman Ivey to Mary Martin, July 26, 1797.
  John F. Wills, BM.
Sam'l Magby to Anney Hamilton, Oct. 25, 1797.
  Jesse Bean, BM.
John Midkiff to Caty Miller, Jan. 2, 1797.
  George Bean, Jr., BM.
Isaac Owen to Catherina Musgrove, June 20, 1797.
  John Owen, BM.
John Owens to Ninse Wilson, Oct. 22, 1797.
  Mathew Black, BM.
John Rhea to Sarah Harris, March 8, 1797.
  Bartin Scrogins, BM.
Cornelous Rodgers to Mary Callum, March 30, 1797.
  David Harbert, BM.
George Russell to Mary Panel, Feb. 15, 1797.
  Thomas Panel, BM.
Bartin Scrogins to Dice Russell, Dec. 27, 1797.
  John Smith, BM.
Ezekiel Shelton to Margaret Davis, Oct. 26, 1797.
  John Davis, BM.
Richard Shelton to Tennessee Street, June 23, 1797.
  Isaiah Midkiff, BM.
Aron Smith to Elizabeth Mitchell, Jan. 2, 1797.
  Yancey Lemar, BM.
Thomas Smith to Mary Ely, June 13, 1797.
  Isaac Newman, BM.
George Stinson to Sarah Arter, Oct. 24, 1797.
  John Arthor, BM.
Richard L. Terry to Ann Murry, Oct. 10, 1797.
  Richard Shelton, BM.
Solomon Web to Rachell Jimon, Aug. 9, 1797.
  Ambrose Yancey & George York, BM.
Samuel West to Lezabeth Thompson, Oct. 24, 1797.
  Duncan Carmichael, BM.
John Woodrum to Elizabeth Bailes, Dec. 11, 1797.
  John Burton, BM.

1798

William Austin to Rebecker Moses (or Messer or Mercer),
  March 22, 1798. Steven Austin, BM.
John Barr to Jenny Dunlap, Sept. 22, 1798.
  Henry Hipshur, BM.
John Bass to Jenney Dunlop, Sept. 22, 1798.
  Henry Hipshur, BM.
George Bean to Peggy Ashart, July 10, 1798.
James Bowen to Polly McGinnis, Oct. 20, 1798.
  John McElheny, BM.
James Bridges to Susannah Mays, Feb. 24, 1798.
  James McCarty, BM.
Samuel Casey to Ann Bealor (or Beatas), Feb. 20, 1798.
  John Casey, BM.

Peter Clauson to Ruth Bailes, July 17, 1798.
(July 17, 1798).
John Copland to Sarah Short, March 25, 1798.
John Smith, BM.
William Countz to Anney Bean, Sept. 10, 1798.
John Countz & Robert Blair, BM.
Stephen Crabb to Delila Daniel, Aug. 18, 1798.
John Rhea, BM.
Enoch Davis to Elizabeth Clerk (or Clark), August 21,
1798. Joab Hill, BM.
Richard Duke to Hanna King, Sept. 2, 1798.
James King, BM.
Handse Hart to Nannie Derur (or Nance Dever),
Jan. 22, 1798. Charles Teaun, BM. (Jan. 11, 1798).
Thos. Hart to Nance Sevier, Jan. 11, 1798.
Chas. Sevier, BM.
Tapley Haygood to Sarah Midkiff, July 24, 1798.
John Midkiff, BM.
James Johnston to Dalila Stewart, Feb. 21, 1798.
John Stewart, BM.
Pleasant Johnston to Polly Kile, March 1, 1798.
Augistine Richardson, BM.
Wm. Kelley to Suanner Robertson, Feb. 20, 1798.
John Clurk, BM. (Feb. 28, 1798).
James McCartey to Susanner Mays, Feb. 24, 1798.
James Bridges, BM.
Frederick Miller to Rody Windham, Dec. 27, 1798.
William Windham, BM.
Daniel Pevehouse to Elizabeth Cass (or Capps), Feb. 7,
1798. Jno. Owen, BM.
Wm. Redus to Rebecka Hodge, Nov. 8, 1798.
Nathan Norton, BM.
Aron Roach to Francis Clifton (or Aron Rock to Fanny
Clifton), July 11, 1798. Edward Jenings, BM.
Hugh Ross to Margret Hugings, Nov. 14, 1798.
Isaiah Midkiff, BM.
James Russell to Elizabeth Bradford, Oct. 26, 1798.
Benj. Bradford, BM.
William Stewart to Jenney Ashert, Oct. 18, 1798.
John Countz, BM. (Oct. 11, 1798).
Edward Thacker to Polley Morgan, July 2, 1798.
John Countz, BM.
James Woodall to Mary Fiers, June 10, 1798.
William Smith & William Fiers, BM.

1799

Samuel Blair to Joanna Perrin, April 10, 1799.
George Combs, BM.
John Buzby to Peggy Martin, Oct. 6, 1799.
David Shelton, BM.
John Cooper to Susanna Howel, June 5, 1799 (see 1797).

William Cox to Margaret Clerk, Sept. 3, 1799.
John Bunch, BM.
Moses Davis to Winefred Wallen, Jan. 26, 1799.
John Dodson to Nancey Kenney, Dec. 29, 1799.
John Ward, BM.
Joseph Dunkin to Rebeccka Vandergriff, Aug. 6, 1799.
Edward Carmack, BM.
Joel Evins to Sarah Fears, March 11, 1799.
Obediah Ginnins, BM. (March 12, 1799).
Thomas Gibbons to Polly Hill, Oct. 27, 1799.
Joab Hill, BM.
Levi Goans to Elizabeth Stations (or Stalians), Nov. 2,
1799. Thos. Stations, BM.
John Hailey to Elizabeth Medlock, Feb. 20, 1799.
Henry Howell, BM.
James Harmon to Serenia Bunch, Aug. 13, 1799.
Isaac Cooper, BM.
Samuel Harris to Isabal May, March 19, 1799.
John Ward, BM.
Reubin Hogg to Jess Lay, Aug. 8, 1799 (Aug. 8, 1799).
Obediah Hogge to Sarah Kennedy, Aug. 2, 1799.
Reubin Hogg & Hess Lay, BM. (Aug. 8, 1799).
Hardeman Hughes to Sinthia Cooke, Feb. 27, 1799.
George S. Smith, BM.
John Hutton to Isabella Dale, Aug. 19, 1799.
Andrew Evans, BM.
Pleasant Johnston to Lettie Owen, Aug. 27, 1799.
Thomas Henderson, BM.
Wm. Kyle to Rebecka Young, Aug. 5, 1799.
Basil Presman, BM.
Thomas Mayes to Elizabeth Bridges, Oct. 11, 1799.
William Cooper, BM.
Charles McEnelley to Polly Shelton, Jan. 14, 1799.
John Burton, BM.
William McGinnis to Nancey Bowen, April 27, 1799.
James Bowen, BM.
Isaac McNamee to Anne Rayl, Aug. 1, 1799.
John Ward, BM.
Henry McPherson to Mary Eaton, Jan. 29, 1799.
John Matlock, BM.
Peter Miller to Polley Smith, Aug. 7, 1799.
John Burton, BM.
Robert Perry to Nancy Midkiff, Dec. 23, 1799.
William Street, BM.
Abraham Robertson to Agnes Russell, May 4, 1799.
Wm. Russel, BM.
George S. Smith to Patsy Cook, March 3, 1799.
John Ward, BM.
John Sullins to Mary Doghead, Dec. 4, 1799.
Harmon Evans, BM.
Thomas Ward to Wonna Sullins, April 3, 1799.
David Evans, BM.
John Warrick to Polley Lane, Aug. 19, 1799.
John Hailey, BM.

John Hailey White to Elizabeth Gilbraith (or Medlock),
Feb. 20, 1799. Henry Howell, BM.
John Wilson to Rachel Windham, Nov. 17, 1799.
William Hill, BM. (Nov. 17, 1799).
George Bean to Prudence Cope, Feb. 11, 1800.
James Ore, BM.
John Bradford to Susanna Story, Jan. 21, 1800.
John Russell, BM.
Raynolds Brogan to Nancey Black, Feb. 3, 1800.
Nehemiah Pettit, BM.
Henry Buckner to Bella Woodall, Aug. 13, 1800.
Thomas Wittson, BM.
John Bull to Nelley Collins, Nov. 23, 1800.
John Bull Senr., BM.
Isham Clark to Isbell Jeffers, April 21, 1800.
Joseph Clerk, BM.
Elisha Cole to Elizabeth Moss (or Mays), Nov. 19, 1800.
William Howorth & John Arnwine, BM.
James Collissen Jr. to Elizabeth Young, July 17, 1800.
John Collison Senr., BM.
Bleir Davison to Darkis Cunningham, Nov. 8, 1800.
James Davison, BM.
David Deveaul to Susanna Guest, March 19, 1800.
John Six, BM.
John Dodson to Sarah Dodson, Jan. 14, 1800.
Samuel Dodson, BM.
John Dora to Suckey Bunch, Nov. 29, 1800.
Harmon Miller, BM.
Matthew English to Nancey Gordon, Oct. 26, 1800.
Robert Gorden, BM.
David Evans to Anney Claxton, March 27, 1800.
Isaiah Kidwell, BM.
Barnabas Gibson to Joyes Artis, Nov. 17, 1800.
Valentine Gibson & Archebus Gibson, BM.
Thomas Hankins to Valentine Hawkins, Sept. 12, 1800.
Edward Hankins, BM.
William Haumack to Lora Brock, Aug. 10, 1800.
Peter Hammack, BM.
William Holt to Milley Claunch, Jan. 2, 1800.
Jeremiah Midkiff, BM.
Jesse Hutcheson to Mary Hutcheson, Aug. 28, 1800.
Paul Hutcheson, BM.
David Jackson to Ann Bowen, July 31, 1800. John Bowen, BM.
Laban James to Rebcah McBride, July 28, 1800.
Joshua Gallion, BM.
John Malson to Fanny Foster, March 5, (or 8), 1800.
George Sprucher, BM.
William Mays to Susanna Bridges, Aug. 31, 1800.
John Dora, BM.
Thomas McDonald to Anney Bean, March 7, 1800.
George Sprecher, BM.
Berry McEnelly to Kiziah Rains, Jan. 27, 1800.
George Bean, BM.

Mathew McKee to Poley Clark, April 23, 1800.
Benjamin Howel, BM.
Isaac Midkiff to Susanna Howel, Jan. 30, 1800.
John Smith & George Stephen, BM.
Julius Miller to Elizabeth Russell, Feb. 15, 1800.
John Donah, BM.
John Millins to Elizabeth Russell, Feb. 15, 1800.
Julius Millins & John Hanah, BM.
Zachariah Mills to Hanna Mendingall, Dec. 16, 1800.
Thomas Murrey to Mary Busby, Jan. 31, 1800.
George Bean, BM.
Robert Parson to Mary Johnston, July 23, 1800.
John Shropsheer, BM.
Jacob Person to Neomi Hays (or Hogg), July 18, 1800.
William Haukins, BM.
Jacob Pevehouse to Rachel Kellums (or Hellums), Aug.
11, 1800. Abraham Pevehouse, BM.
John Russell to Mary Bradford, Jan. 14, 1800.
Benjamin Bradford, BM.
John Sanders to Olevey Cunningham, Dec. 7, 1800.
Bartlett Marshal, BM.
John Shelton Jr., to Elizabeth Smith, March 19, 1800.
William Shelton, BM.
Richard Smith to Margaret Lockwood, Aug. 18, 1800.
Ezekiel Smith, BM.
Robert Southern to Nancy Neal, May 27, 1800.
William Neal, BM.
Robert Stone to Susanah Everet, Jan. 19, 1800.
Bartholomew Smith, BM.
William Street to Nancey Shelton, Jan. 23, 1800.
Richard Shelton, BM.
George Stubblefield to Polley Jeffers, Jan. 2, 1800.
R. Lackey Stubblefield
John Thompson to Anney Goulding, Feb. 14, 1800.
Wm. Murphey, BM.
Wily Warwrick to Margret Lane, Oct. 16, 1800.
James Lane, BM.
Thomas Williams to Hanna Hubbard, Aug. 11, 1800.
Charles Smith, BM.
John S. Wills to Ruth McEnelley, Aug. 5, 1800.
Elijah Donathan, BM.
Jacob Wyer to Polly Jarnigan, April 7, 1800.
Isaac Jarnigan, BM.
Robt. Yancey to J. Coulter, _____, 1800. Jas. Ore, BM.

1801

Daniel Bailes to Elizabeth Hawkins, Feb. 16, 1801.
Henry Hawkins, BM.
John Byrd to Polly McCoy, Aug. 2, 1801. Neal McCoy, BM.
John Carson to Sally Estes, Dec. 5, 1801. John Estes, BM.
William Carter to Ruthey Bean, July 18, 1801.
Washington Bean, BM.

Benjamin Coats to Elizabeth Brock, Sept. 9, 1801.
John Margran, BM.
David Collins to Mary Dodson, Feb. 6, 1801.
Charles McEnelly of Grainger County, BM.
William Cooper to Mary Moore, March 16, 1801.
Isaac Cooper, BM.
James Eastridge to Lucy Boling, Oct. 16, 1801.
Joseph Boling, BM. (Sept. 13, 1801).
John Elsey to Lucinda Morgan, July 18, 1801.
Samuel Terrey, BM.
John Gibbs to Agnes Miller, Feb. 11, 1801. John Gibbs, BM.
William Hammack to Sarah Brock, Aug. 10, 1801.
William Haskins to Elizabeth Reedy, July 1, 1801.
Shadrick Reedy & William Hancock, BM.
Richard Hankins to Barberry Cooke, May 28, 1801.
Abel Hankins, BM.
John Hawkins to Mary Woodall, Jan. 26, 1801.
John Woodall, BM.
John Helms to Elizabeth Turley, Aug. 23, 1801.
Jonathan Helms, BM.
Richard Hits to Drucella Stubblefield, Aug. 6, 1801.
Jas. Stubblefield, BM.
Abraham Howard to Elizabeth Bean, Sept. 19, 1801.
Joel Bean, BM.
Thomas Huddleston to Tabitha McBee, April 25, 1801.
Samuel McBee, BM.
Ezekiel Hudson to Fareby Rhea, March 3, 1801.
Mosses Rhea, BM.
Robert Hughs to _____Perrion (or Perry), _____, 1801.
Robert Smith & James Penjour, BM.
Phillip Ivy to Liddy Dannil, Nov. 7, 1801.
Moses Hodges, BM.
Thomas Jinings to Agnes Dyer, June 22, 1801.
John Horner, BM.
William Love to Sarah Gains, Aug. 23, 1801.
William McPhetridge, BM.
Thomas McBroom to Oney Christian, Feb. 9, 1801.
Allen Christian, BM.
Eli McVay to Mary Blair, June 20, 1801. Aquilla Jones, BM.
John Nau to Agnes Owen, July 12, 1801. Lamken Hall, BM.
Wm. Norton to Hannah Riggs, Aug. 18, 1801.
David Shelton, BM.
Robert Parson to Mary Johnston, July 23, 1801.
Levi Rice to Jane Simmons, Dec. 4, 1801.
Jeremiah Chamberlain, BM.
John Simmons to Jeminah Conley, Dec. 11, 1801.
John Criner & David Elmore, BM.
David Smith to Elizabeth Rice, Dec. 23, 1801.
Henry Rice, BM.
Henry Solomon to Mary Brown, April 18, 1801.
Joseph Shipe, BM.
George Southerlin & Mary Gipson, Dec. 15, 1801.
Valentine Gipson, BM.

GRAINGER COUNTY MARRIAGES

Robert Taylor to Rachel Jennings, Dec. 23, 1801.
  Nathanile Davis, BM.
John Wall to Agness Owen, July 12, 1801.
Thomas Ward to Sarah Sandress, Feb. 25, 1801.
  Bartlett Marsall, BM.
Jacob Weyer to Polly Jarnagin, April 7, 1801.
John S. Wills to Ruth McEnelly, Aug. 5, 1801.
  Elijah Donathan, BM.

1802

Richard Acuff to Patey Hailey, Jan. 18, 1802.
  Cain Acuff, BM.
Randolph Allsop to Elizabeth O. Danniel, July 17, 1802.
  Robert Allsop, BM.
John Arnwin to Clary Rector, Dec. 24, 1802.
  Bartin McFerron, BM.
John Bailes to Sarah Hawkins, Oct. 12, 1802.
  Henry Hawkins, BM.
John Beeler to Hannah Vandergriff, April 19, 1802.
  Thomas Dunn, BM.
Richard Blevens to Mary Duyless, May 6, 1802.
  William Barton, BM.
Edward Brown to Ann Dyer, Aug. 4, 1802.
  James Dyer, Junior, BM.
Isaac Brown to Fanney Clark, May 26, 1802.
  Aroon Roach & William Brown, BM.
George Bull to Elizabeth Grayson, Feb. 4, 1802.
  John Bull, BM.
William Bunch to Elizabeth Buggs, April 8, 1802.
  John Hall, BM.
Wm. Carter to Ruthy Bean, July 18, 1802.
  Washington Bean, BM.
Reubin Churchman to Marget Eaton, Jan. 1, 1802.
  Joseph Eaton, BM. Beck(?) remembered that the name
  Jas. Eaton was subscribed to the above bond by
  Rubin Churchman by the express direction of the said
  Jas. Barton and afterwards acknowledged by him.
Eleazar Clay to Mary Dumvelle, Jan. 19, 1802.
  William Clay, BM.
Abner Davidson to Anney Evans, Aug. 18, 1802.
  Joseph Davidson, BM.
Elias David to Margat Cockrum, June 15, 1802.
  John Stiffee & George McCombs, BM.
Isaac Davis to Elizabeth Mulky, Aug. 21, 1802.
  John Hutton, BM.
William Debord to Merine Ball, Sept. 10, 1802.
  Joseph O'Eilly, BM.
Solomon Dodson to Peggy Collins, Feb. 15, 1802.
  David Collins, BM.
James Dyer to Elizabeth Garroth, Oct. 11, 1802.
  Frederick Moyers, BM.

8

GRAINGER COUNTY MARRIAGES

Matthew Elliot to Ruth Underhill, Feb. 26, 1802.
   William Elliot, BM.
John Ernwine to Clacy Rector, Dec. 24, 1802.
   Barton McFerson, BM.
David Gaines to Elizabeth Howard, March 23, 1802.
   William Howard, BM. (March 23, 1802).
Thomas Gilbert to Ann Alsop, July 27, 1802.
   Randolph Alsop, BM.
Benjamin Grove to Holly Jarnagin, Nov. 11, 1802.
   Captain Thomas Mann, BM.
John Hall, Junr. to Franky Acuff, Feb. 17, 1802.
   John Hall, Senr., BM.
William Henderson to Nancy A. Windham, March 2, 1802.
James Hill to Eles _____, July 17, 1802.
   John Lix & Thomas Owen, BM.
James Holt to Lucy Hodge, May 11, 1802. John Holt, BM.
John Holt to Mancy Midkiff, Jan. 24, 1802. James Holt, BM.
Robert Jackson to Ann Smith, Aug. 28, 1802.
   David Jackson, BM.
Newberry James to Elizabeth Gilmore, Jan. 12, 1802.
   John Gilmore, BM.
William James to Rachel Dennis, Nov. 16, 1802.
   Daniel Clayton & Thomas Dennis, BM.
William James, Junr. to Elizabeth Morris, Oct. 16, 1802.
   Thomas James, BM.
Drury Jarnagin to Nancey Groves, Dec. 11, 1802.
   John Cocke & Daniel Clay Cox, BM.
Jesse Kitchens to Catherine Acuff, April 22, 1802.
   James Perkins, BM.
Wm. Lane to Sarah Hains, Aug. 23, 1802.
   Wm. McPhetridge, BM.
David Lea to Nancy Clay, Feb. 2, 1802. Eliazer Clay, BM.
Zacheriah Lea to Sabrine Clay, Jan. 19, 1802. John Lea, BM.
James Mann to Sarah Vandergriff, March 23, 1802.
   Jno. Homeall, BM.
John Maulsly to Betsy Grisom, July 27, 1802.
   James Haworth, BM.
John McCubbin to Jane Sweeten, Sept. 18, 1802.
   Alexander Davidson & Joseph Britt, BM.
Thomas McDonald to Rebecca Britt, Sept. 18, 1802.
   Joseph Britt, BM.
Samuel Moore to Elsey Mendinghall, May 25, 1802.
William Phillips to Jinny Hunnycut, Jan. 31, 1802.
   Henry Bowen, BM.
James Randolph to Nancy Gowen, Nov. 22, 1802.
   Drury Gowen, BM.
Daniel Reece to Mary Hooser, Oct. 15, 1802.
   David William, BM.
Benjamin Rhea to Sally Coffee, Feb. 9, 1802.
   Merriel Coffee, BM.
Thomas Rhea to Elizabeth Maxwell, Feb. 3, 1802.
   Joseph Rhea, BM.
Joseph Rich to Catherine Noe, April 8, 1802.
   George Nor, BM.

William Robinson to Anna Beeler, Nov. 12, 1802.
William Burton, BM.
Philip Sanders to Elizabeth Ford, April 9, 1802.
Philip Sanders, BM.
David Shelton to Nancy Rodgers, Aug. 19, 1802.
George Noe, BM.
Joel Shelton to Elizabeth Phillips, July 13, 1802.
William Strut, BM.
John Spring to Nancy Moore, April 8, 1802. John Hall, BM.
Anthony Street to Jenny Dyer, Feb. 17, 1802.
Joseph Rich, BM.
Hardiman Taylor to Rebecca Shelton, June 11, 1802.
Richard Shelton to Richard Yancey, BM.
Peter Tuttle to Elizabeth Smith, May 21, 1802.
Thomas James, BM.
Hugh Wooddard to Jean Cox, Jan. 11, 1802. John Lea, BM.
James Zachery to Tabitha Hailey, Feb. 17, 1802.
John Hailey, BM.
Osbourne Ball to Patsey Thomason, Sept. 26, 1803.
Thomas Bunch, BM.
Melon Bishop to Rose Furgeson, Aug. 12, 1803.
William Bishop & James Fergeson, BM.
Allen Brock to Elisabeth Parker, Sept. 22, 1803.
Carnelious Archer, BM.
Jesse (or Joseph) Brock to Elisabeth Clark, July 16,
1803. Peter Hammack, BM.
David Brown to Pateance Southerlin, Sept. 5, 1803.
Henry Bowen, Jun., BM.
David Bunde to _____, Sept. 28, 1803.
David Campbell to Sally Mayson, Aug. 30, 1803.
John McElheny, BM.
Lewis Combs to Jinny Smith, July 5, 1803.
John Correthers to Elizabeth Hankins, Oct. 18, 1803.
John Hankins, BM.
Isaac Countz to Patsey M. Murry, March 14, 1803.
John Countz & James Bowen, BM.
Alexander Davidson to Patsy Smith, Nov. 17, 1803.
James Davis to Ellenore Woods, Aug. 5, 1803.
Jesse & James Daniel Pew, BM.
Elisha Dodson to Polley Midlock, Nov. 3, 1803.
John Ogle, BM.
Alexander Donelson to Patsey Smith, Nov. 7, 1803.
John McElheney, BM.
John Duke to Susannah Easely, July 14, 1803.
Richard Forrest to Sarah Medlock, June 4, 1803.
Aron Roak, BM.
James Harris to Kesiah Taylor, Jan. 17, 1803.
Peter Harris, BM.
William Henderson to Nancy A. Windham, March 2, 1803.
John F. Jack, BM.
Joshua Hickey to Polley Bunch, May 14, 1803.
John Bunch, BM.
John Hodges to Mary Hudson, Jan. 28, 1803.
James Hudson & John Cocke, BM.

Jesse Jinnings to Agnes Alsop, Nov. 23, 1803.
  Robert Taylor, BM.
Michael Kearns, Junr. to Mary Bowing, March 2, 1803.
  James Bowen, BM.
Hillsman King to Elizabeth Crabb, Dec. 18, 1803.
  Spencer Griffin, BM.
Gardner Mays to Chatharine Vineyard, Feb. 23, 1803.
  John Lea & John Vineyard, BM.
Carnelous McCoy to Milley Richardson, Sept. 26, 1803.
  John Walker, BM.
Wm. McPhetridge to Elizabeth Haines, _____, 1803.
David Milliken to Mary Southerland, Dec. 21, 1803.
  William Smith, BM.
John Moore to Elizabeth Gallion, Nov. 23, 1803.
  Samuel Williams, BM.
Samuel Moore to Elsay Mandinghall, May 25, 1803.
  Jonathan Williams, BM.
Martain Morris to Ailcey Dickiner, March 12, 1803.
George Noe to Nancy Duke, Jan. 8, 1803.
  Robert Yancey, BM.
Herculus Ogle to Tressie Clark, June 4, 1803.
  Isaac Brason, BM.
Robert Parcker to Polley Gibson, June 17, 1803.
  Daniel Clayton & Miller W. Easley, BM.
Robert Parks to Nancy Easeley, May 22, 1803.
  Robert Yancey & Miller W. Easeley, BM.
Nathan Phillips to Winefred Martin, April 21, 1803.
  Edward Brown, BM.
Richard Rector to Fanny Smith, Aug. 30, 1803.
  William Murphy, BM.
Archibald Roane to Jenny Smith, July 5, 1803.
  Spencer Griffin & Daniel Clayton, BM.
Archibald Roane to Susannah Easely, July 14, 1803.
  Edward Epps & John Burton, BM.
William Roberts to Mary Crewe, Nov. 27, 1803.
  Sam'l Yancey, BM.
Powell Scott to Nancey McCarty, Jan. 5, 1803.
  Robert Yancey to Enoch McCarty, BM.
Stephen W. Senter to Elizabeth Ore, April 23, 1803.
  Spencer Griffin, BM.
Nicholas Sharp to Nancey Robertson, March 14, 1803.
  John Countz, BM.
Joshua Simmons to Delany James, March or Nov. 13, 1803.
  Abraham James, BM.
William Sims to Ellender Dumbille, June 17, 1803.
  Ennouch Winder, BM.
Joseph Stephenson to Hannah Cox, June 20, 1803.
  Charles Smith (or Cox), BM.
Kisiah Taylor to James Harris, Jan. 17, 1803.
Joel Witt to Franky Dyer, Jan. 8, 1803. Hugh Taylor, BM.

1804

William Acuff to Magdaline Hall, Jan. 28, 1804.
John Hall, Junior, BM.
Lewis Adkins to Elizabeth Monroe, Jan. 24, 1804.
John Calvin, BM.
John Anderson to Usley Campbell, July 12, 1804.
Alexander Campbell, BM.
David Bowling to Rolly Rail, Dec. 13, 1804.
William Rail, BM.
Beaverage Brannum to Sally Brannum, Nov. 7, 1804.
James Brannum to Sally Brannum, Nov. 7, 1804.
Beverage Brannum, BM.
James Campbell to Lucy Howard, Dec. 15, 1804.
John Anderson, BM.
William Condry to Mancy Stanley, Nov. 15, 1804.
Mathew Talley, BM.
Dennie Conway to Mary Marcheall, April 1, 1804.
Jackson Smith, BM.
William Davidson to Hannah Oaks, Jan. 16, 1804.
Henry Ballenger, BM.
John Denny to Sally Beavers, Dec. 27, 1804.
John Dodson, BM.
Martin Dodson to Polly Acuff, May 29, 1804.
Richard Acuff, BM.
Charles Drake to Clarisa James, Oct. 20, 1804.
Jesse James, BM.
John Gray to Sally Morgan, June 23, 1804.
Jonathan Mosey, BM.
William Hall & Nancey Acuff, Jan. 28, 1804.
John Hall, Junior, BM.
George Hauk to Mary McCarrus, March 16, 1804.
Barnabas Butcher, BM.
John Haukins to Polley Gallant, July 25, 1804.
Thomas Haukins, BM.
Richard Howard to Sally Delosure, Oct. 19, 1804.
James Elkins, BM.
Robert Leford to Polley Nall, April 11, 1804.
Larkin Nall, BM.
Zara Magee to Polly Harris, Jan. 24, 1804.
Lewis McDonald, BM.
Nimrod Maxwell to Jinny Huddleston, Aug. 25, 1804.
Michael Coom, BM.
John McPeters to Rachel Robertson, July 28, 1804.
Thomas Robertson, BM.
Solomon Milligan to Naney Morgan, Jan. 5, 1804.
Charles Smith, BM.
James Mitchell to Teamour Groves, April 14, 1804.
Reubin Groves, BM.
George Monrow to Elizabeth Peters, Jan. 17, 1804.
John Calvin, BM.
William Mooney to Lucinda Hayse, Oct. 5, 1804.
John Dobtson, BM.

James Moore to Charity Mills, Sept. 6, 1804.
  Samuel Peary, BM.
Levi Moore to Rachael Haines, Sept. 8, 1804.
  John Margrove, BM.
Samuel Moore to Ann Stubblefield, Jan. 21, 1804.
  David McAnally, Junior, BM.
Thomas Morgan to Sally Willet, May 18, 1804.
  Francis Willet, BM.
Shadrick Morris to Nancy Riggs, March 6, 1804.
  Gideon Morris, BM.
Thomas Ogle to Betsey Dennis, Feb. 14, 1804.
  Herculus Ogle, BM.
James Parker to Elizabeth Lane, April 26, 1804.
  Cornelious Archer, BM.
Winston Partin to Nancy Mason, July 23, 1804.
  John McElhemy, BM.
Robert Randolph to Polley Sisley, July 25, 1804.
  Micheal O. Daniel, BM.
Nicholas Sharp to Rachael Moyers, March 24, 1804.
  John Countz & Michael Moyer, BM.
Britan Smith to Rebecka Acuff, Feb. 28, 1804.
  James Bowan, BM.
Jackson Smith to Elizabeth Thompson, June 24, 1804.
  Peter Harris, BM.
Samuel Taylor to Susanna Countz, Dec. 13, 1804.
  Henry Bowen, Junr., BM.
Isaac Thompson to Charity Miller, Sept. 6, 1804.
  James Moore & Sam'l Perry, BM.
Richard Thornbury to Agey Asher, Sept. 3, 1804.
  Andrew McPheeters, BM.
Leonard Vandergriff to Sally Roberts, Aug. 10, 1804.
  John Hunter, BM.
Rice Whiteacre to Nancey Hunter, Aug. 14, 1804.
  Mathew Hunter & William Hunter, BM.

1805

Benjamin Acuff to Viney Harman, April 4, 1805.
  John Hall, BM.
Richard Adkins to Polley Monroe, Nov. 15, 1805.
  Davis Ray, BM.
William Baker to Mary Sturdivent Jones, April 22, 1805.
  John Moore, BM.
Jesse Beadwell to Sarah Callume, Dec. 21, 1805.
  William Patton, BM.
Hazard Bean to Nancy Howard, Nov. 25, 1805.
  Abraham Howard, BM.
Abraham Bird to Amey Adkins, Dec. 24, 1805.
  Joel Martin, BM.
John Blackburn to Jemima Boulter, Dec. 18, 1805.
  Samuel Branson, BM.
Robert Blain to Aelcey Willson, March 8, 1805.
  James Willson, BM.

Benjamin Bond to Barbara Dale, Aug. 6, 1805.
  William Harmon, BM.
John Boulton to Elizabeth Hamock, Aug. 21, 1805.
  John Hammack, BM.
James Bowen to Nancey Ledbetter, May 15, 1805.
  Henry Bowen, Senr., BM.
Richard Bull to Fanney Bray, May 11, 1805.
  John Ogan, BM.
Richard Burke to Elizabeth Roeolin, May 20, 1805.
  Ryland Burke, BM.
Isaiah Collins to Betsy Mason, Nov. 20, 1805.
  David McAnally, Esqr., BM.
Rubin Cothill to Judith Dickerson, July 24, 1805.
Henry Crouce to Polly Greer, Jan. 23, 1805.
  John Winyard, BM.
John Dotson to Betsey Burk, March 8, 1805.
  Rilaw Burk, BM.
Henry Dresser to Nancy Irwin, May 10, 1805.
  Alexander Hamelton, BM.
William Dyer to Anney Clifton, March 24, 1805.
  Joel Dyer & Robert Henry, BM.
Thomas Galyon to Sarah Huckeyby, Oct. 15, 1805.
  Jacob Galyon, BM. (Oct. 15, 1805).
Squire Harlon to Racheal McElhiney, April 11, 1805.
  William Harlon, BM.
Nehemiah Harris to Sarah Stubblefield, Jan. 26, 1805.
  Peter Harris, BM.
Henry Holt to Elizabeth Bowman, July 1, 1805.
  James Walsey, BM.
James Hornback to Ellender Dyer, Jan. 5, 1805.
  William Martin, BM.
Benjamin Howell to Catharine Morgan, Feb. 25, 1805.
  James Hodges, BM.
William Hunley to Patsey Cooper, Feb. 20, 1805.
William Hutchinson to Mary Burnham, Oct. 25, 1805.
  Colman Hutchinson, BM.
Thomas Ivey to Susanna Hudson, April 12, 1805.
  Moses Hodges, BM.
William James to Mary Crouse, May 14, 1805.
  Mathias Crouse, BM.
William Keith to Sarah Coons, Dec. 18, 1805.
  John Cocke, BM.
Stephen Kirkingdall to Elizabeth Durham, Dec. 19, 1805.
  William Durharam, BM.
George Kitchen to Lucy Cox, July 7, 1805 (or 1806).
  Edward Hailey, BM. (July 7, 1805 (or 1806)).
Littleberry Lay to Isbel Gilmore, Jan. 15, 1805.
  Hugh Gilmore, BM.
John Maize to Nancey Maize, Jan. 11, 1805.
  William Cooper & Daniel Classton, BM.
John Mardock to Anny Wright, Aug. 2, 1805.
  John Thomas, BM.
Robert Martin to Amey Adkins, Dec. 23, 1805.
  Nathan Phillips, BM.

Edmund Mayples to Susanna Hammack, Dec. 7, 1805.
  Jacob Gallian, BM.
John Miller to Rebecca Spradling, Nov. 18, 1805.
  Joseph Stubblefield, BM.
Nathan Morgan to Sevier Smith, June 24, 1805.
  John Jackett, BM.
William Norris to Sue Peetres, May 16, 1805.
  George Norris, BM.
Levi Ody to Mimey Ferguson, March 30, 1805.
  Greenberry Mitchell, BM.
Arthur Overton to Nancey Bragg, Aug. 22, 1805.
  John Ogan, BM.
Joseph Peeters to Nancy Hutchinson, Feb. 19, 1805.
  Charles Hutchinson, BM.
Daniel Prigmore to Nancy Smith, Aug. 2, 1805.
  Mirideth Coffy, BM.
William Rodgers to Patsey Cross, May 3, 1805.
  John Nau, BM.
John Sharp to Anney Clown, June 4, 1805.
  Sam'l Yancey, J.P., BM.
Joseph Slults to Amy Witcher, Nov. 20, 1805.
  Michael Griss, BM.
David Watson to Levina Harmon, March 29, 1805.
  John Acuff, BM.
Robert Willis to Mary McVay, May 17, 1805.
  William Jones, BM. (May 17, 1805).

1806

John Archey to Sarah Claxton, Jan. 16, 1806.
  Josiah Kidwell, BM.
David Branson to Susannah Bolton, Sept. 22, 1806.
  Abraham Prewitt, BM.
Samuel Branson to June Watson, May 20, 1806.
  Abraham Brunt, BM.
Samuel Brown to June Watson, May 20, 1806.
  Abraham Pruit, BM.
John Bull & Fetney Bean, April 3, 1806.
  Bartley Marshall, BM.
Jesse Bunch to Nancy Scot, Jan. 16, 1806.
William Clasop to Patsey Cox, Sept. 8, 1806.
Richard Clemmons to Elizabeth Brown, Aug. 29, 1806.
  William Brown, BM.
Dowell Collins to Mary Ennis, Sept. 22, 1806.
  Griffin Collins, BM.
Hezekiah Cook to Lucinda Watson, June 17, 1806.
  Aron Rook, BM.
Ralien Cotrill to Judith Dickerson, July 24, 1806.
David Countz to Elizabeth Howell, Nov. 8, 1806.
  Henry Bowen, BM.
Jeramiah Cox to Hannah Reece, Feb. 3, 1806.
  Thomas Reece, Junior, BM.

GRAINGER COUNTY MARRIAGES

Joseph Daniel to Rebecca Hodges, Dec. 21, 1806.
John Pratt & Thos. Turley, BM.
Jeremiah Dixon to Grace Ellis, Sept. 4, 1806.
Philip Free, BM.
Joseph Dyer to Nancey Metter, March 17, 1806.
Joseph Long, BM.
Andrew Elder to Elizabeth Snider, May 22, 1806.
Charles McEnelley, BM.
Henry George to Elizabeth Ashart, Feb. 24, 1806.
Jesse Beadwell, BM.
William Gibson to Polly Mitchel, March 4, 1806.
George Sparkman, BM.
William Grayham to Peggy Chamberlin, Aug. 25, 1806.
Robert D. Eaton, BM.
Stephen Greer to Polly Vineyard, Jan. 25, 1806.
John Hamil, BM.
Rubin Groves to Nancy Mays, Feb. 19, 1806.
Enoch Windes, BM.
John Harris to Easther Pew, Oct. 16, 1806.
Daniel Pew, BM.
Robert Huddleston to Theny Dunkin, Nov. 17, 1806.
David Huddleston, BM. (Nov. 17, 1806).
John Hutcheson to Mary Seglar, Nov. 25, 1806.
Charles Hurcheson, Esqr., BM.
Hartwell Keeling to Sally Crain, Jan. 5, 1806.
John Mullins, BM.
Thomas Kelly to Nancy Peters, April 11, 1806.
Joseph Peters, BM.
James Kemp to Elizabeth Hankins, Oct. 25, 1806.
Eli Hankins, BM. (Oct. 25, 1806).
Ezekial King to Sally Cheek, July 21, 1806.
Jesse Cheek, BM.
Elijah Long to Anney Gradley, Feb. 10, 1806.
John Rhinehart, BM.
Thomas Mann to Ceale Estes, Feb. 17, 1806.
John Moffit, BM.
Joel Martin to Elizabeth Adkins, Aug. 15, 1806.
James Adkins, BM.
Dudley Mayes to Elizabeth Price, Feb. 9, 1806.
John McCarty, BM.
Dudley Mays to Elizabeth Daniel, Feb. 9, 1806.
John McCarty, BM.
Levi Miller to Jenney Coffee, Sept. 23, 1806.
Meredith Coffee, BM.
Greenberry Mitchel to Susann Vineyard, Dec. 20, 1806.
John Vinyard, BM.
James Nall to Elizabeth Waggenor, Sept. 18, 1806.
John Kerdith (or Ridith), BM.
Laban Nations to Sally Owen, Sept. 22, 1806.
James Owen, BM.
Benjamin Overton to Rebecca Price, Nov. 23, 1806.
Tapley Haywood, BM.
George Parkeypile to Jenny Classop, Sept. 8, 1806.
William Clasop, BM.

James Perkins to Margret Toping, Feb. 17, 1806.
Abraham Powel to Susanna McCormack, Dec. 27, 1806.
John Smith, BM.
David Ray to Winney Caffey, April 12, 1806.
Thomas Ray, BM.
Caleb Reece to Margit Riggs, April 9, 1806.
Thomas Reece, Junyer, BM.
Hezekiah Rook to Susanna Watson, June 17, 1806.
Aron Rook, BM.
Joseph Seat to Caty Lewis, July 1, 1806.
Merrey Little, BM.
John Sharp to Anney Clower, June 4, 1806.
Thomas Margrave, BM.
Calib Shockley to Hanna Perry, Jan. 20, 1806.
Benjamin Yates, BM.
Philip Southerlin to Elizabeth Campbell, Sept. 20, 1806.
Thomas Smith, BM.
Edward Sweny to Caty Hobs, Nov. 19, 1806.
Benjamin Hudson, BM.
John Turner to Vaney Hopper, Aug. 24, 1806.
John Webb to Elizabeth Reese, Aug. 6, 1806.
Abraham Wilson, BM.
Robert Willson to Nancey Hays, Aug. 12, 1806.
Thomas Copland, BM.
Jacob Yeaden to Racheal Capps, Aug. 18, 1806.
Joseph Yeaden, BM.

1807

Zachariah Astin to Patsey Thomson, Aug. 26, 1807.
John Moore, BM.
William Boatman to Elizabeth Howell, Feb. 19, 1807.
Benjamin Howell, BM.
Johnathan Branson to Elizabeth Hammack, May 10, 1807.
Thomas Bolton, BM.
Josiah Bryan to Polley Redding, March 19, 1807.
Mathew Redding & Richard Shelton, BM.
John Bunch, Jr. to Margret Clay, Aug. 25, 1807.
John Moore, BM.
Joshua Burnham to Elizabeth Elliott, April 20, 1807.
Abner Elliott, BM.
Kinsey Coats to Sinthey Merchant, Feb. 10, 1807.
John Combs to Jinney Jackson, July 15, 1807.
Lewis Combs, BM.
Thomas Davis to Polley Yeats, Aug. 12, 1807.
Thomas Ray, BM.
John Deakins to Elizabeth Watson, March 13, 1807.
Robert Watson, BM.
Lewis Edwards to Mary Chamberlain, Jan. 29, 1807.
W. Hall, BM.
Elijah Evans to Ruthey Holt, Feb. 28, 1807.
John Bunch, Jr., BM.

GRAINGER COUNTY MARRIAGES

Josiah Galyon to Sally Simmons, Oct. 28, 1807.
  John Simmons, BM.
William Garratt to Caty Ray, Jan. 27, 1807.
  John Garratt, BM.
Thomas Gresson to Elizabeth Clounch, Aug. 5, 1807.
  Samuel Dodson, BM.
William Hains to Sally Smith, April 11, 1807.
  Thomas Dunn, BM.
Jesse Hall to Polley Defoe, Aug. 1, 1807.
  Shedrick Brown, BM.
John Hammack, Jr. to Sally Harvey, Sept. 23, 1807.
  John Hammack, Senr., BM.
Elijah Hornback to Polley Ashburn, Aug. 7, 1807.
  Phillip Combs, BM.
William Howerton to Kitty Willinton, Sept. __, 1807.
  Samuel Bristow, BM.
Benjamin Ivey to Jenney Mays, April 25, 1807.
  William Hodges, BM.
Jesse Jentry to Elizabeth Galyon, Jan. 28, 1807.
Thomas Kitchen to Rosanna Cook, Dec. 12, 1807.
  Rinhart Coffman, BM.
Daniel Lebow to Sally Thompson, July 28, 1807.
  William Stubblefield, BM.
John Long to Sarah Witcher, Dec. 1, 1807.
  Jacob Showman, BM.
Josiah Mayples to Mary Ann Dyer, Sept. 16, 1807.
  William Dyer, BM.
William Mays to Elizabeth Moody, Jan. 9, 1807.
  John Mays, BM.
Campbell McCarrur to Nancey Rose, Jan. 1, 1807.
  John Crabb & John Littrell, BM.
Moses Midlock to Frankey Canhill, Sept. 3, 1807.
  Garrot Norris & John Hill, BM.
Charles Mooney to Frankey Hays, Feb. 24, 1807.
  William Brown, BM.
G. Morris to Rebecka Crow, Feb. 22, 1807.
  John Crow, BM.
William Parkison to Salley Anderson, Oct. 21, 1807.
  Lewis Edwards, BM.
John Petree to Anney Casey, March 20, 1807.
  John Beelor, BM.
Mathew Privett to Mary Crawford, Aug. 8, 1807.
  William Reece, BM.
Jacob Ray to Phereby Bidwell, Oct. 20, 1807.
  Thomas Ray, BM.
John Rector to Polley Davis, Feb. 18, 1807.
  James Davis, BM.
Thomas Reece to Polley Glasgow, May 28, 1807.
  John Bunch, Jr., BM.
Andrew Seabolt to Sarah Sward, Feb. 18, 1807.
  Philip Sward, BM. (Feb. 17, 1807).
William Selvage to Polley Garret, Jan. 3, 1807.
  John Garret, BM.

William Street to Eliza Burnet, Sept. 13, 1807.
Henry Howell, BM.
John Taylor to Mary B. Selvage, Jan. 11, 1807.
Jeremiah Selvage, BM.
John Trotman to Fanny Oday, July 31, 1807.
Levy Oday, BM.
Thomas Turley to Susey Duke, Feb. 25, 1807.
George Noe, BM.
Thomas Vetito to Elizabeth Dyer, June 20, 1807.
James Dyer, BM.
Samuel Waggoner to Susannah Hammack, May 19, 1807.
David Branson, BM.
James White to Margrett Cox, Jan. 17, 1807.
Jeremiah Cox, BM.
Joseph Wyett to Nancey Morris, Sept. 12, 1807.
Welcome Hodges, BM.

1808

Henry Acuff to Mary Sandris, April 4, 1808.
William Acuff, BM.
William Bean to Polley McElheny, July 23, 1808.
John McElheny, BM.
Samuel Boatright to Jain Ruth, Nov. 7, 1808.
James Boatright, BM.
William Boatright to Jamima Bowen, July 22, 1808.
John Moore, BM. (July 22, 1808).
Thornton Cheshir to Memey Gibson, March 8, 1808.
Samuel Ousley, BM.
George Clark to Nancy Kirk, March 8, 1808.
William Kirk, BM.
John Crisby to Betsey Lafin, July 25, 1808.
Griffy Griffits, BM.
Gibbons Cross to Jenney Hill, July 13, 1808.
Henry Matlock, BM.
Seth Cutter to Elizabeth Easley, June 16, 1808.
Frederick Mayers, BM.
Jonathan Dale to Polley Cotton, March 22, 1808.
David Ethons, BM.
Reubin Dalton, Junr. to Nancy Shockley, Jan. 4, 1808.
Reubin Dalton, Senr., BM.
Samuel Dodson to Eliner Grison, March 14, 1808.
Jesse Dodson, BM.
Berryman Douglass to Susannah Bailes, Oct. 19, 1808.
Anthony Underwood, BM.
Spilsby Dyer to Betsey Conley, Jan. 23, 1808.
Robert Martin, BM.
James Fears to Catherine Duglass, May 15, 1808.
Nelson Horton, BM.
William H. Gains to Eliza Ruth Braint, March 22, 1808.
James Braint, BM.
John Hagerty to Ezabella Cunningham, April 1, 1808.
Ambrose Yancey, BM.

William Harlowand to Jenney McElheny, Feb. 11, 1808.
John McElheny, BM.
Peter Harris to Mary Whitlock, May 19, 1808.
James Harris, BM.
John Hill to Nancy Nall, Sept. 24, 1808.
Joseph Dennis, BM.
James Hodges to Peggy Moran, Nov. 11, 1808.
William Morgan, BM. (Nov. 11, 1808).
Welcome Hodges to Elizabeth Corothers, Dec. 17, 1808.
James Hodges, BM. (Dec. 17, 1808).
John Howell to Christian Reece, Sept. 30, 1808.
Yarnell Reece, BM.
Lewis Hutchison to Nancy Hutchison, Dec. 24, 1808.
Joseph Peters, BM.
Zacheriah Keith to Peggy Countz, Jan. 16, 1808.
David Countz, BM.
David Knox to Nancy Coffman, May 19, 1808.
John Knox, BM.
Henry Margian to Mary Riggs, Jan. 25, 1808.
Shadrick Morriss, BM.
Solomon Masingale to Polley Chamberlin, May 7, 1808.
Dudley Cox, BM.
John Maxwell to Patsey Jones, March 4, 1808.
David Huddleston, BM.
Gooding Mays to Elizabeth Corrithers, Jan. 15, 1808.
John McCarty, BM.
Joshua McCarver to Jenny Hill, July 7, 1808.
Thomas Dunn, BM.
Alexander Milligan to Elizabeth Russel, Sept. 17, 1808.
Edward Tate, BM.
Able Morgan to Mary King, Feb. 9, 1808.
William Morgan, BM.
James Morrow to Jain Campbell, Dec. 13, 1808.
John Moore, BM.
Fair Owen to Nancy Farr, Sept. 27, 1808.
Herman Wynne, BM.
William Petterson to Ailsey Kirk, July 30, 1808.
Arnstid Kirk, BM.
Hezekiah Robertson to Anney Grantham, Feb. 8, 1808.
Benjamin Davis, BM.
Micagah Seamore to Nancy Sparkman, Sept. 21, 1808.
John Linch, BM.
Stephen Stubblefield to Elizabeth Moore, July 30, 1808.
Samuel Moore & James Conn, BM.
George Turner to Fanney Oakes, April 13, 1808.
Samuel Williams to Rebecka Morgan, Jan. 23, 1808.
Isaac Williams, BM.
David Willson to Elizabeth Winslow, Aug. 12, 1808.
Robert Winslow, BM.
John Woodall to Nancy Cordell, April 20, 1808.
Willis Dossett, BM.
John Wright to Betsy Smith, Sept. 5, 1808.
Captain John Moore, BM.

GRAINGER COUNTY MARRIAGES

Robert Young to Elizabeth Britian, May 17, 1808.
Francis Young, BM.

1809

Abner Bason to Mary Hinshaw, Oct. 14, 1809.
Robert Fields, BM.
Thomas Bolton to Elizabeth James, Sept. 16, 1809.
John Blackburn, BM.
John Brigs to Nelley Shockley, Feb. 1, 1809.
Aaren Rook, BM.
Thomas Bristow to Peggy Claunch, Dec. 19, 1809.
John Griffitts, BM.
John Bryan to Nancey Moore, Dec. 6, 1809.
Joseph Bryan, BM.
Elijah Bullock to Polley Norris, Feb. 21, 1809.
Jeremiah Norris, BM.
Anderson Bunch to Sally Bunch, Feb. 1, 1809.
Thomas Bunch, BM.
William Bunch to Delilah Bunch, Aug. 4, 1809.
Claiborne Burnett, BM.
William Bunch to Nancy Jones, June 3, 1809.
David Watson, BM.
William Bunch to Nelly Rook, June 2, 1809.
John Bunch, BM.
James Burnett to Rebeccah Needham, Aug. 26, 1809.
Henry Acuff, BM.
Richard Burnett to Polly James, July 1, 1809.
James Burnet, BM.
John Butcher to Nancy Sevard, May 25, 1809.
Justice Null, BM.
Samuel Callison to Elley Morgan, Dec. 22, 1809.
William Morgan, BM.
Stephen Cantrell to Elizabeth Sturd (or Hurd), May 11,
1809.
Asbury Chandlers to Mary Harris, Aug. 19, 1809.
Robert Massengill, BM.
Peter Clear to Peggy Damewood, Aug. 16, 1809.
Kinsey Coats, BM.
Daniel Clowen to Polley Fargerson, Nov. 16, 1809.
Robert Gaines, BM.
William Fears to Polley Douglass, Sept. __, 1809.
James Fears, BM.
Abyram Gibson to Mary Ballard, Dec. 11, 1809.
Thornton Chesher, BM.
Samuel Gillmore to Amy Housely, Sept. 18, 1809.
Newberry James, BM.
Hugh Gilmore to Sarah Gallion, Dec. 18, 1809.
Newberry James, BM.
James Greenlee to Ruth Southerland, Aug. 3, 1809.
Isaiah Midkiff, BM.
Joel Hall to Judith Mallicoat, Dec. 2, 1809.
William Hall, BM.

GRAINGER COUNTY MARRIAGES

John Hickman to Polly Hunter, June 25, 1809.
John Conner, BM.
Michall Holt to Marget Midkiff, Jan. 4, 1809.
Isaiah Midkiff, BM.
William B. Hones to Minny Jarnagin, March 19, 1809.
Miller Easly, BM.
William Hutchenson to Peggy Sigler, July 15, 1809.
Philip Sigler, BM.
John Keller to Polley Callison, Jan. 20, 1809.
John Graves, BM.
William Kirby to Elizabeth Hopson, May 27, 1809.
John Kirley & Richard Kirby, BM.
George Lovel to Rebecca Mickings, Sept. 25, 1809.
William Dotson, BM.
Goodwin Mays to Cily Mitchell, Nov. 8, 1809.
John Bright & Joel Haworth, BM.
John I. McNess to Jenny Murfy, Oct. 22, 1809.
John Bailey, BM.
Benjamin Moore to Jinny Hankins, July 9, 1809.
Thomas Hankins, BM.
Thomas Morris to Sally Vandergriff, Oct. 20, 1809.
Anderson Adkins, BM.
John Mullins to Betsey Stanley, Jan. 15, 1809.
James Malicoat, BM.
Jacob Noe to Margarette Tate, Jan. 6, 1809.
Edward Tate, BM.
John Justice Null to Elizabeth Newman, Dec. 16, 1809.
John Cocke, BM.
Archibald Neal Rhea to Charlotte Davis, June 17, 1809.
Jesse Issell, BM.
David Sharp to Sally Maples, Oct. 5, 1809.
Thomas Sharp & Thomas Newgen, BM.
Sterling Smith to Lavina Kearns, Aug. 11, 1809.
Nicholas Kearns, BM.
James Sterling to Janet Chamberlain, April 24, 1809.
Ninion Chamberlaim, BM.
Edward Tate to Lucy Moody, Dec. 25, 1809.
David Tate, Junr., BM.
Robert Watson to Sally Ogles, Oct. 10, 1809.
David Watson, BM.
John Whaling to Rhoda Chambers, Aug. 29, 1809.
William Keith, John Moore & James Campbell, BM.
Richard Whaling to Anny Chambers, Oct. 10, 1809.
James Whaling, BM.
Etheldred Williams to Mary Copeland, July 17, 1809.
John Herril, BM.
Isaac Williams to Peggy Arnold, Feb. 25, 1809.
Thomas Williams, BM.
Samuel Williams to Susannah Harris, March 10, 1809.
Richard Harris, BM.
James Wilson to Nancy Gillmore, Sept. 18, 1809.
Newberry James, BM.
John Wilson to Nancy Humes, Aug. 19, 1809.
Amos Sharp, BM.

1810

James Acuff to Nancy Hutcherson, May 15, 1810.
Robert Watson, BM.
Thomas Acuff to Martha Sowders, Dec. 11, 1810.
Richard Acuff, BM.
Martin Albert to Elizabeth Chamberlian, Aug. 7, 1810.
William Keith, BM.
Thomas Allsup to Margaret Moore, Nov. 9, 1810.
John McBroom, BM.
Daniel Arnwine to Polley Rector, Oct. 1, 1810.
Albartis Arnwine, BM.
Samuel Bayles to Susanah Hawkins, Dec. 24, 1810.
Henry Hawkins, BM.
George Beeler, Junr. to Polley Hammock, Jan. 30, 1810.
George Beeler, Senr., BM.
William Bingham to Polley Bingham, May 21, 1810.
James Fowler, BM.
Leonard Brock to Elizabeth Sharp, Oct. 4, 1810.
John Mynett, BM.
Joseph Bull to Nancey Bray, June 7, 1810.
Stagner Bray, BM.
James Clark to Elizabeth Daniel, Feb. 17, 1810.
James Conn, BM.
James Conn to Jain Henderson, Oct. 17, 1810.
William Windham, BM.
Edmond Cox to Polly Davis, Nov. 17, 1810.
William Glassop, BM.
Michael Dyche to Rebecca Churchman, Aug. 11, 1810.
Thomas Churchman, BM.
James Elkins to Sytha Chesher, Feb. 26, 1810.
Thornton Chesher, BM.
William Gray to Mary Hammock, Feb. 28, 1810.
Richard Atkins, BM.
Isaac Harris to Rebecca Smith, Dec. 14, 1810.
Joseph Goldin, BM.
William Harris to Moarning Taylor, Oct. 22, 1810.
Sterling Cocke, BM.
John Hathcoat to Elizabeth Musteen, Aug. 13, 1810.
John Bruvinton, BM.
Sterling Haynes to Lucey Lay, July 25, 1810.
Edward Dennis, BM.
George Henderson to Nancey Larimore, Jan. 1, 1810.
William Henderson & James Condry, BM.
Alexander Heneate to Sally Woolfinbarger, Dec. 10, 1810.
Jacob Woolfinbarger, BM.
Eli Hodges to Elizabeth Holestan, July 9, 1810.
Benjamin Davis, BM.
David Huddleston to Jemimah Simmons, Feb. 14, 1810.
Seamore York, BM.
Hiram Hurst to Mary Thompson, March 10, 1810.
Daniel Leabo, BM.

John Ivey to Betsey Kidwell, Feb. 20, 1810.
Caleb Howell, BM.
John King to Elizabeth Johnston, Aug. 14, 1810.
William Cook, BM.
Ezekiel Kirk to Dolly Simpson, Jan. 14, 1810.
William Patterson, BM.
John Lane to Elizabeth Lovel, April 4, 1810.
William Dodson, BM.
John Lay to Nancy Cook, Jan. 22, 1810.
Thomas Lay, BM.
Joseph Leabow to Nancey Stubblefield, Nov. 17, 1810.
John Leabow, BM.
Jacob Long to Catherine Perry, Feb. 15, 1810.
Frederick Moyers, BM.
Robert Martin to Mary Adkins, Oct. 10, 1810.
Joel Dyer, BM.
Elijah Mitchell to Elizabeth Vineyard, Feb. 25, 1810.
Henry Howell, BM.
William Moore to Clay Clayton, Nov. 21, 1810.
Joseph Gain, BM.
Chesley Morgan to Marion Hall, Dec. 15, 1810.
Samuel Williams, BM.
Henry Moyers to Mary Beeler, Jan. 23, 1810.
Joseph Beeler, BM.
William Nall to Betsey Hill, Oct. 24, 1810.
Philip Sigler, BM.
Thomas Newberry to Jane Thacker, April 2, 1810.
Aaron Rooks, BM.
David Nicely to Doris Norris, Oct. 4, 1810.
John Nicely & Thomas Norris, BM.
Lewis Norris to Martha Fry, Aug. 21, 1810.
William Norris, BM.
James Perry to Nancy Witt, Feb. 1, 1810.
Joseph Long, BM.
Thomas Purcifield to Nancey Spires, Jan. 17, 1810.
John Hacker, BM.
Richard Richards to Mary Elkins, July 29, 1810.
John Richards, BM.
William Rollins to Ebby Haynes, Dec. 8, 1810.
John Smith, BM.
William Shockley to Polly Crawly, Dec. 29, 1810.
Henry Crawley, BM.
William Stone to Nancey Highlander, Dec. 18, 1810.
Charles Kidwell, BM.
Jesse Waggoner to Lucy Hutchison, Nov. 6, 1810.
Thomas Bolton & Spencer Hutchinson, BM.
James Webb to Rachel Certain, June 7, 1810.
John W. Roach, BM.
Larkin Webb to Sarah Bray, June 7, 1810.
John Webb, BM.
Isham Williams to Patsy Cobb, May 29, 1810.
Thomas Cobb, BM. (May 29, 1810).
John Wyrick to Margaret Monroe, Aug. 7, 1810.
John Kitts, BM.

GRAINGER COUNTY MARRIAGES

William Zackary to Suckey Richardson, June 7, 1810.
Joseph Walker, BM.

1811

John Alford to Jeney McElhatten, Jan. 13, 1811.
Thomas Turley, BM.
Willby Blake to Mary Midkiff, March 19, 1811.
Isaiah Midkiff, BM.
Robert Bomar to Sally Shelton, Jan. 8, 1811.
Ralph Shelton, BM.
Edward Daniel to Precilla Mays, Dec. 22, 1811.
John McCarty, BM.
James Dockery to Elizabeth Berry, Dec. 23, 1811.
Pearson Barney, BM.
John Donelson to Ceily Jourdon, Oct. 14, 1811.
Thomas Whiteside, BM.
Worsham Easley to Caty Countz, March 9, 1811.
David Noe, BM.
Joseph Eaton to Pricilla Cravs, Oct. 16, 1811.
Moses Gray to Elizabeth Hamock, April 4, 1811.
William Gray, BM.
William Gray to Polly Lebow, Oct. 24, 1811.
John Gray, BM.
John Howell to Temprence Midkiff, Oct. 7, 1811.
George Jarnagin to Penelope Tate, Nov. 4, 1811.
Samuel Moffet, BM.
Marques Littleton to Mary Walker, June 27, 1811.
James Conn, BM.
Benjamin Maxwell to Catharn Humbert, Jan. 26, 1811.
Samuel Richardson, BM.
James Mays to Jenney Howell, _____, 1811.
John Cocke, BM.
Rollin McGill to Jeney Ivy, Aug. 1, 1811.
Caleb Howel, BM.
Burton Peter to Sarah Hill, Feb. 9, 1811.
Abraham Hill, BM.
Abner Ray to Polley Sparkman, Jan. 8, 1811.
Samuel Ray, BM.
Thomas Richardson Mullins to Franky Cobb, Aug. 30, 1811.
Chrispen Shelton to Sarah Williams, Oct. 1, 1811.
Ralph Shelton, BM.
Isham Smith to Betsey Hodges, July 2, 1811.
William Midall, BM.
Joseph Smith to Elizabeth Housley, Aug. 31, 1811.
Thomas Smith, BM.
Daniel Sollomon to Jenny Bryant, Aug. 28, 1811.
James Bryant, BM.
Abraham Solomon to Elizabeth Chetty, June 13, 1811.
John Seamons, BM.
Levi Sparkman to Anny Ray, April 13, 1811.
Abner Ray, BM.

James Stephen to Anna Kidwell, June 8, 1811.
James Kidwell, BM.
Solomon Sutherland to Betsey Mays, April 29, 1811.
Sterling Cocke, BM.
Thomas Troutman to Artemis Barber, Oct. 3, 1811.
Berry Mitchell, BM.
Thomas Turley to Desdemony Taylor, June 5, 1811.
Thomas Whiteside, BM.
Gilbert Vandergriff to Dicy Brock, Oct. 19, 1811.
George Brock, BM.
Frederick Warick to Feby Jack, Aug. 28, 1811.
Martin Thornberry, BM.
David Watson to Martha Williams, Aug. 19, 1811.
Jonathan Williams, BM.
Erick York to Mary Hill, Dec. 18, 1811.
Joseph Hill, BM.

1812

Richard Ballard to Nancy Grayson, Sept. 16, 1812.
John Simmons, BM.
Nathaniel Branson to Mary Dalton, Jan. 14, 1812.
Charlton Dyer, BM.
John Cabbage to Catherine Moyers, July 20, 1812.
John Moyers, BM.
Abraham Cameron to Betsey Gallian, March 7, 1812.
John Stiffy, BM.
Eleakin Case to Nancy Grimes, Feb. 6, 1812.
Enos Hamers, BM.
John Clark to Mary Young, June 20 (or 28), 1812.
Nathan Humphrey, BM.
Mathius Condray to Rebecca Anderson, Jan. 5, 1812.
James Seamore, BM.
Elisha Cox to Anny Cox, Oct. 21, 1812.
David Reece, BM.
Philip Denham to Rebecca Goin, Dec. 22, 1812.
Baxter Ivie, BM.
Edward Dennis to Ruth Beason, May 21, 1812.
John Dennis, BM.
Joel Donelson to Sally Acuff, Oct. 6, 1812.
William Glassop, BM.
William Dyre to Mary Witcher, July 20, 1812.
Andrew C. Evans to Sally Yeadon, April 9, 1812.
William G. Yeadon, BM.
Jack Fears to Alsey Holt, Feb. 17, 1812.
James Cotton, BM.
Aaron Harbison to Nancy Dyer, Oct. 13, 1812.
Isaac Dyer, BM.
William Hart to Temperance Davis, July 31, 1812.
Silas Isreal & Isham Simmons, BM.
Meseander Helton to Abby Terry, Dec. 15, 1812.
John Noe, BM.

GRAINGER COUNTY MARRIAGES

Joseph Hollinsworth to Rebecca Whaling, Aug. 29, 1812.
    Richard Whaling, BM.
Nathan Humphrey to Elizabeth Young, July 11, 1812.
    John Clark, BM. (July 13, 1812).
John Hunter to Lucy Drake, April 3, 1812.
    Edward Dennis, BM.
William Jack to Mary Oaks, March 20, 1812.
    Robert Fields, BM.
William Jonston to Ruth Longacre, Sept. 12, 1812.
    Matthew Perrin, BM.
Peter Kills to Amy Bird, May 11, 1812.
    William Dyer, BM.
Nathaniel Levi to Merriam Smith, Sept. 7, 1812.
    Samuel Milligan, BM.
William Line to Polly Howel, Nov. 21, 1812.
    Benjamin Case, BM.
Philip Mallicoat to Nancy Combs, Dec. 24, 1812.
    David Huddleston, BM.
Robert Massingill to Elizabeth Paul, Aug. 2, 1812.
    Solomon Mays, BM.
Thomas McMillen to Rachel Dennis, Dec. 31, 1812.
    Edward Dennis, BM.
Augdon Miller to Jane Richerson, July 23, 1812.
    James Richardson, BM.
Brick Mitchel to Elizabeth Perry, Feb. 29, 1812.
    William S. Dyer, BM.
John Monrow to Eave Wyrick, Nov. 24, 1812.
    George Monrow, BM.
John Moody to Elizabeth Mayes, Oct. 17, 1812.
    David Tate, BM.
Thomas R. Mullins to Franky Cobb, Aug. 30, 1812.
    Harrold Cobb, BM.
John Nance to Sally Ore, Feb. 25, 1812.
    Samuel Bunch, BM.
John Needham to Polly Brock, Sept. 1, 1812.
    James Burnet, BM.
James Norris to Anna Crows, Nov. 15, 1812.
    William Norris, BM.
John Oaks to Nancy Selvage, Jan. 18, 1812.
    John Galyon, BM.
Richard Oaks to Sarah Taylor, Nov. 5, 1812.
    John Taylor, BM.
Moses Pain to Nancy Rucker, April 23, 1812.
    Isaac Pain, BM.
William Poindexter to Nancey Cannon, Oct. 1, 1812.
    Hughes Taylor, BM.
James Richardson to Isabella Moore, _____ 1812.
    Edward Tate, BM.
Ninion Riggs to Elizabeth Boatman, Oct. 12, 1812.
    David Tate, Senr., BM.
Thomas Simmons to Rebeccah Wilson, Aug. 23, 1812.
    Isham Simmons, BM.
Drury Solomon to Elizabeth Greenlee, Oct. 28, 1812.
    Henry Solomon, BM.

James Sunderland to Rebecca Daniel, Oct. 8, 1812.
Abraham Sunderland, BM.
Andrew Vineyard to Sally Clowers, Aug. 18, 1812.
John Vineyard, BM.
John Vineyard to Jeney Dent, Feb. 25, 1812.
Elijah Mitchell, BM.
James Whaling to Sally Chambers, March 4, 1812.
Richard Whaling, BM.
Wm. Whitecotton to Patsey Elkins, Feb. 18, 1812.
James Brown & William Cooper, BM.
William Whitecotton to Polly Goan, May 20, 1812.
John Cocke, BM.
Amos Willson to Barbara James, May 26, 1812.
Hugh Gilmore, BM.
Henry Wyrick Jun. to Mary Nipp, Dec. 25, 1812.
Henry Wyrick, BM.

1813

John Anderson to Ruth Blackley, Aug. 16, 1813.
James Husk, BM.
William Ball to Margaret Widner, May 1, 1813.
Isaac Dyer, BM.
John Brockers to Mary Smith, Feb. 17, 1813.
John Simmons, BM.
John Brooks to Elizabeth Brooks, July 4, 1813.
Charles Brooks, BM.
Thomas Bryan to Eliza Ore, June 10, 1813.
Joseph Bryan, BM.
William Burnett to Patsey Burnett, March 1, 1813.
James Burnett, BM.
James Butcher to Jeany Huddleston, June 24, 1813.
Robert Huddleston, BM.
Benjamin Capps to Zelphy Haynes, Nov. 17, 1813.
William Lane, BM.
Elijah Cayton to Elizabeth W. Roch, Nov. 11, 1813.
John W. Roch, BM.
Eli Clark to Polly Hollinsworth, May 1, 1813.
Levi Clark, BM.
David Coffman to Susanah Bunch, Aug. 20, 1813.
Philip Free, BM.
Michael Coffman to Polly Henderson, May 9, 1813.
Thomas Ogle, BM.
Martin Cotner to Sally Ballard, Feb. 6, 1813.
Nathan Ballard, BM.
Nicholas Countz to Patsey Hammers, Aug. 29, 1813.
Zachariah Keith, BM.
Harmond Cox to Sarah Colson, Oct. 21, 1813.
James Hughes, BM.
Meridia Dalton to Dolphy Rucker, Feb. 3, 1813.
Rubin Dalton, BM.
Edward Dennis to Betsey More, Dec. 6, 1813.
Joseph Hall, BM.

GRAINGER COUNTY MARRIAGES

William Dennis to Mary Fields, Aug. 4, 1813.
Joseph Fields, BM.
Abner Duncan to Rody Robertson, Jan. 19, 1813.
Thomas Breeden, BM.
Joseph Eaton to Precilla Craves, Oct. 16, 1813.
William Eaton, BM.
Brown Edwards to Sally Harrison, March 18, 1813.
Richard Whalen, BM.
James Gallant to Rachel Hankins, Feb. 27, 1813.
William Hankins, BM.
Thomas Harriss to Isabella Goins, Jan. 6, 1813.
David Tate, BM.
Thomas Henderson to Mary James, May 1, 1813.
Nathaniel Smith, BM.
William Howell to Mary Evans, Oct. 8, 1813.
Elexander Millakin, BM.
John Hubbs to Nancy Churchman, March 3, 1813.
Thomas Churchman, BM.
James Hust to Elizabeth Jones, June 20, 1813.
Isaiah Midkiff, BM.
Abraham James to Anny Gilmore, Oct. 28, 1813.
David Tate, BM.
William James to Mary Edger, May 31, 1813.
William Bunch, BM.
Lewis Jarnagin to Betsey Richardson, March 29, 1813.
James Richardson, BM.
William Lay to Sarah Capps, Nov. 2, 1813.
Starling Hayns, BM.
John Mayes to Mary Dannel, Jan. 29, 1813.
Mark Lacy, BM.
Stephen McBroom to Hanah Chamber, Feb. 22, 1813.
John McBroom, BM.
Merry Mitchell to Polly Hickson, Jan. 22, 1813.
John Mayes, BM.
William Mitchell to Mary Bunch, Jan. 24, 1813.
Ninian Chamberlin, BM.
George Muchelberry to Lucy Pollard, Aug. 3, 1813.
Samuel Pollard, BM.
Thomas Neugin to Phebe Bates, Jan. 6, 1813.
David Sharp, BM.
William Norris to Joan Norris, June 13, 1813.
William Norris, BM.
John Nunn to Catherine Gray, March 23, 1813.
William Gray, BM.
David Owens to Elizabeth Blair, Jan. 4, 1813.
Fare Owens, BM.
John Owen to Mary Hill, June 9, 1813.
James Phipps, BM.
Thomas Patterson to Mary Blair, Jan. 22, 1813.
William Windham, BM.
James Pilant to Sarah Henderson, Aug. 17, 1813.
Stephen W. Senter, BM.
John Powell to Easter Beeler, Feb. 21, 1813.
Peter Beeler, BM.

GRAINGER COUNTY MARRIAGES

John Prator to Polly Harmon, Oct. 7, 1813.
  Gilbert Vandogriff, BM.
John Ramsey to Nancy Kidwell, Oct. 19, 1813.
  Nathaniel Smith, BM.
John Readman to Nancy Hamilton, Dec. 29, 1813.
  John Perin, BM.
Field Robertson to Susannah Shelton, Sept. 7, 1813.
  Nathaniel Smith, BM.
William Robertson to Polly Bowen, Sept. 27, 1813.
  Arnsted Kirk, BM.
Joseph Routh to Elizabeth Stone, Nov. 23, 1813.
  Aron Rock, BM.
Mathew Russell to Susannah Howell, Dec. 23, 1813.
  Alexander Millican, BM.
Hosia Saterfield to Betsey Simmons, Jan. 6, 1813.
  John Simmons, Jr., BM.
James Selvage to Betsey Oaks, Feb. 9, 1813.
  John Kitchen, BM.
John Sharp to Charity Bond, May 1, 1813.
  Benjamin Bond, BM.
Aaron Shipley to Rosannah Burch, June 26, 1813.
  Adam Shipley, BM.
Richard Simmons to Ruth Dail, April 14, 1813.
  Abel Dial, BM.
Alexander Simms to Barbara Cotner, Feb. 27, 1813.
  John H. Tate, BM.
Josiah Smith to Nancey Condry, Oct. 8, 1813.
  James Buther, BM. (Oct. 9, 1813).
Spencer Sullivan to Saudel Condry, Dec. 25, 1813.
  Dennis Condry, BM.
Thomas Waggoner to Elizabeth Bolton, Feb. 15, 1813.
  Samuel McBee, BM.
Jacob Widener to Polly Bull, July 27, 1813.
  Lewis Widener, BM.
Peter Wyrick to Nancy Norris, Nov. 14, 1813.
  Samuel Etter, BM.
Frank Young to Jane Williams, Feb. 12, 1813.
  William Clark, BM.

1814

Robert Allstall to Sally Long, Feb. 19, 1814.
  Nicholas Beans, BM.
Thomas Anderson to Elizabeth Harris, July 24, 1814.
  Richard Harris, BM.
William Anderson to Annie Smith, May 3, 1814.
  William Stansberry, BM.
Spencer Bassett to Febly Lebow, Sept. 20, 1814.
  Benjamin Mumpower, BM.
Isaac Bethrem to Elizabeth Biggs,   , 1814.
  Samuel Lewis, BM.
James Blair, Junr. to Mary Kelso, May 25, 1814.
  James Blair, Senr., BM.

Samuel Box to Jimima Murphy, June 9, 1814.
James Ezell, BM.
Hagner Bray to Sally Waters, Aug. 12, 1814.
Henry Bray, BM.
William Brown to Polly Sherrel, Aug. 26, 1814.
William Sherrel, BM.
James Campbell to Elizabeth Hawkins, Dec. 17, 1814.
Peter Moses, BM.
Levi Clark to Susana McVay, Aug. 27, 1814.
Elisha Hall, BM.
Sterling Coke to Eliza Massingill, Aug. 25, 1814.
(Sept. 6, 1814).
Elijah Cornwall to Elizabeth Poindexter, July 13, 1814.
Richard Bragg, BM.
Edward Daniel to Phebe Mays, July 23, 1814.
John Daniel, BM. (July 24, 1814).
Jacob Davidson to Sarah Selvage, Jan. 30, 1814.
James Selvage, BM.
Robertson Denniston to Nancy Bradshaw, Aug. 21, 1814.
William Davidson, BM.
James Dyor to Polly Harmon, Sept. 7, 1814.
William Ball, BM.
Garret Gibson to Patsey Gyton, June 18, 1814.
Nathan Ballard, BM. (June 22, 1814).
Thomas Giffin to Edy Sharp, Jan. 12, 1814.
William Griffin, BM.
John Gray to Sarah Madlock, June 8, 1814.
Jesse Patterson, BM.
John Helton to Violet Philips, May 25, 1814.
Joseph Rich, BM.
Philip Hodge to Condis Howell, Jan. 18, 1814.
Jesse Hodge, BM.
Charles Hopper to Susannah Penn, Jan. 10, 1814.
Archabald Hopper, BM.
John Howell to Susan Moore, Aug. 16, 1814.
Richard Shelton, BM.
David Ivey to Nancy Robertson, Sept. 23, 1814.
Jurdon Smith, BM.
Thomas Janes to Jane Windham, March 12, 1814.
(March 14, 1816).
William Kennedy to Hannah Milligan, Nov. 1, 1814.
Samuel Milligan, BM.
James King to Mary Jane Cocke, Feb. 8, 1814.
William C. Mynatt, BM.
Samuel Lane to Polly Lovel, April 5, 1814.
Thomas Brocus, BM.
Edward Mayse to Nanie Greenlee, Dec. 23, 1814.
William Lacy, BM.
James Mayse to Milley Vinyard, Oct. 17, 1814.
Andrew Vinyard, BM.
Samuel Merit to Barbary Wolfenbarger, Feb. 20, 1814.
Peter Wolfenbarger, BM.
George Miller to Nancy Hunter, Sept. 9, 1814.
Francis Hunter, BM.

Genl. Sullavan Loyd Monroe to Nancy Harris, Dec. 9, 1814.
John Harris, BM.
Talifaro Partin to Lucy Hallford, Sept. 8, 1814.
Jacob Hallford, BM.
Willie Reed to Nancy Spoons, Feb. 20, 1814.
Thomas __gges, BM.
William R. Saney to Nancy Cyrus, March 24, 1814.
Henry Moulder, BM.
John Shelton to Theana W. Brock, Sept. 7, 1814.
Miller Shelton, BM.
James Simmons to Barbery McGinnigats, Sept. 12, 1814.
Isham Simmons, BM.
Joel Smith to Hannah Long, Aug. 27, 1814.
Hezekiah Brown, BM.
Gilbert Vandagrift to Aggy Dalton, Feb. 28, 1814.
Charleston Dyer, BM.
William Whitecotton to Patsey Elkins, Oct. 2, 1814.
James Elkin, BM.
John Williams to Elizabeth Arwine, Aug. 16, 1814.
John Arwine,BM.

1815

William B. Bowen to Polly Brown, Dec. 3, 1815.
Robert Alstot, BM.
Obediah Brock to Nancy Vandergriff, June 1, 1815.
Jacob Vandergriff, BM.
John Brown to Rebeckah Cocke, Dec. 11, 1815.
William E. Cocke, BM.
William Burton to Sarah Shockley, Nov. 4, 1815.
Richard Shockley, BM.
Joshua Casy to Alley Harris, Dec. 23, 1815.
Samuel Richardison, BM. (Jan. 14, 1816).
Thomas Chersher to Matilda Smith, Dec. 21, 1815.
Fredrick Smith, BM.
James Clowes to Polly Sharp, Dec. 9, 1815.
Thomas Griffin, BM.
John Cox to Sarah Cline, Sept. 12, 1815.
Abraham Cox, BM.
Charles Crain to Margret Trogdon, Oct. 10, 1815.
Charles Crain, Senr., BM. (Oct. 10, 1815).
John Creyton to Agnes Dalton, June 10, 1815.
William Clark, BM.
Jacob Danner to Watson, Dec. 20, 1815.
Henery Watson, BM.
Joshua Dyer to Winny Dyer, June 21, 1815.
Joshua Washburn & Charlton Dyer, BM.
Benjamin Emmery to Sarah Morris, Dec. 30, 1815.
Moses Willis, BM.
John Fry to Elizabeth Mansfield, Aug. 30, 1815.
William Griffits, BM.
William Gains to Cintha Howell, July 5, 1815.
Henry Brown, BM.

David T. Hall to Caty Adkins, Dec. 2, 1815.
    Isaac Dyer, BM.
Samuel P. Harbin to Elizabeth Chusher, July 29, 1815.
    Edward Harbin, BM.
Epephroditus Hightower to Nancy Clay, Jan. 25, 1815.
    Caswell Jarnagin, BM.
George Hinshaw to Anna Goldin, Dec. 16, 1815.
    John Cocke, BM.
James Hix to Patsey Stubblefield, Jan. 4, 1815.
    Wyet Stubblefield, BM.
Charles Hopper to Sarah Willis, Nov. 12, 1815.
    Thomas Willis, BM.
Solman Humphrey to Sarah Smith, June 17, 1815.
    Henry Humphreys, BM. (June 19, 1815).
Elijah James to Rachel Long, Feb. 1, 1815.
    (Feb. 2, 1815).
Jermiah Jarnagin to Patsey Bunch, Jan. 9, 1815.
    John Brown, BM.
Thomas Jeffres to Patsey Shelton, Oct. 12, 1815.
    Crispin E. Shelton, BM.
Joseph Lefew to Polly Jones, Aug. 5, 1815.
    Thomas Griffits, BM.
James Massingill to Odsey Stone, Sept. 5, 1815.
    Sterling Cocke, BM.
Charles Matlock to Mary Baker, Nov. 18, 1815.
    John Brown, BM.
Edward Mayse to Nancy Greenlee, Dec. 23, 1815.
John McBee to Susanah Breaden, Dec. 16, 1815.
    William Breaden, BM.
Robert McCristian to Mary Bowen, Aug. 13, 1815.
    Aaron Counce, BM.
Robert McMillen to Betsy Chandler, June 21, 1815.
    Daniel Chandler, BM.
Wm. S. Merchant to Hisey Reece, May 9, 1815.
    Thomas Hankins, BM.
Aquilla Mitchel to Elizabeth Fargerson, May 23, 1815.
    Elijah Mitchell, BM.
William Morris to Hannah R. R. Ross, May 16, 1815.
    Thomas James, BM.
William Morris to Lucy Willis, Nov. 12, 1815.
    Harmon Morris, BM.
Larkin Norman to Nancy Shoemaker, Sept. 12, 1815.
    Pleasant Norman, BM.
Benton Peter to _____, Nov. 7, 1815.
    Isaac Thompson, BM.
Thomas Ray to Mary Arnett, Aug. 25, 1815.
    Joseph Ray, BM.
Seamore Reece to Sally Adams, April 14, 1815.
    James Fears, BM.
William Rucker to Ruth Dodson, Nov. 4, 1815.
    Samuel Dodson, BM.
Jonathan Seamans to Elizabeth Sparksman, June 14, 1815.
    William Sparksman, BM.

GRAINGER COUNTY MARRIAGES

Samuel Sharp to Sarah Dennis, Dec. 12, 1815.
  Lenard Brock, BM.
James Shelton to Polly Bristo, Nov. 9, 1815.
  Samuel Shelton & John Shelton, BM.
Solomon Trogdon to Elizabeth Minice, July 6, 1815.
  Samuel Richardson, BM.
Henry Watson to Jane Hock, Nov. 17, 1815.
  Aaron Rooks, BM.
James Williams to Mary Jackson, May 11, 1815.
  Jacob Jackson, BM.
John Williams to Elizabeth Arwine, Aug. 7, 1815.
  John Arwine, BM.
Moses Willis to Susannah Fields, Dec. 30, 1815.
  Allin Davidson, BM.
Peter Wolfenbarger to Nancy Dyer, Dec. 19, 1815.
  George Dyer, BM.
John York to Jane Overton, Oct. 8, 1815.

1816

Abraham Beeler to Mary Jack, Sept. 26, 1816.
  Joseph Beeler, BM.
Andrew Bowen to Catherine Hawith, Aug. 26, 1816.
  Eli Clark, BM.
Richard Bragg to Debby Jones, July 24, 1816.
  William Morrison, BM. (July 25, 1816).
John Burnet to Susanna Wolfenbarger, Sept. 4, 1816.
  John Acuff, BM. (Sept. 24, 1816).
James Cannon to Rebecca Bowen, May 31, 1816.
  Winphrey Robertson, BM. (June 2, 1816).
Thomas Churchman to Margaret Williams, June 21, 1816.
Hopkins Cox to Eliza Ore, Sept. 18, 1816.
  Richard Braden, BM.
Enock Cyrus to Rebecca Cook, Aug. 31, 1816.
  Nimrod Cyrus, BM.
Briant Davidson to Sarah Janes, Nov. 17, 1816.
  John Davidson, BM. (Nov. 17, 1816).
Solomon Ezel to Mary Patterson, April 24, 1816.
  James Ezell, BM. (April 25, 1816).
Jesse Ezell to Allie Seamans, July 2, 1816.
  James Ezell, BM. (July 2, 1816).
James Farmer to Betsey Shockley, Aug. 8, 1816.
  Thomas Shockley, BM.
William George to Polly Webb, March 10, 1816.
  David McAnally, BM.
William Hankins to Elizabeth Carpenter, April 24, 1816.
  John Large, BM.
Coalman Harrell to May Long, March 16, 1816.
  Nathl. Smith, BM.
Joseph Heavins to Deliah Baker, Oct. 18, 1816.
Edmon Hodges to Betty Smith, June 8, 1816.
  William McGill, BM. (June 10, 1816).

Thomas Hunter to Elizabeth Drake, Oct. 12, 1816.
(Oct. 24, 1816).
William Inclebarger to Sarah Campbell, Sept. 11, 1816.
Nathl. Smith, BM. (Sept. 11, 1816).
Thomas Janes to Jane Windham, March 12, 1816.
James Johnston, BM.
Eligha Leffew to Anney McCinsy, Aug. 15, 1816.
Thomas Mays to Sarah Daniel, Jan. 27, 1816.
Thomas Morgan, BM. (Jan. 28, 1816).
Nelson Miller to Sarah Lord, Oct. 31, 1816.
Stephen Miller, BM. (Nov. 6, 1816).
James Nipper to Catherian Lerimere, Dec. 16, 1816.
Jordan Nipper to Jane Snodgrass, Aug. 26, 1816.
William Zachary, BM.
Elum Partin to Lindy Clayton, May 7, 1816.
John Clayton, BM.
Morgan Pendexter to Polly Blair, July 11, 1816.
James Blair, BM.
_____ Phara to Elizabeth Reece, June 22, 1816.
Martin O'Hara & James S. Moore, BM. (Phara may be
O'Hara).
Andrew Philips to Jane Bucher, Feb. 19, 1816.
Simon York, BM.
Roger Reece to Nancy OHarror, June 30, 1816.
Martin O'Harror, BM. (July 1, 1816).
William Reed to Anney Eustice, Dec. 8, 1816 (or 1815).
Washington Eustice, BM. (Dec. 12, 1816).
Ellis Riggs to Adeline Read, July 20, 1816.
Lunis Riggs, BM. (July 23, 1816).
Levi Riggs to Sarah Boatman, Aug. 19, 1816.
Henry Boatman, BM.
Kiah Robertson to Abitha Grantham, Dec. 8, 1816.
John Kirkhim, BM.
Laten Romine to Fanny Carnutt, July 31, 1816.
William Carnutt, BM.
James Shelton to Nancy Gentry, Aug. 19, 1816.
Isaac Harny, BM.
Miller Shelton to Elizabeth Webb, Oct. 2, 1816.
(Sept. 24, 1817).
David Tate to Mary Massengill, Feb. 25, 1816.
Edward Tate, BM. (Feb. 25, 1816).
John K. Tate to Rachel Carmical, Dec. 5, 1816.
Edward Tate, BM. (Dec. 5, 1816).
Jacob Vandegriff to Winny Brock, May 4, 1816.
Daniel Beelor, BM.
Baseton Waters to Betsey Young, April 26, 1816.
Girland Morris, BM.
James Whitlock to Sarah Smith, Jan. 28, 1816.
Daniel Prigmore, BM. (Jan. 28, 1816).
Robert Willis to Betty Bumpower, Feb. 12, 1816.
(Feb. 14, 1816).
James Wood to Catharine Reece, Nov. 3, 1816.
David Reece, BM. (Nov. 5, 1816).

1817

John Acuff to Nancy Harmon, Dec. 17, 1817.
  Nathan Kelly, BM.
Willis Akins to Polly B. Floyd, Jan. 7, 1817.
  Reas Williams, BM.
Henry Alsup to Mary Harris, Dec. 14, 1817.
  John Brown, BM. (Dec. 24, 1817).
William Balard to Rosana Cotner, Jan. 1, 1817.
  (Jan. 2, 1817).
Robert Bean to Cristina Miller, Oct. 7, 1817.
  William B. Bowen, BM.
James Brock to Elizabeth Beeler, Nov. 29, 1817.
  Isaac Dyer, BM.
Thomas Brockers to Nancy Norris, Oct. 19, 1817.
  William Norris, BM. (Oct. 19, 1817).
Thomas Brocks to Susannah Helton, Dec. 24, 1817.
  James Helton, BM. (Dec. 25, 1817).
David W. Bunch to Heister Midkiff, April 17, 1817.
  John Bunch, BM. (Sept. 24, 1817).
William Carnutt to Lucindia Dent, Dec. 2, 1817.
  David Smith, BM.
Daniel Chambers to Nancy Simmons, Sept. 25, 1817.
  Joel Smith, BM.
William Cheek to Lucindia Dyer, Dec. 2, 1817.
  Lenord Brock, BM.
Daniel Cluck to Jane Kidwell, Oct. 26, 1817 (or 1816).
  David Kidwell, BM. (Oct. 30, 1817).
Arron Countz to Ruth Hammers, Sept. 23, 1817.
  Winphrey Robertson, BM.
Benjamin Cox to Sally Noe, Oct. 8, 1817.
  Elexander Millekin, BM.
David Dalton to Polly Dyer, Aug. 16, 1817.
  Joshua Washam, BM. (Aug. 17, 1817).
John Davis to Margaret Griffitts, Aug. 7, 1817.
  Ninion Riggs, BM. (Aug. 14, 1817).
James Dodson to Rachel Grantham, July 25, 1817.
  James Robertson, BM. (July 29, 1817).
John Edward to Nancy Vitito, July 11, 1817.
  Thomas Vitito, BM. (Sept. 24, 1817).
William Ellis to Pheby Lacy, Nov. 16, 1817.
  John Cocke, BM.
William Epps to Francis Easley, Oct. 2, 1817.
  William E. Cocke, BM.
Joel Fields to Pheby Hill, Dec. 19, 1817.
  Charles Hardin, BM. (Dec. 23, 1817).
Robert Fry to Frances Burnet, Aug. 15, 1817.
  John Burnet, BM. (Sept. 24, 1817).
William Gallion to Jane King, Sept. 10, 1817.
  Hugh Gilmore, BM. (Sept. 12, 1817).
Lindsy Gibson to Susanah Hurt, Oct. 23, 1817.
  Archilles Page, BM.

GRAINGER COUNTY MARRIAGES

Drury Goans to Mary Goans, Aug. 23, 1817.
Edward Riggs, BM.
William Hamilton to Susanah Willis, Dec. 7, 1817.
John Cocke, BM.
Richard Hawkins to Betsy Wiles, Aug. 7, 1817.
Benjamin Hencily to Mary Gallion, Sept. 17, 1817.
William Gallion, BM. (Sept. 17, 1817).
John Hicks to Elizabeth Stubblefield, Nov. 28, 1817.
Robert Stubblefield, BM.
Abel Hill to Susanah Jones, Oct. 19, 1817.
Thomas Brown, BM. (Oct. 19, 1817).
James Hill to Sarah Moulder, Feb. 6, 1817.
William Sharp, BM.
Joseph Hill to Nancy Cockrim, Jan. 9, 1817.
(Jan. 11, 1817).
William Hilton to Rachel Pendextor, Jan. 7, 1817.
Henry Byrd, BM.
William Hunter to Tempey Hill, Sept. 4, 1817.
Francis Hunter, BM. (Sept. 7, 1817).
Charles Jones to Sally Jones, Nov. 29, 1817.
James Moore, BM.
David Lacy to Nancy Moody, March 15, 1817.
Dodson Morgan, BM. (March 16, 1817).
William Lawry to Abinida Sigler, April 2, 1817.
St. Clair F. Caldwell, BM. (June 24, 1817).
Samuel Lockhart to Elizabeth Atkins, April 26, 1817.
St. Clair F. Caldwell, BM.
John Long to Charity May, Oct. 25, 1817.
William Morrison, BM.
Joel McCoy to Sally Andrican, Oct. 23, 1817.
David McCoy, BM.
John McHaffie to Elizabeth Dyer, Sept. 15, 1817.
John Bull, BM. (Sept. 24, 1817).
John Molder to Rachel Syrus, May 19, 1817.
Henry Moulder, BM.
Cardwell C. Moore to Lidy C. Moore, Sept. 9, 1817.
William Dunning, BM. (Sept. 11, 1817).
James Moore to Rheda Grantham, Dec. 3, 1817.
William Moore, BM. (Dec. 18, 1817).
Robert Moore to Catherine Atkins, Nov. 6, 1817.
Thomas Pierce, BM. (Nov. 6, 1817).
John Morgan to Nancy James, Oct. 8, 1817.
John Galian, BM. (Oct. 8, 1817).
Samuel Morrison to Anna Bragg, Nov. 1, 1817.
John Cocke, BM. (Nov. 6, 1817).
Gallent Norris to Sarah Colby, March 16, 1817.
William Norris, BM.
Thomas Norris to Mary Kitts, June 1, 1817.
William Norris, BM.
John J. Null to Rheda Wheeling, April 26, 1817.
John Cocke, BM.
Richard Oaks to Anny Longmire, Jan. 25, 1817.
Michael O'Conner to Nancy Alsop, July 13, 1817.
Emond Been, BM.

GRAINGER COUNTY MARRIAGES

John Perrin to Polly Churchman, May 21, 1817.
   William E. Cocke, BM.
John Proffit to Rachel Briant, Dec. 27, 1817.
   David Proffit, BM.
Samuel Ray to Angy Sparkman, Feb. 1, 1817.
   Thomas Ray, BM. (Sept. 3, 1817).
Jesse Rayle to Elsa Bunch, March 15, 1817.
   George Rayle, BM. (Sept. 24, 1817).
Alexander Reeder to Malinda Moss, May 29, 1817.
   William Reeder, BM.
John Robertson to Polly Houlston, May 24, 1817.
   James Dodson, BM. (May 27, 1817).
Samy Seaman to Peggy Hamilton, Jan. 14, 1817.
   Lenord Brock, BM. (Jan. 26, 1817).
John Seamore to Catherine Woods, Dec. 21, 1817.
   Jesse Ezell, BM. (Dec. 23, 1817).
James Sellers to Elizabeth Brock, April 22, 1817.
   George Brock, BM. (Sept. 24, 1817).
James Senter to Elizabeth Harris, Dec. 15, 1817.
   Nathaniel Smith, BM. (Dec. 16, 1817).
Joseph Shannon to Elinor Moffit, Jan. 28, 1817.
   (Jan. 28, 1817).
Joseph Shedrick to Francis Grayson, Dec. 10, 1817.
   Richard Ballard, BM. (Dec. 11, 1817).
Isam Smith to Betsy Hodges, July 2, 1817.
Masey Smith to Barthena Miller, Aug. 18, 1817.
   Joseph Dyer, BM. (Aug. 19, 1817).
John Stubblefield to Elizabeth Grason, Dec. 30, 1817.
   Zera McGee, BM. (Dec. 30, 1817).
Daniel Taylor to Martha Thomason, Dec. 10, 1817.
   Philip Traverse, BM. (Dec. 16, 1817).
Abner Trogden to Patience Lemmons, Jan. 2, 1817.
   Robert Ore, BM. (Jan. 2, 1817).
Daniel Underhill to Winney Ball, Oct. 18, 1817.
   Levi Dennis, BM. (Oct. 21, 1817).
Daniel Vinyard to Polly Dent, Aug. 31, 1817.
   John Vinyard, BM. (Sept. 2, 1817).
Nicholas Vinyard to Betsey Walker, March 31, 1817.
   Caswell L. Walker, BM. (April 1, 1817).
Joseph Williams to Jane Southerland, April 26, 1817.
   Edward Williams, BM. (April 27, 1817).
William F. Williams to Anna K. Copland, Dec. 2, 1817.
   Hugh Huston, BM. (Dec. 4, 1817).
Michel Wyrick to Lucindia Jones, Feb. 8, 1817.
   Henry Wyrick, BM. (Feb. 13, 1817).
William Young to Elizabeth James, Dec. 19, 1817.
   James Galian, BM. (Dec. 20, 1817).

1818

James Aytes to Jane Miller, Sept. 26, 1818.
   William Inglebarger, BM. (Sept. 27, 1818).

William Barnett to Cynthia Clay, June 29, 1818.
Epaphroditus Hightower, Junr., BM.
George Bedsaul to Dicey Howell, Aug. 1, 1818.
Welcom Howel, BM.
Moses Blackman to Betty King, Oct. 22, 1818.
John W. Blake to Margaret B. Kidwell, Nov. 19, 1818.
John Ramsey, BM. (Nov. 26, 1818).
Chasley H. Boatright to Louisa Taylor, March 21, 1818.
John Harris, BM. (March 29, 1818).
Samuel Box to Catherine Ricketts, Oct. 25, 1818.
Archibald Pugh, BM. (Nov. 8, 1818).
Jacob Cabbage to Frances Bolton, Feb. 7, 1818.
Peter Bolton, BM. (Feb. 7, 1818).
David Caps to Barbary Long, Sept. 2, 1818.
John Long, BM. (Sept. 3, 1818).
Jacob Caps to Jemima Long, Oct. 20, 1818.
Peter Boulton, BM.
Daniel Cardwell to Elizabeth Abbott, May 11, 1818.
Stephen Cocke, BM. (May 19, 1818).
Samuel Cates to Mary Richardson, July 9, 1818.
John Richardson, BM. (July 19, 1818).
Thompson Chamberlan to Mary West, July 25, 1818.
John Braem, BM. (July 28, 1818).
Thomas Chandler to Hannah Fletcher, Aug. 27, 1818.
Robert McMillan, BM. (Aug. 27, 1818).
Henry Cluck to Hannah Kidwell, April 4, 1818.
Daniel Cluck, BM. (April 10, 1818).
John Dennis to Letty Fields, Aug. 1, 1818.
William Dennis, BM. (Aug. 6, 1818).
William Dunning to Anna Hamilton, Aug. 7, 1818.
Lenord Brock, BM. (Aug. 7, 1818).
Isaac B. Dyer to Rachel Hall, July 6, 1818.
Thomas Dyer, BM. (July 6, 1818).
Worsham Easley to Elizabeth Lathim, Sept. 1, 1818.
Stephen Cocke, BM.
John Fincher to Nancy Derham, June 26, 1818.
David Noe, BM. (June 27, 1818).
Jacob H. Fort to Jacinthea Copeland, Nov. 30, 1818.
Ethelrid Williams, BM. (Dec. 3, 1818).
John Gallian to Rhoda Mitchell, March 10, 1818.
Hugh Gilmore, BM. (March 11, 1818).
John Gallian to Vedy Smith, Feb. 19, 1818.
John Cocke, BM.
John Glasgow to Elizabeth Reece, Feb. 13, 1818.
Isaiah Reece, BM. (Feb. 15, 1818).
Valentine Hacker to Polly Spires, Aug. 11, 1818.
William Coffman, BM. (Aug. 13, 1818).
Enos Hammers to Francis Thomas, Nov. 19, 1818.
Nicholas Counce, BM. (Nov. 19, 1818).
Joel Hammers to Polly Cannon, May 15, 1818.
Nicholas Counce, BM. (May 15, 1818).
Daniel Hammock to Elizabeth Spires, Aug. 18, 1818.
William Hammock, BM. (Aug. 18, 1818).

Robert Hanes to Nancy Mullins, Jan. 24, 1818.
William P. Yeadon, BM.
John C. Harvey to Nancy Wiseman, Sept. 24, 1818.
Nathanel Smith, BM.
Malkjah Hines to Sarah Elkins, Dec. 18, 1818.
William Hines, BM. (Dec. 19, 1818).
Benjamin Howell to Agneys Grisham, Oct. 31, 1818.
John Howell, BM. (Nov. 1, 1818).
William Inclebarger to Sarah Aytes, Aug. 4, 1818.
Daniel Cardwell, BM. (Aug. 5, 1818).
Cazwill Jarnagin to Elizabeth Thompson, Jan. 7, 1818.
Thomas Jarnagin, BM.
Alexander Kirk to Caty Bolinger, March 11, 1818.
Winfrey Robertson, BM. (March 11, 1818).
Isaac Kline to Sally Quinner, Dec. 31, 1818.
John Brown, BM.
John Maples to Elizabeth Sharp, Feb. 7, 1818.
Thomas Griffin, BM.
Thomas McCloud to Thena Draper, April 21, 1818.
William Noles, BM.
Thomas Midkiff to Vilet Manning, Aug. 22, 1818.
Isaiah Midkiff, BM.
Allen Dodson Morgan to Roda Churchman, Feb. 11, 1818.
Elias David, BM.
James Patterson to Susanah Sandery, March 10, 1818.
Rubin Nance, BM.
George Rhinehart to Sarah Moore, Dec. 5, 1818.
John Rhineheart, BM. (Dec. 5, 1818).
Winfrey Robertson to Margaret Kirk, April 13, 1818.
Stephen Cocke, BM. (April 16, 1818).
Brown B. Rookard to Nancy Norris, Feb. 14, 1818.
William Dodson, BM.
Moses Smith to Armerilla Midkiff, Aug. 8, 1818.
Thomas Midkiff, BM.
Joseph Stubblefield to America Bond, Feb. 9, 1818.
Benjamin Davis, BM.
Goodin Stutt to Lida Bean, Nov. 17, 1818.
Baxter Ivy, BM.
Patties Thacker to Sally Coxe, Nov. 12, 1818.
John James, BM.
James Thomson to Jane Read, Oct. 27, 1818.
Daniel Robertson, BM. (Oct. 29, 1818).
Anthony Underwood to Sarah Rolings, July 19, 1818.
Stephen Greer, BM.
Caswell Walker to Carolina McCinny, Dec. 22, 1818.
William Inglebarger, BM. (Dec. 7, 1819).
Christian Wyrick to Elizabeth Gassage, July 11, 1818.
Henry Wyrick, BM.

1819

Richard Adkins to Nancy Wirick, Dec. 17, 1819.
Martin Thornburg, BM.

GRAINGER COUNTY MARRIAGES

Jacob Arnet to Ann Coffy, Nov. 3, 1819.
  John Coffy, BM. (Dec. 11, 1819).
John Ball to Catherine Headrick, Sept. 8, 1819.
  Daniel Underhill, BM. (Sept. 9, 1819).
Peter Boulton to Salomy Coffman, Feb. 1, 1819).
  Thomas Waggoner, BM. (Feb. 5, 1819).
Jonathan Box to Jane McNiece, Feb. 3, 1819.
  Robert Box, BM. (Feb. 7, 1819).
William Brockus to Elizabeth Ramsey, March 15, 1819.
  Jeremiah Lovell, BM.
Adam Cabbage to Catherine Long, Aug. 30, 1819.
  David Capps, BM. (Aug. 22, 1819).
Charles Campbell to Sarah Burket, July 8, 1819.
  John Stiffy, BM. (July 8, 1819).
Asbury Chammes to Mary Harris, Aug. 19, 1819.
  (Aug. 23, 1819).
David Coats to Mary Hinshaw, Oct. 23, 1819.
  (Jefferson County) (Grainger County)
  Josiah Grasty (Jonah Grasly), BM. (Oct. 24, 1819).
William Coffiman to Polly Wirick, March 22, 1819.
  Peter Boulton, BM. (March 23, 1819).
Andrew Coffman to Anny Kirkpatrick, Sept. 7, 1819.
  Thomas Coffman, BM. (Sept. 9, 1819).
Thomas Craig to Mary Ann Pope, Jan. 7, 1819.
  Jonathan Dale, BM.
Elish Dotson to Fanna Thompson, Oct. 31, 1819.
  James Robertson, BM. (Nov. 4, 1819).
Thomas Dyer to Sarah Hammers, Aug. 10, 1819.
  James Malicoat, BM. (Aug. 10, 1819).
James Gallion to Avia Smith, July 28, 1819.
  Dixon Smith, BM. (July 28, 1819).
Joseph Gaults to Luda Higgs, Nov. 3, 1819.
  Jesse Creech, BM. (Nov. 3, 1819).
Caleb Gibson to Barbary Kirk, Oct. 9, 1819.
  Lizy Gibson, BM. (Oct. 10, 1819).
James Greenlee to Pheby Mays, Sept. 18, 1819.
  Edward Mays, BM. (Sept. 19, 1819).
William Greer to Mary Hines, Aug. 28, 1819.
  Thomas Waggoner, BM. (Aug. 29, 1819).
John Gregory to Charlotte Hall, Oct. 27, 1819.
  Isaac Ruth, BM.
Malon Harris to Mary Holland, Sept. 4, 1819.
  Fair Owen, BM.
William Hipshire to Polly McCoy, Dec. 23, 1819.
  Charles McAnally, BM. (Dec. 23, 1819).
Charles Hopper to Susanah Garland, Dec. 21, 1819.
  Walter Evans, BM. (Dec. 23, 1819).
Peter James to Jane Thacker, Dec. 3, 1819.
  Henry Tanner, BM.
Sanford Johnson to Louise Lebo, Oct. 25, 1819.
  Thomas Johnson, BM.
Henry Kneedham to Anna Brock, Aug. 15, 1819.
  James Burnett, BM.

41

Thomas Large to Hannah Minter, Sept. 11, 1819.
William Large, BM. (Sept. 12, 1819).
David McCouster to Evi Bowen, June 26, 1819.
Nicholas Nolson, BM.
James McDaniel to Sally Griffin, Aug. 11, 1819.
John Griffin, BM. (Aug. 12, 1819).
Daniel Miller to Peggy Hunter, April 22, 1819.
William Hunter, BM. (April 22, 1819).
John Mills to Nancy Mumpower, Sept. 24, 1819.
Isaac Leabow, BM.
William Nicely to Elizabeth Aytes, May 8, 1819.
Linsey Gibson, BM. (May 9, 1819).
Thomas Norris to Mary Miller, Feb. 4, 1819.
William Norris, BM. (Feb. 4, 1819).
Aquila Payn to Rachel James, Aug. 3, 1819.
John James, BM. (Aug. 3, 1819).
William Reece to Charlotte Glassop, Feb. 6, 1819.
Isaiah Reece, BM. (Feb. 7, 1819).
Joseph Rutherford to Elizabeth Baker, March 24, 1819.
Joseph Harvey, BM.
David Sharp to Betsy Carthers, Oct. 31, 1819.
James Pilor, BM.
Adam Shipley to Katherine Mann, June 26, 1819.
John Long, BM.
Booker Shockly to Haniah Dalton, Dec. 22, 1819.
Goodin Solomon to Peggy Hill, Jan. 8, 1819.
Henry Solomon, BM.
Thomas D. Starling to Elizabeth Bryan, Dec. 15, 1819.
Thomas Maddon, BM.
Jacob Thompson to Mary Eastise, Sept. 28, 1819.
Adam Shiply, BM. (Sept. 28, 1819).
William Vittito to Isabel McNey, Oct. 18, 1819.
Joseph Holinsworth, BM. (Oct. 18, 1819).
Samuel Woods to Elizabeth Rayons, Aug. 17, 1819.
Welcome Hodge, BM.

1820

David Acuff to Faney Malicoat, Nov. 8, 1820.
John Acuff, BM.
Elza Barby to Polly Maples, May 23, 1820.
John Perrin, BM. (May 23, 1820).
Marcus D. Bearden to Anny E. Cocke, July 25, 1820.
W. H. Stockton, BM.
Danial Bolton to Dicy Smiddy, April 2, 1820.
Daniel Woldridge, BM. (April 6, 1820).
John Brock to _____ Bowman (?), Dec. 22, 1820.
Robert Bose, BM.
Joseph Brown to Sally Hilton, Dec. 23, 1820.
James Bryant, BM. (Dec. 26, 1820).
William Brown to Matilda Hawkins, Jan. 18, 1820.
John Bryant, BM. (Jan. 18, 1820).

Joseph Bryan to Elizabeth Hill, Feb. 15, 1820.
  Thomas D. Karling, BM. (Feb. 17, 1820).
Samuel Bunch to Amanda Anderson, Oct. 22, 1820.
  John Bunch, BM.
William T. Cardin to Winford Dyer, Sept. 16, 1820.
  Owen Dyer, BM. (Sept. 21, 1820).
William Cardwell to Calia Harper, Jan. 7, 1820.
  John Cardwell, BM.
James Carrol to Polly Bond, Sept. 1, 1820.
  John Carrol, BM.
Pherncy Condry to Sarah Moulder, March 23, 1820.
  G. W. L. Moulder, BM.
John Cook to Alvina Kearns, Aug. 20, 1820.
Solomon Cox to Dicy Glasgow, June 10, 1820.
  Harmon Cox, BM. (June 11, 1820).
Joseph Daniel to Mary Long, Dec. 13, 1820.
  Sterling Cocke, BM.
James Davidson to Nancy Braden, Nov. 18, 1820.
  William Davidson, BM.
Samuel Davis to Liddy Murphy, Feb. 22, 1820.
  (Feb. 27, 1820).
Samuel Dodson to Mary Williams, Aug. 3, 1820.
  Samuel Dodson & William Moore, BM. (Aug. 3, 1820).
W. Estis to Betsy Perky, July 15, 1820.
  Hugh O. Taylor, BM.
George Evans to Matilda Lathum, Jan. 18, 1820.
  William Evans, BM. (Jan. 21, 1820).
Thomas Ferguson to Rebecca Davis, Oct. 14, 1820.
  (Oct. 15, 1820).
William Gilmore to Precia Gallion, May 6, 1820.
  William Smith, BM. (May 7, 1820).
Caleb Gowing to Polly Dunkin, June 10, 1820.
  Claborn Gowing, BM.
David Gowing to Nancy Dinckin, March 8, 1820.
  William McGill, BM. (March 9, 1820).
David Graham to Polly Fargerson, July 11, 1820.
  John Perrin, BM. (July 16, 1820).
John Grey to Levinia Pinkston, June 10, 1820.
  Carter Henderson, BM.
George Guinn to Elizabeth Brummet, March 15, 1820.
  Elijah Brummet, BM. (April 16, 1820).
Allmand Hall to Polly Corum, March 29, 1820.
  (March 30, 1820).
John Hammac to Sally Sharp, Feb. 20, 1820.
  John B. Stagner, BM. (Feb. 21, 1820).
Ephraim Hammock to Jane Long, Sept. 2, 1820.
  Ephraim Hammock & William Gray, BM.
John Hammock to Dicy Selvedge, Jan. 21, 1820.
  Martin Hammock, BM.
John Hand to Sally Haun, Sept. 12, 1820.
  Jacob Haun, BM. (Sept. 14, 1820).
John Hedrick to Elizabeth Ball, April 6, 1820.
  James Ball, BM. (April 9, 1820).

Edmond Hodge to Sary Noe, April 6, 1820.
  John Hodge, BM.
Jesse Howell to Elinor Millikan, Aug. 25, 1820.
  John Howell, BM. (Aug. 21, 1820).
William Humbard to Elizabeth Golden, March 4, 1820.
  Benjamin Maxfield, BM. (March 5, 1820).
Tandy James to Betsy Cloud, Sept. 23, 1820.
  Thomas Waggoner,BM. (Sept. 30, 1820).
William James to Sally Fox, April 24, 1820.
  George Fox, BM. (April 27, 1820).
Benjamin Johnson to Sally Bledsoe, Dec. 4, 1820.
John Kenedy to Sarah Humbard, March 25, 1820.
  William McCoy, BM. (March 26, 1820).
William Kennedy to Betsy Jonson, Sept. 5, 1820.
  Thomas Johnston, BM. (Sept. 6, 1820).
John Kidwell to Catherine Davis, Jan. 3, 1820.
  William Buckacre,BM.
John Kidwell to Nancy Philips, Dec. 9, 1820.
  John Ramsey, BM. (Dec. 10, 1820).
John W. Lide to Mary E. P. Lipscombe, March 4, 1820.
  Thomas D. Arnold, BM.
Jermiah Lovel to Sarah Smith, March 7, 1820.
  Nathanell Smith, BM.
George H. Macby to Patsy Willis, Sept. 20, 1820.
  Silas Macby, BM. (Sept. 21, 1820).
Edward Maples to Betsey Brock, May 24, 1820.
  William Hammock, BM. (May 24, 1820).
Alxr. McElhany to Polly Payn, April 2, 1820.
  Charles Payn, BM.
John McPhetridge to Margaret Irwin, June 2, 1820.
  William Clark, BM.
Stephen Miller to Jamimah Stubblefield, Sept. 2, 1820.
  David Miller, BM. (Sept. 3, 1820).
John Mullins to Elizabeth Dail, Jan. 13, 1820.
  Abner Dail, BM.
Martin S. Mynatt to Isabel Roberts, June 20, 1820.
  Balser Shirley, BM. (June 20, 1820).
Benjamin Nealy to Patsy Elkins, May 20, 1820.
  Joseph Elkins, BM. (May 21, 1820).
Joseph Noe to Kitty Purkeyfield, Jan. 10, 1820.
  Henry Counce, BM. (Jan. 11, 1820).
William Odle to Peggy Beelor, June 14, 1820.
  Joseph Beelor, BM. (June 16, 1820).
William C. Ore to Elizabeth Moore, Oct. 21, 1820.
  William C. Ore & William Dickson, BM.
Thomas Ray to Betsy Rays, July 5, 1820.
  William T. Tate, BM. (July 9, 1820).
George G. Reed to Charlotte Jarnagin, June 29, 1820.
  Thomas Roddy, BM.
James Roberson to Catharun Mann, April 6, 1820.
  Rolly Dotson, BM.
William Sams to Dicy Dunhaw, March 2, 1820.
  William McGill, BM. (March 2, 1820).

John Scott to Patsey Ivy, Nov. 11, 1820.
Thomas Midkiff, BM. (Nov. 12, 1820).
Booker Shockley to Hannah Dalton, _____, 1820.
Carter Dalton, BM.
James Smith to Nancy Carney, Feb. 9, 1820.
James Smith & Garrot Norris, BM.
John Smith to Eliz th Harris, Nov. 20, 1820.
Jesse Harris, BM (Nov. 23, 1820).
Mathas Vinyard to . rthy Vinyard, March 10, 1820.
Mathias Vinyard & Allman Hall, BM.
Brackston Waters to Malinda Kein, Jan. 22, 1820.
Anderson Kein, BM. (Jan. 22, 1820).
Timnethy Weaver to S rah Smeddy, Jan. 15, 1820.
John Weaver, BM. Jan. 16, 1820).
John Whitlock to Kit y Quinn, Aug. 3, 1820.
Jacob Goldin, BM. (Aug. 10, 1820).
James Yates to Susan Ticely, July 20, 1820.
William Nicely, BM. (July 6, 1820).
Meredy Yates to Delil. h Ray, Aug. 29, 1820.
Samuel Cates, BM. Aug. 29, 1820).

1821

John Acuff to Sabra M: lcoat, Sept. 5, 1821.
Thomas Acuff, BM.
Benjamin Armstrong to Nancy Mitchell, Oct. 8, 1821.
Benjamin Mitchell, BM. (Oct. 8, 1821).
James Arwine to Nancy Lively, Sept. 15, 1821.
Alburtis Arwine, BM. (Sept. 16, 1821).
William L. Atkinson to Eliza Cobb, Sept. 19, 1821.
William J. Anderson, BM.
James Ball to Clarine Rice, Feb. 6, 1821.
John Ball, BM. (Feb. 8, 1821).
Elijah Bibbins to Franky Soloman, Oct. 17, 1821.
John Soloman, BM. (Oct. 18, 1821).
William Boatright to Nancy Morgan, April 28, 1821.
Edward Tate, BM. (April 29, 1821).
Joseph Bullen to Betsy Dolson, June 19, 1821.
Joseph Beeler & Benjamin Fry, BM.
Davis Campbell to Patsey James, Nov. 5, 1821.
John James, BM.
Daniel Cardwell to Martha Easley, Dec. 31, 1821.
T. D. Knight, BM.
John Carney to Elizabeth Chamberling, Dec. 1, 1821.
John Combs, BM. (Dec. 6, 1821).
Samuel Cloud to Betsey Cabbage, April 9, 1821.
Isaac Mayes, BM.
Jesse Cobb to Nancy Mullins, Jan. 30, 1821.
Alexander Bearden - Alex. Rankin, BM.
John Coffey to Rebecah Ragsdel, Feb. 24, 1821.
Jacob Arnett, BM. (Feb. 27, 1821).
John Collins to Lydia Toner, Oct. 8, 1821.
Griffin Collins, BM.

GRAINGER COUNTY MARRIAGES

Pherney Condrey to Peggy Condrey, July 27, 1821.
George Moulder, BM.
Brewis Cox to Susanna Hankins, Dec. 8, 1821.
Ezra Buckner, BM.
Edward Culvehouse to Nancy Coody, Dec. 12, 1821.
Gallant Harris, BM. (Dec. 13, 1821):
William Daniel to Martha Mayse, Nov. 3, 1821.
William E. Cocke, BM. (Nov. 4, 1821).
James Davis to Luise Cockrum, April 13, 1821.
John Davis, BM. (April 22, 1821).
Joseph Dennis to Anna Irvine, May 25, 1821.
John Irvine, BM. (June 10, 1821).
John Dennon to Lifty Hodge, Nov. 5, 1821.
William McGill, BM. (Nov. 15, 1821).
Alexander Dobb to Milly Smith, Feb. 27, 1821.
James Smith, BM.
Benjamin Duncomb to Vita Foster, Dec. 23, 1821.
(Dec. 25, 1821).
Philip Duncomb to Polly Crawford, Oct. 25, 1821.
Benjamin Duncomb, BM. (Oct. 25, 1821).
Philip Dunham to Nancy Price, May 25, 1821.
Lewis Riggs, BM.
James Dyer to Milley Needham, Dec. 6, 1821.
George Dyer, BM. (Dec. 6, 1821).
John Edington to Margat Smith, Dec. 18, 1821.
Allen Smith, BM. (Dec. 19, 1821).
William Elkins to Mary Ann Davis, April 28, 1821.
Anthony Cardwell, BM.
Samuel A. Findley to Lucinda Holt, Jan. 4, 1821.
Thomas Turly, BM. (Jan. 4, 1821).
Benjamin Frye to Elizabeth Burnett, Jan. 13, 1821.
Robert Davis, BM.
Rubin Harris to Dacy Minett, July 1, 1821.
Henry Allsup, BM. (July 1, 1821).
Zepheniah Heins to Anny Chesher, Jan. 17, 1821.
Samuel Humbard, BM. (Jan. 17, 1821).
James Helton to Carry Rail, March 12, 1821.
Aaron Counts, BM.
Rowland Henderson to Elizabeth Cox, Oct. 3, 1821.
Daniel Taylor, BM.
John Hinchey to Patsey Booths, March 31, 1821.
Meredith Coffer, BM. (April 22, 1821).
Francis Hunter to Mary Neill, Dec. 19, 1821.
John Brown, BM.
Thomas Kimbrow to Elizabeth K. Batis, Dec. 31, 1821.
John Newman, BM.
Jacob Lebow to Louisa Henderson, Aug. 20, 1821.
James Mayes, BM.
William Lewis to Martha Smith, Sept. 24, 1821.
Joseph Smith, BM. (Sept. 24, 1821).
John Long to Caty Bealor, Oct. 14, 1821.
William H. Odle, BM.
John Long to Nancy Stubblefield, June 29, 1821.
William Murray, BM.

Silas McBee to Sarah Dyer, Jan. 20, 1821.
  Silas McBee & Owen Dyer, BM. (Feb. 1, 1821).
Jacob McConnel to Betsy Godwin, Nov. 10, 1821.
  Hugh Jones, BM. (Nov. 12, 1821).
John McDowell to Rebecca Capps, Oct. 25, 1821.
  Alexander Williams, BM.
David Meltin to Deedama Hodge, April 18, 1821.
  Richard Blair, BM.
Thomas Midkiff to Almira Midkiff, Feb. 15, 1821.
  Robert Bean, BM. (Feb. 18, 1821).
George Milikin to Betsey Coffman, Jan. 13, 1821.
  Jesse Howell, BM. (Jan. 18, 1821).
Benjamin Mitchell to Anny Lloid, Feb. 10, 1821.
  William Mitchell, BM. (Feb. 17, 1821).
James Nicely to Susan Norris, Jan. 18, 1821.
  John Nicley, BM. (Jan. 18, 1821).
James Parker to Tempy Lane, Sept. 27, 1821.
  John Brown, BM. (Sept. 27, 1821).
Gilbert Percyfield to Sally Spires, March 13, 1821.
  Daniel Hammock, BM.
Leroy Pullen to Hannah Cox, Sept. 25, 1821.
  Francis Williams, BM. (Sept. 27, 1821).
William B. Reese to Sarah McCocke, May 1, 1821.
  William B. Reese, BM.
Daniel Rice to Anny Ray, July 17, 1821.
  Edward Chesser, BM. (July 18, 1821).
Lewis Riggs to Nancy Estis, March 5, 1821.
  Joshua Hicky, BM. (March 6, 1821).
Wiley Robinson to Elizabeth Campbell, Aug. 30, 1821.
  Jesse Countz, BM.
Stanford L. Saunders to Martha Lebow, May 11, 1821.
  Richard Richards, BM.
William Sears to Susanah Childres, Jan. 15, 1821.
  John Perrin, BM. (Jan. 15, 1821).
William Short to Nancy Cassady, May 26, 1821.
  Dixon Smith, BM. (May 26, 1821).
Edward Smith to Elizabeth Dent, Sept. 24, 1821.
  Joseph Smith, BM. (Sept. 25, 1821).
John Sparksman to Ragina Nicely, May 25, 1821.
  James Yates, BM. (May 27, 1821).
Samuel Spencer to Caty Prophett, March 16, 1821.
  David Prophett, BM.
Samuel Thomas to Frances Boman, Feb. 17, 1821.
  Jonathan Dail, BM. (Feb. 18, 1821).
William Thomason to Nancy Yates, Feb. 19, 1821.
  Henry Alsop, BM. (Feb. 20, 1821).
James Vance to Rebecca Robinson, Nov. 1, 1821.
  John Purkipile, BM. (Nov. 1, 1821).
David P. Walker to Jane McKinney, Jan. 29, 1821.
  Caswell Walker, BM. (Feb. 7, 1821).
Thomas Walters to Nancy Walters, Dec. 3, 1821.
  John Waters, BM.
Isaac J. Watkins to Margaret Chamberlin, Aug. 3, 1821.
  Geo. M. Combs, BM. (Aug. 14, 1821).

Seth Webber to Delilah Manly, Dec. 17, 1821.
William Anglea, BM. (Dec. 22, 1821).

1822

Jaramiah Barnett to Sarah York, April 27, 1822.
Andrew Philips, BM. (April 27, 1822).
William Blanset to Patsy Lane, Oct. 2, 1822.
Hugh Jones, BM. (Oct. 2, 1822).
Giles J. Bledsoe to Rody Jarnagin, Dec. 3, 1822.
John Jarnagin, BM.
George Booker to Sally Bond, Jan. 2, 1822.
Thomas Devault, BM. (Jan. 2, 1822).
Nicholas Bowen to Polly May, Nov. 16, 1822.
Armsted Kirk, BM.
Moses Brock to Zephrona Dennis, May 10, 1822.
Edward Brock, BM. (May 12, 1822).
Jerry Brocker to Nancy Culvyhouse, Feb. 22, 1822 (or
Feb. 27, 1822). Garland Norris, BM.
Anthony Cardwell to Mary Perrimon, Nov. 14, 1822.
James Chaney to Sarah Bull, April 27, 1822.
Nathan Shipley, BM. (April 29, 1822).
Elijah Colvin to Susan Moulder, Dec. 3, 1822.
Hayman Claridge, BM. (Dec. 3, 1822).
William Crow to Sarah Taylor, Oct. 19, 1822.
Marrel M. Midkiff, BM.
Carter Dalten to Polly Viditoe, Feb. 25, 1822.
Charlton Dyer, BM. (Feb. 26, 1822).
Rolly Dotson to Marth Johnson, Jan. 4, 1822.
Jaramiah Johnston, BM.
Stephen Dotson to Nancy Parker, Sept. 29, 1822.
John Brown, BM. (Sept. 29, 1822).
Lewis Evans to Barthena Smith, March 25, 1822.
W. M. Smith, BM. (March 25, 1822).
Andrew Ferguson to Nancy Zechery, Dec. 15, 1822.
Edward Churchman, BM. (Dec. 15, 1822).
Thomas Ferguson to Rebecca Davis, Oct. 14, 1822.
Lemuel Floyd to Jane Sutherland, Dec. 30, 1822.
Robert Thomason, BM. (Dec. 31, 1822).
John Frost to Nancey Pate, Jan. 10, 1822.
Charles Chais, BM. (Jan. 10, 1822).
John Garret to Sarah Brevare, July 6, 1822.
Peter Godwin, BM. (July 6, 1822).
John Granlee to Polly Mayse, Jan. 12, 1822.
E. Mayses, BM. (Jan. 12, 1822).
James Hankins to Polly Breaden, Sept. 4, 1822.
Bremas Cox, BM. (Sept. 4, 1822).
Hiram Henderson to Nancey Lewis, Sept. 10, 1822.
Andrew S. McPheters, BM. (Sept. 10, 1822).
Benjamin Howell to Temple Hodge, March 20, 1822.
Jesse Raye, BM.
Samuel Hubberd to Dacas Yates, Aug. 9, 1822.
Jacob Hubberd, BM. (Aug. 9, 1822).

John Hubbs to Nancy Hill, Aug. 8, 1822.
   John Hill, BM. (Aug. 8, 1822).
Charles Hume to Elizabeth Memo, Nov. 20, 1822.
   Thomas McBroom, BM. (Nov. 22, 1822).
James Ivy to Sarah Philips, Dec. 24, 1822.
   James Hail, BM. (Dec. 24, 1822).
James Jack to Easter Dennis, May 21, 1822.
   Levi Dennis, BM. (May 24, 1822).
Thomas Jarnagin to Mary Walker, Nov. 21, 1822.
   William Walker, BM.
John Jennings to Jane Griffits, May 17, 1822.
   Wm. D. Jennings, BM.
Tristram D. Knight to Eliza Gill, March 30, 1822.
   John Brown, BM.
Joseph Leffew to Polly Miller, July 24, 1822.
   William Bunch, BM.
James Lewis to Elizabeth Erby, Sept. 23, 1822.
   Charles Erby, BM.
John Lilley to Elender Brock, Aug. 27, 1822.
   Samuel Casey, BM. (Aug. 27, 1822).
Thomas Loveles to Barthena Russell, June 20, 1822.
   Herman Cox, BM.
Isaac Mansfield to Teney Bowling, Nov. 19, 1822.
   William Reece, BM. (Nov. 19, 1822).
David McAnally, Jr., to Nancy Taylor, April 22, 1822.
   John Long, BM. (April 22, 1822).
Abraham McConnel to Mahala Godwin, May 26, 1822.
   Wm. E. Cocke, BM. (May 26, 1822).
Dan McPheters to Sarah Acuff, Dec. 18, 1822.
   Andrew McPheters, BM. (Dec. 18, 1822).
Manuel Midkiff to Wenney Dyer, Nov. 26, 1822.
   Thomas Dyer, BM.
Martin Miller to Nancy Jennkings, Dec. 27, 1822.
   Joseph Dyer, BM. (Dec. 29, 1822).
Thomas Morris to Polly Golder, Dec. 10, 1822.
   Isaac Harris, BM. (Dec. 10, 1822).
John Orm to Anna Carathers, Feb. 14, 1822.
   David Sharp, BM. (Feb. 14, 1822).
John Petree to Elizabeth Long, Nov. 16, 1822.
   John Long, BM. (Nov. 16, 1822).
John Philips to Sally Mynatt, July 12, 1822.
   James Wilson, BM. (July 12, 1822).
John Polley to Rebecca Channey, Sept. 14, 1822.
   Caleb Gibson, BM. (Sept. 14, 1822).
Washington Rayl to Keziah Howell, April 26, 1822.
   Wm. E. Cocke, BM. (April 26, 1822).
Hardy Schaderick to Caty Miller, July 16, 1822.
   Alfred Carole, BM. (July 16, 1822).
John Sharp to Betsy Bond, Nov. 19, 1822.
   James Clowers, BM. (Nov. 19, 1822).
Sampson Sharp to Katherine Hill, Sept. 19, 1822.
   John Sharp, BM. (Sept. 19, 1822).
Adam Shipley to Lydia Taylor, Dec. 12, 1822.
   John Easterly, BM.

GRAINGER COUNTY MARRIAGES

Archlus Smith to Patsy Warricke, Feb. 15, 1822.
Elias Warricke, BM. (Feb. 15, 1822).
Dickson Smith to Susan McDannel, Nov. 18, 1822.
John Gray, BM. (Nov. 18, 1822).
Charles Sparkman to Sally Bunch, Aug. 19, 1822.
Moses Bright, BM. (Aug. 19, 1822).
George Stubblefield to Elizabeth Kirkham, Aug. 19, 1822.
Raleigh Stubblefield, BM.
George Stubblefield to Mary Johnson, May 15, 1822.
Robert Stubblefield, BM.
James Tallent to Eliza Stone, Aug. 12, 1822.
Mitchel Stone, BM. (Aug. 12, 1822).
Isham Thompson to Rebecca Haulston, Sept. 22, 1822.
Henry Counts, BM.
Robert Tomison to Prudence Crain, Sept. 17, 1822.
William Tomison, BM.
Peter Widner to Polly Lane, Jan. 10, 1822.
Sampson Sharp, BM.
Joseph Wirack to Nancy Rooks, Aug. 8, 1822.
Mitchell Wirick, BM. (Aug. 8, 1822).
John Yates to Frances Carnutt, July 24, 1822.
William Carnutt, BM. (July 24, 1822).

1823

John Atkins to Nelly McElhaney, May 28, 1823.
Joel Philips, BM. (May 28, 1823).
John Beeler to Anna Mefford, Feb. 24, 1823.
Daniel Cardwell, BM.
Henry Bowen to Rachel Mayse, May 6, 1823.
William F. Tate, BM. (May 6, 1823).
John Bowen to Jane Bridgeman, Nov. 7, 1823.
Reese Bowen, BM. (Nov. 7, 1823).
Nicholas Bowen to Polly May, Nov. 16, 1823.
Benard Burnett to Jane Whaling, May 26, 1823.
Josiah Hillinsworth, BM.
Joseph Bushong to Elizabeth Owens, Oct. 2, 1823.
James Hines, BM. (Oct. 2, 1823).
Thomas G. Cardwell to Sarah Easley, May 5, 1823.
Wesley Barton, BM. (May 5, 1823).
Anderson Cates to Elizabeth Combs, Dec. 27, 1823.
Samuel B. Tate, BM. (Dec. 27, 1823).
Stephen Cates to Elizabeth Cassady, Aug. 8, 1823.
James Cassady, BM. (Aug. 8, 1823).
John Clark to Frances Acuff, Feb. 3, 1823.
Joseph Clark, BM. (Feb. 3, 1823).
Joseph Clark to Susan Latham, Dec. 10, 1823.
William Clark, BM.
William Clark to Elizabeth Jennings, June 10, 1823.
Joseph Clark, BM.
William Coleman to Sophy Perryman, Nov. 8, 1823.
Henry Condry, BM. (Nov. 8, 1823).

GRAINGER COUNTY MARRIAGES

John Connor to Fanny Atkins, July 16, 1823.
Enos Hammer, BM. (July 16, 1823).
Moses Crawford to Melinda Churchman, Dec. 29, 1823.
Dotson Morgan, BM. (Dec. 30, 1823).
Wilson C. Denerant to Polly Waddle, Nov. 17, 1823.
John Henderson, BM. (Nov. 17, 1823).
Joseph Dennis to Polly Brown, March 6, 1823.
Meredith Sharp, BM. (March 6, 1823).
John Dent to Nancy Nemoe, Nov. 20, 1823.
Martin Vinyard, BM. (Nov. 20, 1823).
Owen Dyer to Elizabeth Condry, Jan. 16, 1823.
John Sharp, BM. (Jan. 16, 1823).
John Estes to Mary Kidwell, July 16, 1823.
William E. Cocke, BM.
James Griffin to Hetty Douglas, June 14, 1823.
Isaac Bradley, BM.
Lewis Harrell to Patsy Lambdin, March 26, 1823.
David Boulton, BM. (March 26, 1823).
John Hickson to Sarah Pollard, April 9, 1823.
James Malicoat, BM. (April 9, 1823).
William Hill to Mary Dennis, Aug. 2, 1823.
Joel Fields, BM. (Aug. 2, 1823).
Frazer Hodge to Betsy Miller, June 21, 1823.
David Counts, BM. (June 21, 1823).
John Horn to Cintha Martin, July 29, 1823.
Nathan Shipley, BM. (July 29, 1823).
William Ivy to Patsy Clark, Jan. 21, 1823.
James Daniel, BM. (Jan. 21, 1823).
David Kidwell to Elizabeth Boyd, June 20, 1823.
John W. Blake, BM. (June 20, 1823).
James Lewis to Elizabeth Erly, Sept. 23, 1823.
Jese Liveston to Honar Noah, Oct. 28, 1823.
David Counts, BM. (Oct. 28, 1823).
James Mallicoat to Elizabeth Gray, April 21, 1823.
James Mallicoat, BM.
John Malicoat to Cassy Adkins, Dec. 23, 1823.
Dedman Malicoat, BM. (Dec. 23, 1823).
John Maples to Susannah Henderson, Oct. 18, 1823.
Wilson Maples, BM. (Oct. 18, 1823).
Wilson Maples to Nancy Jinnings, April 26, 1823.
Robert Martin to Nancy Handcock, Oct. 7, 1823.
Joel Martin, BM.
John Merrit to Sarah Vittitoe, June 10, 1823.
Joseph Clark, BM. (June 10, 1823).
Robert Martin to Nancy Handcock, Oct. 7, 1823.
Joel Martin, BM.
John Merrit to Sarah Vittitoe, June 10, 1823.
Joseph Clark, BM. (June 10, 1823).
Huch Nance to Pricilla Norris, Oct. 14, 1823.
Richard Richards, BM. (Oct. 14, 1823).
John Nicely to Patsy Cabbage, May 2, 1823.
David Nicely, BM. (May 2, 1823).
Mathias Nicholas to Nansy Ragsdale, July 20, 1823.
Jacob Annett, BM. (July 20, 1823).

John Oakly to Susan Hopper, Jan. 12, 1823.
James Hail, BM. (Jan. 12, 1823).
Andrew Patterson to Milly Goulden, May 13, 1823.
Yathe Smith, BM. (May 14, 1823).
Joab Perrin to Rebecca Churchman, Oct. 11, 1823.
James Clowers, BM.
Joel Philips to Linsey McElhaney, Oct. 8, 1823.
Aaron Counts, BM. (Oct. 8, 1823).
Robert Ray to Sally Inklebarger, Dec. 30, 1823.
Meredith Yates, BM. (Dec. 30, 1823).
David Rentfrow to Letita Mobly, May 5, 1823.
Thomas Havely, BM. (May 5, 1823).
George Rich to Elizabeth Long, Sept. 6, 1823.
Jacob Noe, BM. (Sept. 6, 1823).
John Roach to Sally Romans, Dec. 22, 1823.
Robert Sellers to Mary Idols, Jan. 30, 1823.
John Sellers, BM. (Jan. 30, 1823).
Isaac Semore to Betsy Norris, April 9, 1823.
Hugh Jones, BM. (April 14, 1823).
Meredith Sharp to Elizabeth Dennis, Feb. 11, 1823.
William Dennis, BM.
John Shields to Mary Gill, Sept. 12, 1823.
Thomas Whiteside, BM.
Thomas Solomon to Mahaly Derham, Oct. 14, 1823.
James Lasey, BM. (Oct. 14, 1823).
Martin Spikes to Rachael Capps, Jan. 4, 1823.
Daniel Hammock, BM.
John Spoon to Mahaly Turner, Dec. 30, 1823.
Jese Livingston, BM.
James Talbert to Elizabeth Right, Aug. 5, 1823.
Hugh W. Taylor to Alice Grantham, Jan. 25, 1823.
John Long, BM. (Jan. 25, 1823).
Elisha Thomason to Magdaline Hammer, Nov. 10, 1823.
Jese Counts, BM. (Nov. 10, 1823).
Samuel Waggoner to Sabinna Murry, Nov. 17, 1823.
William P. McBee, BM. (Nov. 17, 1823).
William Walker to Elizabeth Crouse, Nov. 21, 1823.
Samuel Low, BM. (Nov. 21, 1823).
Thomas West to Elizabeth Orr, May 5, 1823.
William Orr, BM. (May 5, 1823).
William Western to Nancy Roberts, Dec. 10, 1823.
David Noe, BM. (Dec. 10, 1823).
John Widener to Hannah Sharp, March 12, 1823.
William Peters, BM. (March 12, 1823).
Ruben Yates to Milly Hughes, Sept. 4, 1823.
James Yates, BM. (Sept. 4, 1823).
Pleasant York to Rachel McFetridge, Nov. 8, 1823.
Jeremiah Burnett, J. P., BM. (Nov. 23, 1823).

1824

Joel Aldridge to Mary Jarnagin, March 2, 1824.
Saml. Lowe - Robert Triston, J.P., BM. (March 2, 1824).

Benjamin Armstrong to Nancy Bratwell, Dec. 18, 1824.
Henry Johns, BM.
Dudley Belton to Janey Rolan, Feb. 29, 1824.
David Counts, BM. (Feb. 29, 1824).
Joab Blake to Debitha Lowe, Dec. 4, 1824.
Jno. Long, BM. (Dec. 4, 1824).
Edmund Boling to Sally Going, Jan. 3, 1824.
Shadrach Going, BM.
Enoch Bowdown to Delilah Hughs, Sept. 24, 1824.
Daniel Cardwell, BM.
George Bowen to Telitha McAnally, Nov. 15, 1824.
T. D. Knight, BM.
Ezekiel Bowling to Nancy Gowing, Dec. 2, 1824.
Pleasant Weston, BM. (Dec. 2, 1824).
William Bowman to Nancy McKahan, Sept. 9, 1824.
David Counts, BM. (Sept. 9, 1824).
Squire Bridges to Elizabeth Powel, Feb. 29, 1824.
Evan Smith, BM. (Feb. 29, 1824).
George Bright to Martha Bowman, Feb. 13, 1824.
Larvos Brocker to Rebecca Grant, Oct. 9, 1824.
William Reeder, BM.
John Brown to Mahala Dennis, Nov. 25, 1824.
Joseph Dennis, BM.
Pryor P. Bunch to Susan Counts, Jan. 12, 1824.
Joseph Loyd, BM. (Jan. 1, 1824).
Winslow W. Bunch to Elizabeth Lyne, Aug. 30, 1824.
William Daniel, BM. (Aug. 30, 1824).
Hughes Cannon to Margaret Irby, Oct. 27, 1824.
James Lewis, BM.
Mary Capps to Mary Evans, July 17, 1824.
John Long, BM. (July 17, 1824).
Joseph Chapman to Elizabeth Walker, May 18, 1824.
Joseph Dyer, BM. (May 18, 1824).
James Clark to Polly Stubblefield, Sept. 25, 1824.
Joseph Stubblefield, BM.
Isaac Cook to Delila Lovel, Aug. 25, 1824.
Jarred Norris, BM.
Henry Counts to Mary Campbell, Nov. 17, 1824.
John Brown, BM. (Nov. 17, 1824).
Jessee Counts to Easter Campbell, Dec. 21, 1824.
Benjamin Craighead, BM.
Henry Crews to Jane Hankins, June 14, 1824.
Thomas Hawley, BM. (June 14, 1824).
John B. Cruise to Anna Cunningham, Feb. 7, 1824.
Robert M. Landrum, BM. (Feb. 7, 1824).
James Damewood to Rachel Seamore, July 7, 1824.
Ebben Dale, BM.
William Davis to Barbary Johnson, July 17, 1824.
Joseph Wyrick, BM. (July 17, 1824).
Greenville Dockery to Sally Davis, Nov. 4, 1824.
Hugh McConnel, BM. (Nov. 4, 1824).
James Dotson to Mary Hommel, Oct. 20, 1824.
John Watkins, BM. (Oct. 20, 1824).

Benjamin Duncomb to Visa Fortner, _____ __, _____
   William Corum, BM.
George Dyer to Dorsey Wilson, Aug. 28, 1824.
   William Dyer, BM. (Aug. 28, 1824).
Elisha Eaton to Dicey Majors, April 19, 1824.
   David Majors, BM.
Archibald Finley to Patsy Hines, March 29, 1824.
   Joseph Renfro, BM. (March 29, 1824).
William Fletcher to Ruth Mitchell, Aug. 24, 1824.
   Paschal Cutts, BM.
Nicholas Gaines to Martha Roberts, Aug. 15, 1824.
   Dennis Roberts, BM.
John Garrison to Sally Houlston, Sept. 13, 1824.
   Ellis Riggs, BM. (Sept. 13, 1824).
Richard F. Griffin to Elizabeth G. Shirley, Dec. 1,
   1824. Daniel Cardwell, BM. (Dec. 1, 1824).
Larkin L. Harrel to Susanna Nash, Feb. 4, 1824.
   William Harrel, BM. (Feb. 4, 1824).
George W. Haun to Jane Martin, Nov. 6, 1824.
   Jno. Haun, BM.
Branham Hill to Sally Moore, March 30, 1824.
John Johns to Sarah Brightwell, Nov. 16, 1824.
   Benjamin Armstrong, BM.
Joshua Johnson to Sarah Dent, July 25, 1824.
   John Dent, BM. (July 25, 1824).
James Jones to Mahala Fortner, Oct. 23, 1824.
William Kennon to Tabitha Ray, Dec. 23, 1824.
William Lemmons to Nancy McCrary, Dec. 20, 1824.
   Abner Trogdon, BM. (Dec. 20, 1824).
John Lovel to Polly Ruckard, Feb. 9, 1824.
   John Lane, BM. (Feb. 9, 1824).
Addison Lowe to Salley Dennis, Sept. 25, 1824.
   Abel Hill, BM. (Sept. 25, 1824).
Henry Mayse to Mary Greenlee, July 10, 1824.
   Edward Mayse, BM. (July 10, 1824).
William Mitchell to Ruth Mitchell, Aug. 24, 1824.
Mitchell Myers to Matilda King, April 19, 1824.
   Peter Harris, BM.
William Mynatt to Margarite Wilson, Aug. 11, 1824.
   Thos. Mynate, BM. (Aug. 11, 1824).
William Newman to Elizabeth Francis, July 31, 1824.
   Griffin Dobbins, BM. (July 31, 1824).
Archibald Nichols to Diedima Mitchell, June 7, 1824.
   Elijah Mitchell, BM.
Isaac Nichols to Jane Thomason, March 2, 1824.
   William Thomas, BM.
George Norris to Elizabeth Robertson, Dec. 7, 1824.
   Hugh Vance, BM. (Dec. 7, 1824).
W. M. Norris, Senr. to Betsy Culvahouse, Oct. 19, 1824.
   Peter Wyrick, BM. (Oct. 19, 1824).
Benjamin Owens to Phebe Parker, May 18, 1824.
   Levi Miller, BM. (May 18, 1824).
James Parker to Mary Yarvis, March 4, 1824.
   William Yarvis, BM. (March 4, 1824).

GRAINGER COUNTY MARRIAGES

William Parker to Anna Hollinsworth, Aug. 5, 1824.
   Josiah Hollinsworth, BM.
Thomas Pharoh to Frances Spencer, Feb. 27, 1824.
   Samuel B. Tate, BM.
William Reynolds to Jane Moore, Jan. 14, 1824.
Russel C. Smallwood to Rhoda Hankins, Sept. 11, 1824.
   Thomas D. Mortan, BM.
Joseph Smith to Elizabeth Tuttle, Nov. 27, 1824.
   Peter Boulton, BM.
Thomas Smith to Mary Johnson, Jan. 27, 1824.
   David Coats, BM.
William Spoonard to Mary Ellis, Oct. 4, 1824.
   John Long, BM. (Oct. 24, 1824).
Samuel Stearns to Pricilla Newman, Sept. 8, 1824.
   Robert Cutts, BM. (Sept. 8, 1824).
Wm. Thomason to Nancy Hinghs, Dec. 27, 1824.
   Hardiman Sparkman, BM. (Dec. 27, 1824).
Jacob Vineyard to Susan Nance, Jan. 3, 1824.
   Martin Vineyard, BM.
Elisha Walker to Rachel Daniel, Aug. 11, 1824.
   Samuel Dotson, BM.
John Watkins to Mourming Johnson, Dec. 23, 1824.
   Wm. E. Cocke, BM.
William Wickliff to Mary Jonas, Feb. 27, 1824.
   Bolser Shirley, BM. (Feb. 27, 1824).
William Williamson to Mahaly Jarnagin, Jan. 27, 1824.
   Wm. Cocke, BM. (Jan. 27, 1824).
Samuel Wyrick to Peggy Wyrick, June 29, 1824.
   Andrew Wyrick, BM. (June 29, 1824).
Henry Young to Meriah Rogers, April 20, 1824.
   Warham Easley, BM. (April 20, 1824).
James Zachery to Elizabeth Elkins, Sept. 28, 1824.
   William Zachery, BM. (Sept. 28, 1824).

1825

Daniel Beeler to Wyney Wolfenbarger, Nov. 25, 1825.
Charles R. Bittle to Elizabeth Greenlee, Dec. 6, 1825.
   Saml. Pollard, BM. (Dec. 6, 1825).
Joseph Blair to Aly Hunter, Nov. 30, 1825.
   Henry Wyrick, BM. (Nov. 30, 1825).
Alexander Boling to Mary Gilmore, Feb. 27, 1825.
   David Coats, BM. (Feb. 27, 1825).
David Bowen to Elizabeth Dennis, Oct. 8, 1825.
   William Carder, BM. (Oct. 8, 1825).
Reece Bowers to Mary Moody, April 4, 1825.
   Warham Easley, BM. (April 4, 1825).
Barry Caits to Delia Briant, April 30, 1825.
   Claiborne Latham, BM. (April 30, 1825).
Milton Cheek to Patsy McCarroll, Dec. 31, 1825.
   John Jennings, BM.
Jesee Coats to Nancy Hammock, Dec. 17, 1825.
   Presley Barret, BM.

Massey Cockram to Rachel Churchman, Oct. 3, 1825.
James Coffee to Sally Fielding, Dec. 14, 1825.
  John Coffee, BM. (Dec. 14, 1825).
Addison Collingsworth to Francis Combs, Dec. 11, 1825.
  Robert Loyd, BM. (Dec. 11, 1825).
James Collins to Elizabeth Martin, Jan. 17, 1825.
  William Benney, BM. (Jan. 17, 1825).
Isaac Condry to Rebeccah Haynes, April 9, 1825.
  William Easley, BM. (April 9, 1825).
Howell Crews to Sarah O. Kirkham, June 28, 1825.
  Rase Bowen, BM.
Isaac Damewood to Mildred Seamore, Sept. 22, 1825.
  James Damewood, BM. (Sept. 22, 1825).
James Davis to Hannah Helton, Jan. 24, 1825.
  John Davis, BM.
Clabourn Dotson to Ellen Mallicoat, Nov. 18, 1825.
  Saml. Dotson, BM.
Jesee Evans to Nancy Counts, April 20, 1825.
  Richard Williams, BM.
Edward Ferguson to Elizabeth Mills, April 8, 1825.
  Thomas Neegin, BM. (April 8, 1825).
Robert Gibbons to Polly Creely, Sept. 23, 1825.
  Abraham Connel, BM.
Zachariah Glassup to Nancy Ivy, Oct. 3, 1825.
  John Satterfield, BM. (Oct. 3, 1825).
Levi Going to Nancy Dickson, Dec. 8, 1825.
  John Satterfield, BM. (Dec. 8, 1825).
Austin H. Green to Jasuetha Barrett, Oct. 8, 1825.
  (Oct. 8, 1825).
Samuel Griffin to Sally Caveriden, Aug. 5, 1825.
  Jacob Daniel, BM. (Aug. 5, 1825).
Henry Grub to Saley Waddell, Sept. 10, 1825.
  Wilson Dunevan, BM.
James R. Haggard to Jane Loyd, June 15, 1825.
  Wm. Moody, BM.
John Harbin to Linda Boling, June 8, 1825.
  Robt. Mitchell, BM. (June 8, 1825).
Henry Harpole to Rachel Parker, Sept. 28, 1825.
  Trestron D. Knight, BM. (Sept. 28, 1825).
Zachariah Hinds to Sally Brastly, Oct. 13, 1825.
  Noel B. Hinds, BM. (Oct. 13, 1825).
William P. Humbard to Margaret Eaton, Feb. 8, 1825.
  Andrew C. Eaton, BM. (Feb. 8, 1825).
Chesley Jarnagin to Martha Gill, Jan. 21, 1825.
  William Winstead, BM. (Jan. 21, 1825).
Francis E. Jarnagin to Elleanor M. Curl, Dec. 19, 1825.
  Andrew C. Eaton, BM. (Dec. 19, 1825).
Samuel Johns to Jane Harris, July 13, 1825.
  Charles N. Peck, BM. (July 13, 1825).
John Johnson to Milla Smith, April 9, 1825.
  Edward Smith, BM. (April 9, 1825).
Wm. P. Kendrick to Macah Clay, April 21, 1825.
  Eph. Hightower, BM.

GRAINGER COUNTY MARRIAGES

William Kirkpatrick to Alice Ferguson, March 12, 1825.
Jno. Marshal, BM. (March 12, 1825).
Pleasant H. Lefew to Nelly Rook, Feb. 21, 1825.
Jacob Ruth, BM.
Jese Lemmons to Nancy Blair, Nov. 20, 1825.
Henry Wyrick, BM.
James Long to Viney Johnson, July 15, 1825.
Ephriam Hammock, BM. (July 15, 1825).
Lauren Long to Polly Shropshire, July 20, 1825.
Jacob Noe, BM. (July 20, 1825).
Samuel Lowe to Catherine Hawkins, March 1, 1825.
Benjamin Craighead, BM. (March 1, 1825).
Robert Martin to Betsy Jack, Nov. 5, 1825.
William Martin, BM.
Isaac F. McCarty to Ellen M. Williams, Dec. 16, 1825.
James B. Williams, BM.
Isaac Neil to Cloe Perrin, Oct. 12, 1825.
Robert Howard, BM.
Hiram M. Nemore to Temple M. Dent, Oct. 1, 1825.
William Carnutt, BM. (Oct. 1, 1825).
Mathias Nichols to Alice Mittan, Dec. 23, 1825.
Andrew McPheters, BM. (Dec. 23, 1825).
Solomon Noe to Mahaly Norman, July 14, 1825.
W. M. Roberts, BM. (July 14, 1825).
Hugh Peters to Mary Pratt, Feb. 17, 1825.
Willis Pratt, BM. (Feb. 17, 1825).
John Popejoy to Elizabeth Widener, Sept. 17, 1825.
Hugh Jones, BM. (Sept. 17, 1825).
John Purkapile to Sarah Estes, Feb. 6, 1825.
Joseph Noe, BM. (Feb. 6, 1825).
Joseph Richards to Flora Mullins, Oct. 22, 1825.
David Beeler, BM. (Oct. 22, 1825).
Thomas Richards to Elizabeth Williams, Aug. 24, 1825.
Robert Franklin, BM. (Aug. 24, 1825).
William Roach to Margaret Watson, May 14, 1825.
John Richard, BM. (May 14, 1825).
Edmund Rucker to Polly Bentley, Sept. 26, 1825.
James Harris, BM. (Sept. 26, 1825).
William Sanders to Jane Thompson, Dec. 12, 1825.
John Talbott, BM. (Dec. 12, 1825).
Daniel Smith to Martha Boman, Dec. 24, 1825.
Aaron Counts, BM.
John Stewart to Jane Williams, June 14, 1825.
William Burge, BM.
Samuel Thomas to Sally McElhaney, Oct. 13, 1825.
Robert Mitchell, BM. (Oct. 13, 1825).
Martin Vineyard to Jane Nance, July 17, 1825.
John Renfro, BM. (July 17, 1825).
William Warden to Delia Edmons, Nov. 16, 1825.
Morgan Poindexter, BM. (Nov. 16, 1825).
James L. Warren to Jane Taylor, May 10, 1825.
William Taylor, BM. (May 10, 1825).
John L. Watson to Mary Turner, Jan. 5, 1825.
Dennis Roberts, BM.

John Williams to Edys Steward, May 7, 1825.
Nineon Riggs, BM. (May 7, 1825).
Joseph Williams to Polly Clark, Sept. 23, 1825.
John Williams, BM. (Sept. 23, 1825).
John Wyrick to Mary Mullins, July 16, 1825.
Philip Wyrick, BM.
Henry Wysnor to Martha Gowins, Jan. 31, 1825.
Drury Gowin, BM. (Jan. 31, 1825).
Meredith Yeats to Patsy Sparkman, Dec. 29, 1825.
Charles Sparkman, BM. (Dec. 29, 1825).

1826

Jeremiah Acuff to Rebeccah Caits, Dec. 8, 1826.
Thos. Acuff, BM.
James Barnard to Peggy Ball, Jan. 1, 1826.
John Mills, BM. (Jan. 1, 1826).
Allen Bates to Mary Helton, June 12, 1826.
Alexander Bates, BM.
Isaac Beeler to Polly Wolfenbarger, Dec. 28, 1826.
Jacob Beeler, BM.
George Bright to Martha Boman, Feb. 13, 1826.
Henry Holt, BM. (Feb. 13, 1826).
Humphrey Brumfield to Mary Ann King, Feb. 20, 1826.
John Philips, BM.
Ezekiel Butcher to Sarah Evans, Jan. 21, 1826.
Isaac Butcher, BM. (Jan. 21, 1826).
Daniel Carmical to Prudance Howell, May 10, 1826.
Joshua Hickey, BM. (May 10, 1826).
Charles Cates to Elizabeth Loyd, April 4, 1826.
Robert Loyd, BM. (April 4, 1826).
James Colvin to Barcary Phipps, Dec. 14, 1826.
James Phipps, BM. (Dec. 14, 1826).
John Combs to Dorcus Cox, Sept. 11, 1826.
John Talbot, BM. (Sept. 11, 1826).
John Culvahouse to Frances Smith, Dec. 23, 1826.
Frederick Smith, BM.
William Daughty to Dolly Spoon, Jan. 26, 1826.
John Spoon, BM.
Henry Donahugh to Sarah Gill, May 22, 1826.
Samuel Jack, BM. (May 22, 1826).
James England to Elizabeth Roe, Feb. 6, 1826.
Martin Johnson, BM. (Feb. 6, 1826).
John Ford to Matilda Ford, June 13, 1826.
Jacob Perkipile, BM. (June 13, 1826).
Jonathan Glosupp to Sarah Aldridge, July 14, 1826.
Wiley B. Roberson, BM.
Philips R. Haley to Sarah Hawkins, May 4, 1826.
Claiborne Acuff, BM.
A. Hall to Polly Coram, March 29, 1826.
Mathias Vineyard, BM.
Benjamin Hancock to Mary Butler, March 24, 1826.
Jas. Hancock, BM. (March 24, 1826).

Henry Hoffar to Sally Hawkins, July 17, 1826.
W. M. Brown, BM. (July 17, 1826).
Thomas Hopper to America Ertic, Sept. 28, 1826.
Robert Mitchel, BM.
James Irby to Elizabeth Cannon, Jan. 18, 1826.
James Lewis, BM.
Caswel Jarnagin to Elizabeth Bowen, Nov. 6, 1826.
Benj. Craighead, BM. (Nov. 6, 1826).
James Joice to Nancy Morse, July 19, 1826.
Dudley Belton, BM.
William Keen to Elendor Walters, Nov. 29, 1826.
John Wealters, BM. (Nov. 29, 1826).
Lawson Long to Mary Long, July 17, 1826.
John Harris, BM. (July 17, 1826).
Samuel Love to Elizabeth West, Nov. 13, 1826.
James West, BM.
Wm. Kennon to Talitha Ray, Dec. 23, 1826.
Robert Ray, BM. (Dec. 24, 1826).
Hugh McElhany to Elizabeth Philips, Feb. 2, 1826.
Henry Counts, BM. (Feb. 2, 1826).
Alexander McFarlin to Jane Long, Sept. 16, 1826.
Wm. Taylor, BM.
Daniel McPhetridge to Rebeccah Hamilton, June 30, 1826.
Edward Clark, BM. (June 30, 1826).
John Miller to Tempy Hunter, Sept. 25, 1826.
Hugh Jones, BM. (Sept. 25, 1826).
Obediah Miller to Susan Breeding, Sept. 6, 1826.
L. B. Combs, BM.
Randolph Murphy to Polly Miller, Sept. 4, 1826.
Frazier Hodge, BM. (Sept. 4, 1826).
William Murphy to Susan Boatright, June 13, 1826.
Hugh Taylor, BM. (June 13, 1826).
William Neal to Amelia Moody, Sept. 25, 1826.
Henry Fry, BM. (Sept. 25, 1826).
John Noe to Mary Percapile, Sept. 27, 1826.
Samuel Carmical, BM. (Sept. 27, 1826).
Jese Parsley to Polly Ray, Aug. 23, 1826.
David Ray, BM.
Charles L. Peck to Louisa Lathim, Sept. 25, 1826.
Wm. E. Coke, BM. (Sept. 25, 1826).
William Philipa to Ruthey McElhaney, May 11, 1826.
Hugh McElhaney, BM. (May 11, 1826).
George Robinson to Anny Norris, Feb. 8, 1826.
George Norris, BM. (Feb. 8, 1826).
Ambrose B. Rookard to Elizabeth Lane, March 5, 1826.
James Norris, BM.
James Shields to Mary Cobb, Sept. 1, 1826.
John Shields, BM.
John Short to Elizabeth Long, July 12, 1826.
Perlemore Long, BM.
Fielding Smiddy to Sarah Hughes, Sept. 15, 1826.
James G. Harris, BM. (Sept. 15, 1826).
John Spoon to Sarah Kidwell, Feb. 15, 1826.
David Counts, BM.

GRAINGER COUNTY MARRIAGES

Amos Stallsley to Catharine Murphy, Dec. 26, 1826.
  Robert Lemmons, BM. (Dec. 26, 1826).
Joshua W. Stephens to Louisa Cain, Sept. 21, 1826.
  William McCallum, BM.
Andrew Stroud to Nancy Livingston, Sept. 9, 1826.
  Thos. Stroud, BM.
Peter Thacker to Catey Fain, April 21, 1826.
  Clabourne Latham, BM. (April 21, 1826).
Martin Vinyard to Dorothy Morris, March 10, 1826.
David Watson to Lucritia Free, Feb. 11, 1826.
  Lemuel Branson, BM. (Feb. 14, 1826).
Pleasant Weston to Mary Jones, June 20, 1826.
  William B. Bowen, BM.
George Witt to Emmy Taylor, Feb. 21, 1826.
  John Kirkham, BM.

1827

Franky Acuff to Maser Garner, March 5, 1827.
  James Mallicoat, BM. (March 5, 1827).
William Atkins to Polly B. Floyd, Jan. 9, 1827.
Thomas Blackburn to Polly Moulder, April 11, 1827.
  Jacob Capps, BM. (April 11, 1827).
Richard Boatman to Sidney Darnold, Nov. 24, 1827.
  William Boatman, BM. (Nov. 24, 1827).
John Bradley to May Humbard, June 16, 1827.
  William Humbard, BM. (June 16, 1827).
Benjamin Bray to Catherine Ogan, April 8, 1827.
  Joseph C. Bunch, BM. (April 8, 1827).
Hugh Cain to Lucinda Holston, Sept. 5, 1827.
  Henry Holston, BM.
George Campbell to Seney Evans, Jan. 8, 1827.
  Pryor Harvey, BM.
John Carden to Sally McPhetridge, Sept. 23, 1827.
  John F. Huddleston, BM.
John Chase to Nancy Campbell, March 20, 1827.
  James Campbell, BM.
Lewis Coats to Parthena Hynds, Oct. 20, 1827.
  James Campbell, BM. (Oct. 20, 1827).
Allen Collins to Biddy Collins, Oct. 24, 1827.
  Moses Collins, BM. (Oct. 24, 1827).
Homar Condry to Myra Branson, Sept. 15, 1827.
  Lathim Blackburn, BM. (Sept. 15, 1827).
Thornton Coram to Anna Gaines, March 9, 1827.
  Milton Yate, BM.
John Cornut to Savary Moser, Feb. 19, 1827.
  Wm. Carnut, BM. (Feb. 19, 1827).
Martin Corum to Rebecca Carruthers, Nov. 10, 1827.
  Thornton Corum, BM.
Benjamin Covender to Sally Nance, Dec. 26, 1827.
  Martin Vineyard, BM.
John Crain, Jr. to Elizabeth Lemmons, March 11, 1827.
  Thomas Ray, Jr., BM. (March 11, 1827).

60

John Culverhouse to Elizabeth Dale, Sept. 14,1827.
Charles Hume, BM. (Sept. 14, 1827).
John Douglas to Rachael West, Feb. 13, 1827.
Samuel West, BM. (Feb. 13, 1827).
William Dove to Delia Clapp, Nov. 5, 1827.
Henry Carr, BM.
William Easley to Elizabeth Curl, Jan. 3, 1827.
Thomas Wier, BM.
Lewis N. Ellis to Sally Jennings, Sept. 4, 1827.
Bechman Bunch, BM. (Sept. 4, 1827).
William Estis to Catharine Levington, Jan. 15, 1827.
Jacob Kline, BM. (Jan. 15, 1827).
Acy Evans to Rebeccah Phipps, Feb. 5, 1827.
James Cheek, BM. (Feb. 5, 1827).
William Fielding to Letty Casey, Nov. 19, 1827.
James Fielding, BM.
Fracom Garison to Heziat White, April 9, 1827.
William White, BM. (April 9, 1827).
Jonathan Glossupp to Sarah Aldridge, July 14, 1827.
John Godwin to Parthena Barton, March 1, 1827.
Joseph Proffitt, BM.
Douglas Grady to Patsy Briant, Oct. 10, 1827.
Charles Pain, BM. (Oct. 10, 1827).
Willis Grantham to Kessire Stubblefield, Aug. 9, 1827.
Lefer Long, BM. (Aug. 9, 1827).
John Grean to Mariah Grant, July 27, 1827.
David Vineyard, BM.
Edwin Hancoke to Nancy Lipscomb, Jan. 6, 1827.
James Hancocke, BM.
Elijah S. Harrell to Susan Hightower, May 8, 1827.
Abner Hightower, BM.
John Hedrick to Lucinda Hipshear, Feb. 13, 1827.
Elijah Hipshear, BM. (Feb. 13, 1827).
Jonathan Henshaw to Happy Jones, Aug. 2, 1827.
James Briant, BM.
Joshua Henshaw to Mary Mitchell, Sept. 23, 1827.
Martin H. Benson, BM. (Sept. 23, 1827).
Jacob Hipshear to Matilda Hays, Nov. 19, 1827.
Thomas Hays, BM.
William Holston to Catherine Dyke, March 27, 1827.
Jacob Dyke, BM. (March 27, 1827).
James Hundley to Sally Savage, March 21, 1827.
Richard Oaks, BM. (March 21, 1827).
James James to Mary Smith, Nov. 13, 1827.
James Purkey, BM. (Nov. 13, 1827).
Isaac Janeway to Jane Smith, Aug. 18, 1827.
William Rader, BM. (Aug. 18, 1827).
Thomas January to Margaret Taylor, Dec. 30, 1827.
Isaac January, BM.
Pleasant Jennings to Abey Cleveland, Jan. 4, 1827.
Stephen Dotson, BM.
James Ketch to Julian Barrow, Aug. 8, 1827.
William Busby, BM.

Clabourn W. Latham to Mary Ann McGinnis, Aug. 16, 1827.
Josiah Bunch, BM.
Isaac Lebow to Sarah Gray, Dec. 4, 1827.
Hugh Holston, BM. (Dec. 4, 1827).
Seth Lewis to Sarah Branson, May 18, 1827.
Benj. Lewis, BM.
Nehemiah Magic to Elizabeth Briant, Oct. 14, 1827.
Wesley Smith, BM. (Oct. 14, 1827).
David McCoy to Carolin Wolf, Oct. 24, 1827.
Andrew McGinnis, BM.
John Miriate to Martha Richardson, Feb. 17, 1827.
James Wilson, BM.
Aquilla Mitchell to Nancy Harris, July 29, 1827.
William Mitchell, BM.
Robert Monroe to Sally Burnet, April 28, 1827.
Presley Burnet, BM.
Joseph Mynatt to Hepsia Brown, Nov. 26, 1827.
Andrew Ferguson, BM. (Nov. 26, 1827).
Clement C. Nance to Elizabeth Philipps, June 11, 1827.
Willis J. Brady, BM.
Deadman Nash to Polly Chandler, Feb. 8, 1827.
Thomas Nash, BM.
Alfred Neadham to Polly Dyer, Nov. 15, 1827.
James Dyer, BM. (Nov. 15, 1827).
Mathias Nickels to Gabarella Perry, Dec. 26, 1827.
Jacob Phips to Sally Kits, Sept. 3, 1827.
Thomas C. Cocke, BM.
Gabriel Proffitt to Catherin Long, Jan. 3, 1827.
John Short, BM.
Joseph Proffitt to Margaret Godwin, March 1, 1827.
John Godwin, BM.
Joseph Purkey to Frances Casady, April 6, 1827.
William Briant, BM. (April 6, 1827).
Jarren Rhea to Berty Thomason, Aug. 26, 1827.
William Thomason, BM. (Aug. 26, 1827).
John Rubble to Elizabeth Mefford, Feb. 5, 1827.
Reece Williams, BM. (Feb. 5, 1827).
Joseph Simmons to Catherine Cotner, July 21, 1827.
Green Spencer, BM.
Moses Smith to Jane Fielding, May 30, 1827.
Thomas Smith, BM. (May 30, 1827).
Hardeman Sparkman to Mira Coffee, Aug. 6, 1827.
John Sparkman, BM. (Aug. 6, 1827).
Micial Sparkman to Jane Ray, Dec. 4, 1827.
Meredith Yates, BM.
John Stalsworth to Amy Mitchell, Oct. 31, 1827.
James Brye, BM. (Oct. 31, 1827).
Michael W. Stone to Sarah Campbell, March 20, 1827.
James Campbell, BM. (March 20, 1827).
Nathaniel Thacker to Mary Malicoat, Jan. 4, 1827.
Josiah Bunch, BM.
Adam Thompson to Malinda Kirk, Oct. 13, 1827.
Samuel Thornburgh to Sarah Moody, May 19, 1827.
Wm. E. Cocke, BM. (May 19, 1827).

GRAINGER COUNTY MARRIAGES

Henry Tindall to Polly Butcher, Feb. 3, 1827.
Isaac Butcher, BM.
William C. Watson to Easter Beeler, Dec. 24, 1827.
Benj. Craighead, BM.
James S. West to Mary Ore, April 11, 1827.
Thomas West, BM. (April 11, 1827).
Alfred Youngblood to Matilda Mann, Feb. 14, 1827.
John Shields, BM. (Feb. 14, 1827).

1828

Winright Atkins to Sally Claunch, Nov. 11, 1828.
John Mallicoat, BM. (Nov. 13, 1828).
Henry T. Booker to Dolly Lane, Jan. 9, 1828.
James Jones, BM. (Jan. 9, 1828).
Edward Breeden to Eve Sowers, Feb. 18, 1828.
John Willis, BM. (Feb. 18, 1828).
Samuel C. Bunch to Parthena P. Jarnagin, Jan. 29, 1828.
William Cardwell, BM. (Jan. 29, 1828).
Barton Coffman to Polly White, March 5, 1828.
David Counts, BM. (March 5, 1828).
Conley Collins to Comfort Nickles, April 26, 1828.
Winston Painter, BM.
George Collins to Mariah Carback, June 7, 1828.
Thomas Carback, BM.
Benjamin Craighead to Orlena P. Bunch, Nov. 11, 1828.
Wm. L. Cardwell, BM. (Nov. 11, 1828).
Lewis Culvehouse to Francis Smith, March 29, 1828.
Nathan Grear, BM.
William H. Curl to Anna Jarnagin, Sept. 22, 1828.
William Aldridge, BM.
Timothy Dalton to Dilpha Coffee, Dec. 29, 1828.
Meredith Dalton, BM.
Robert Daniel to Elizabeth Grant, Oct. 22, 1828.
W. Bradshaw, BM.
James Davis, Jr. to Polly Stalsworth, July 15, 1828.
Samuel Holston, BM.
Joseph Dennis, Jr. to Bohamas Hardin, Feb. 25, 1828.
David Bowers, BM. (Feb. 25, 1828).
William Dotson to Matilda McAnally, Jan. 14, 1828.
William L. Cardwell, BM.
James Dyer, Junr. to Stacy Elkins, Feb. 5, 1828.
William T. Carden, BM. (Feb. 5, 1828).
Richard Ferguson to Elender Willis, Nov. 20, 1828.
Robert Loyd, BM. (Nov. 20, 1828).
Robert Franklin to Mary Blain, Sept. 26, 1828.
Hugh Houston, BM. (Sept. 26, 1828).
Nathan Grear to Jinsey Grant, Aug. 2, 1828.
John Crouse, BM. (Aug. 3, 1828).
Madison Griffin to Synthia McBride, Jan. 5, 1828.
Jacob Griffin, BM. (Jan. 5, 1828).
James Hancock to Elizabeth Martin, Jan. 17, 1828.
Isaac Dyer, BM. (Jan. 17, 1828).

Samuel Harmon to Patsy Acuff, Dec. 16, 1828.
 Andrew S. McPheters, BM.
John C. Harris (or Harrison) to Lucinda Right,
 Sept. 10, 1828. David Johnson, BM. (Sept. 10, 1828
 or Sept. 14).
Alexander Higgs to Sarah Hynds, Jan. 13, 1828.
Milton Irby to Jane Thacker, Aug. 9, 1828.
 John Irby, BM.
Ewel Jordan to Elizabeth McCoy, June 13, 1828.
 George Wolf, BM.
Joshua Kidwell to Jane Mayes, Oct. 14, 1828.
 John Ivey, BM. (Oct. 14, 1828).
Thomas Lamon to Eliza McKinny, Jan. 29, 1828.
 William Lamon, BM. (Jan. 29, 1828).
William Lephew to Barbary Grady, March 31, 1828.
 (March 31, 1828).
David Lively to Catharin Arnwine, Feb. 25, 1828.
 James Arwine, BM.
James K. Mallicoat to Nancy Martin, March 11, 1828.
 W. M. Mallicoat, BM.
James Manis to Polly Holt, April 15, 1828.
 Isaiah Midkiff, BM. (April 15, 1828).
James Martin to Nancy Spoon, Feb. 8, 1828.
 David Counts, BM. (Feb. 8, 1828).
Jonathan Martin to Peggy Hickman, Dec. 27, 1828.
 William Boatright, BM.
James McDaniel to Nancy Hayes, April 17, 1828.
 James Jackson, BM.
Jesse McPheters to Cynthia Posey, Dec. 22, 1828.
 Thos. Stokley, BM. (Dec. 22, 1828).
James W. Netherland to Ann Virginia Lipscomb,
 June 5, 1828. John W. Lyde, BM.
John Perry to Mary E. C. McConnel, June 15, 1828.
 James Tomlinson, BM.
William Price to Mary Ann Large,' June 4, 1828.
 Thomas Hawley, BM. (June 4, 1828).
John Purkey to Mary Hodge, May 7, 1828.
 James Hodge, BM.
Lewis Raines to Elizabeth Proffitt, Dec. 25, 1828.
 Joseph Proffitt, BM.
Lewis Reynolds to Elender Ball, Dec. 1, 1828.
 Joshua Hickey, BM. (Dec. 1, 1828).
William Reynolds to Sally Waddle, Dec. 1, 1828.
 David Waddle, BM. (Dec. 1, 1828).
John Rice to Winneyford Stubblefield, March 24, 1828.
 Young L. Long, BM.
John W. Rogers to Kesizah Harris, Jan. 8, 1828.
 Thomas Robertson, BM.
Henry Salling to Elizabeth Branston, Oct. 22, 1828.
 Solomon Branson, BM. (Oct. 22, 1828).
Ambrose Sanderland to Martha Findley, April 22, 1828.
 James Davis, BM.
Harmon Sanders to Mary Bettis, July 8, 1828.
 John Sanders, BM. (July 8, 1828).

Samuel Smith to Elizabeth Dyer, May 28, 1828.
Thomas Smith, BM. (May 28, 1828).
Abraham Spoon to Betsy Ford, Sept. 10, 1828.
.Jonathan Noe, BM. (Sept. 10, 1828).
James Strange to Mary Strange, Jan. 12, 1828.
John Lafferty, BM.
John Talbott to Barsheba Cobb, May 13, 1828.
Jacob P. Chase, BM. (May 13, 1828).
Samuel B. Tate to Caroline Senter, May 8, 1828.
Wm. L. Cardwell, BM. (May 8, 1828).
Richard Taylor to Anney Shipley, Nov. 19, 1828.
Frances Williams, BM. (Nov. 19, 1828).
John Thomason to Polly Nickles, Nov. 20, 1828.
Abraham Nickles, BM.
Abraham Thompson to Malinda Kirk, Oct. 13, 1828.
Daniel Widdows, BM.
James Trout to Elizabeth Lane, March 13, 1828.
James Cassady, BM. (March 13, 1828).
Samuel Watson to Mariah Ann Carback, Sept. 17, 1828.
William Roach, BM. (Sept. 17, 1828).
David Williamson to Alta Mincy Henderson, March 27, 1828.
Robert Wyrick to Anny Grear, May 10, 1828.
William Coffman, BM.

1829

Charles Acuff to Elizabeth Long, Nov. 14, 1829.
Andrew C. Eaton, BM.
George Adkins to Catherine Kitts, Feb. 3, 1829.
Alexander McElhaney, BM. (Feb. 3, 1829).
Isaac Agy to Hannah Bounds, Oct. 7, 1829.
John Archer, BM. (Oct. 7, 1829).
John Anderson to Mary Cothern, April 16, 1829.
Balser Sherley, BM.
Moses Atkins to Polly Phipps, April 27, 1829.
Hugh Jones, BM. (April 27, 1829).
Aaron Bean to Catherine Carwiles, Feb. 22, 1829.
Robt. Mitchell, BM.
John Bowers to Cloe Arwine, March 11, 1829.
Andrew Bowers, BM.
John Bradley to Hannah Churchman, Sept. 9, 1829.
Pierce Bradshaw, BM.
Isaac Bullin to Mary Dotson, Nov. 3, 1829.
Joseph Bullin, BM.
Stephen Butler to Mary A. Shirley, Sept. 27, 1829.
Andy E. Eaton, BM. (Sept. 27, 1829).
John Campbell to Sarah Burnett, Jan. 25, 1829.
Josiah C. Bunch, BM. (Jan. 25, 1829).
Wm. L. Cardwell to Mary Ann G. Bittle, Dec. 15, 1829.
Robt. Masengill, BM.
William B. Carmichal to Margaret Patterson, Nov. 7, 1829.
Thomas Patterson, BM. (Nov. 12, 1829).

David Carnutt to Drucilla Johnston, Feb. 20, 1829.
William Carnutt, BM.
Joseph Clipper to Nancy Beverly, Aug. 15, 1829.
Isaac Kline, BM.
Joel Coffee to Elizabeth Grubb, Feb. 5, 1829.
Jacob Grubb, BM.
John Davis to Elizabeth Goins, Aug. 18, 1829.
Henry Alsup, BM. (Aug. 19, 1829).
John Davis to Mary Ann Manley, Dec. 12, 1829.
Madison Kirk, BM. (Dec. 13, 1829).
William Dennis to Hannah Dyer, June 10, 1829.
Isaac Damewood, BM.
Samuel Dotson, Jr. to Syntha Sellers, Jan. 22, 1829.
Ruben Dotson, BM.
Wilson Dyer to Rebecca Morgan, Nov. 14, 1829.
William Dyer, BM.
Ambrose Evans to Louisa Magee, Jan. 10, 1829.
James Briant, BM.
Hiram Floyd to Sarah Row, Oct. 13, 1829.
Johnathan Floyd, BM. (Oct. 13, 1829).
John Frost to Nancy Popejoy, Dec. 29, 1829.
John Hubbs, BM. (Dec. 29, 1829).
Thomas Gamewell to Rebecca Hammel, Jan. 17, 1829.
James C. Cocke, BM.
Jacob Godwin to Caroline H. Easley, Sept. 21, 1829.
Thomas Cocke, BM.
Jeremiah R. Goin to Levenia Renfro, Feb. 28, 1829.
Stephen C. Renfro, BM.
Preston Gowin to Betsy Gowin, Dec. 9, 1829.
Nathan Gowin, BM. (Dec. 9, 1829).
James Gray to Mary Collins, April 18, 1829.
Pendleton Taylor, BM.
Eli Greenlea to Mary Daniel, Feb. 14, 1829.
Jese Counts, BM. (Feb. 14, 1829).
Jacob Grubb to Sarah S. Seaver, May 18, 1829.
Joseph Seaver, BM. (May 24, 1829).
Ezra Hammers to Kesiah Cannon, June 10, 1829.
John Cannon, BM.
George Haney to Nancy Nash, May 6, 1829.
Peter Hulstine, BM.
Pryor Harvey to Anna Mumpower, Oct. 8, 1829.
Hiram Samsel, BM.
Alexander Higgs to Sarah Hynds, Jan. 13, 1829.
Abraham Trogdan, BM. (See same names in 1828).
Henry Hipshere to Ruthy Mack, Nov. 27, 1829.
John Creech, BM.
William Hodge to Mary Joice, Dec. 1, 1829.
James Counts, BM. (Dec. 1, 1829).
Peter Holston to Sarah Haynes, Aug. 12, 1829.
Madison Kirk, BM.
John Holt to Katherine Densar, Jan. 29, 1829.
Edward Hodge, BM.
Thomas Hunley to Sarah Killer, Feb. 25, 1829.
Rody Savage, BM. (Feb. 25, 1829).

GRAINGER COUNTY MARRIAGES

James Jarnagin to Dolly Corum, Dec. 2, 1829.
 William Jarnagin, BM. (Dec. 3, 1829).
Thomas Joice to Elizabeth Colson, Jan. 2, 1829.
 Frederic May, BM.
Wortham Joice to Dinah Daniel, Dec. 22, 1829.
 Edward Hodge, BM. (Dec. 24, 1829).
Hugh Jones to Jane Woody, Feb. 5, 1829.
 James R. Cocke, BM. (Feb. 5, 1829).
Partemon Long to Mary Ann Proffett, June 25, 1829.
 Anthon Long, BM.
Thomas Low to Lucinda Thompson, Dec. 17, 1829.
 Andrew C. Eaton, BM. (Dec. 17, 1829).
Enoch Mackey to Mary Harvey, Jan. 28, 1829.
 Nelson Perle, BM.
Robert Martin to Sarah Mincey, Sept. 23, 1829.
 Hugh Jones, BM. (Sept. 23, 1829).
Robert Martin, Jr. to Eli Atkin, Feb. 23, 1829.
 George Atkin, BM.
William Martin to Elza Davis, Aug. 11, 1829.
 Jesse Rhea, BM.
Frederic May to Elizabeth Mays, Sept. 20, 1829.
 Aaron Counts, BM.
Berry Mayse to Nancy Ivy, Nov. 16, 1829.
 Joshua Kidwell, BM.
William McBee to Susan Hawkins, March 13, 1829.
 Jno. S. Waters, BM.
William P. McBee to Nancy Dyer, April 7, 1829.
 Benjamin Nealy, BM.
Absalom Miller to Jane Roberts, Dec. 26, 1829.
 James Miller, BM.
Noah Miller to Anna M. Sparkman, July 9, 1829.
 John Davis, BM.
Green Mitchell to Amelia Brown, June 15, 1829.
 Jubel Mitchel, BM.
John Mullins to Sarah Starnes, May 15, 1829.
 William Sharp, BM.
John Needham to Nancy Chandler, June 5, 1829.
 John Chandler, BM.
William Nickelson to Gabnella Perry, Dec. 26, 1829.
 John Thomason, BM.
Richard Oaks to Sarah Butcher, Jan. 12, 1829.
 Holston Butcher, BM. (Jan. 15, 1829).
William Orr to Mary Rodgers, April 13, 1829.
 Thomas Turley, BM.
Charles M. Perryman to Louisa Colinsworth, Aug. 31,
 1829. John Easley, BM. (Aug. 31, 1829).
Francis Rayl to Sarah Shropshear, July 28, 1829.
 George Rayl, BM.
Ephram Repas to Mary A. Haymore, June 19, 1829.
 Joseph Severs, BM. (June 19, 1829).
Willis Rook to Rebecca Carroll, Feb. 16, 1829.
 Hezekiah Rook, BM. (Feb. 22, 1829).
William Rookard to Nancy Brockus, Jan. 8, 1829.
 Brown B. Rookard, BM.

Jacob Row to Disey Fields, Feb. 4, 1829.
Hiram Floyd, BM.
Roddy Savage to Margret Hundley, Feb. 25, 1829.
T. P. Hunley, BM.
George Seamore to Letty Dennis, Dec. 1, 1829.
John Wyrick, BM. (Dec. 1, 1829).
Wm. C. Shipley to Susana Nelson, Aug. 6, 1829.
Andrew C. Eaton, BM.
David Shropshear to Sally Long, Aug. 14, 1829.
Reuben Long, BM.
Eli Spoon to Mary Terry, Dec. 3, 1829.
John Spoon, BM.
Ambrose Sutherland to Syntha Mynatt, Jan. 20, 1829.
William Lewis, BM.
Abraham Trodgen to Mary K. Hinds, Dec. 23, 1829.
John Simmons, BM. (Dec. 23, 1829).
Pascal Turner to Catherin Purkey, Dec. 16, 1829.
John Spoon, BM.
Obediah Waters to Polly Powell, Jan. 2, 1829.
William Hall, BM.
Claiborn Watkins to Rhody Harris, Sept. 9, 1829.
Thomas Smith, BM.
Thomas Watson to Sarah Roberts, Oct. 15, 1829.
Absolem Molder, BM. (Oct. 15, 1829).
James A. Whiteside to Mary J. Massengill, Feb. 5, 1829.
Gray Garrett, BM. (Feb. 5, 1829).
Jacob Woods to Matilda Harris, Nov. 16, 1829.
Thomas Rush, BM. (Nov. 17, 1829).
William Wrinkles to Catherine Reed, July 6, 1829.
Christopher Stroud, BM.
Robert Yancey to Mary Kirkham, Aug. 7, 1829.
Pharoah B. Cobb, BM.

1830

Alfred Acuff to Margaret Vitetoe, Oct. 4, 1830.
Pleasant Watson, BM.
Clabourn Acuff to Martha Hammers, March 27, 1830.
Richard Acuff, BM.
James Acuff to Sarah E. Harrell, Dec. 21, 1830.
Thomas Acuff, BM.
Nathan Atkins to Anna Needham, Aug. 7, 1830.
James F. Hooper, BM.
Aron Ballinger to Sarah Dobbin, Aug. 18, 1830.
James Coffee, BM.
John Beeler to Anna Shelton, June 23, 1830.
Joseph Petre, BM. (June 23, 1830).
Pryor Biba to Elizabeth Smith, Aug. 14, 1830.
Claiborn Godwin, BM.
William Bradley to Sarah Perrin, Aug. 18, 1830.
Archy Smith, BM.
Martin Bridgeman to Anna Dyer, Nov. 8, 1830.
Elijah S. Harrell, BM. (Nov. 8, 1830).

James Campbell to Margery Blain, May 29, 1830.
Andrew C. Eaton, BM.
John Cardwell to Sarah Smith, Feb. 20, 1830.
Clements York, BM.
Andrew Chamberlain to Mary Cardwell, Oct. 11, 1830.
Robert Boza, BM.
Colby (Cobby ?) Coffee to Mary Adams, May 22, 1830.
John Rucker, BM.
Pleasant Combs to Mary Hayworth, Feb. 16, 1830.
Joseph Combs, BM.
John Copeland to Elizabeth Fielding, Aug. 11, 1830.
Andrew Chamberlain, BM.
Jese Cox to Mary Williams, June 30, 1830.
Jese Riggs, BM.
Nemoe Crouse to Margaret Swaggerty, July 28, 1830.
Armstead Clark, BM.
Timothy Dalton to Susannah Adams, Aug. 18, 1830.
William Dalton, BM.
James Deer to Margaret Frye, Aug. 17, 1830.
Jacob Shoats, BM.
Levi Dennis to Delila Dunnahew, Nov. 25, 1830.
Samuel Jack, BM.
Thomas Ferguson to Mary McElhaney, Sept. 28, 1830.
John Paint, BM.
Isaac Flora to Prudence Carroll, Dec. 4, 1830.
John Wade, BM.
Cornelius Goforth to Alice Cardivile, Aug. 16, 1830.
Joel Duncan, BM. (Aug. 19, 1830).
Edward Hankin to Rushey Coram, March 23, 1830.
Merchant Hankins, BM.
William Hankins to Anna Milhanks, March 20, 1830.
John Large, BM. (March 21, 1830).
Richard Harrison to Mariah Holly, Feb. 6, 1830.
Henry Gowin, BM.
John Hill to Nancy Dennis, Nov. 23, 1830.
Samuel Jack, BM.
Henry I. Hodge to Jane Ivy, Oct. 2, 1830.
James S. Campbell, BM.
Zacharias Hollis to Mary Whalen, Feb. 11, 1830.
Armstead Clark, BM.
Caleb Holly to Elizabeth Pin, Sept. 4, 1830.
Richard Harrison, BM.
James Hubbard to Mary Large, Dec. 18, 1830.
Jese Cleveland, BM.
Joseph Kitts to Agens Bullock, Dec. 25, 1830.
Peter Kitts, BM.
Jacob Long to Malvina Bridgeman, Nov. 10, 1830.
William Brown, BM.
William Maples to Sarah Jonas, Oct. 4, 1830.
William Taylor, BM.
John McDaniel to Nancy Dale, April 8, 1830.
William Dyer, BM.
Moses McElhany to Elizabeth Cawley, Aug. 11, 1830.
William Philips, BM. (Aug. 12, 1830).

Alfred McGee to Sarah Mann, June 3, 1830.
James McVey, BM.
Winfry McGee to Mima Daniel, June 12, 1830.
Ambrose Evans, BM.
John McKennon to Elizabeth Fletcher, June 6, 1830.
John Chandler, BM. (June 6, 1830).
Roderick McKennon to Mary Brown, May 1, 1830.
James Barton, BM. (May 1, 1830).
Daniel Noe to Polly Riggs, March 6, 1830.
David Noe, BM.
John Noe to Jane Reed, Jan. 2, 1830.
Jonathan Noe, BM.
William H. Nole to Sarah Tate, May 19, 1830.
Jacob Godwin, BM.
Thomas Perry to Nancy Kennon, Feb. 18, 1830.
James Irby, BM.
Isaac Philips to Susannah Willis, Jan. 20, 1830.
Jas. Cheek, BM. (Jan. 20, 1830).
Willis L. Pratt to Delila Myers, Feb. 10, 1830.
Stephen Jones, BM.
Jeremiah Reed to Prudence Shipley, Dec. 16, 1830.
William Rogers, BM. (Dec. 16, 1830).
Simeon Rutherford to Catherine Denson, Feb. 22, 1830.
James Rutherford, BM. (Feb. 22, 1830).
Thomas Shipley to Elenor Rogers, Aug. 19, 1830.
Richard Taylor, BM. (Aug. 19, 1830).
Robert Simmons to Nancy Walker, June 12, 1830.
Lea Dyer, BM. (June 12, 1830).
Thomas Smith to Agnes Dyer, Jan. 21, 1830.
Henry Alsup, BM.
Green Spencer to Elizabeth Childres, June 4, 1830.
James Simmons, BM.
Nathaniel Spencer to Jane Chillis, March 8, 1830.
Samuel Watson, BM.
Eben Taylor to Mary Collinsworth, Sept. 12, 1830.
Addison Collinsworth, BM.
Elika A. Taylor to Elizabeth Mayes, March 23, 1830.
James Kennon, BM. (March 23, 1830).
John P. Warwick to Elenar Smith, Aug. 12, 1830.
Thomas Smith, BM. (Aug. 12, 1830).
James Watson to Clarenda Davis, Oct. 14, 1830.
Charles Perryman, BM. (Oct. 14, 1830).
Pleasant Whitlow to Isabella Jones, March 30, 1830.
Wm. Jones, BM.
David Williamson to Catherine Henderson, March 27, 1830.
George Henderson, BM.
Weston Willis to Elizabeth Vitetoe, Nov. 3, 1830.
George W. Vitetoe, BM.
Lacey Witcher to Mary Mallicoat, Dec. 1, 1830.
Andrew C. Eaton, BM. (Dec. 1, 1830).
Clabourn Witcher to Eliza Jane Beckham, Aug. 5, 1830.
Andrew C. Eaton, BM.

1831

John Acuff to Winney Kitts, Oct. 6, 1831.
John Acuff, Jr., BM. (Oct. 6, 1831).
Barnabas Adkins to Sarah Routh, Sept. 28, 1831.
John Chandler, BM. (Oct. 5, 1831).
James R. Allsup to Parthena Harris, Sept. 10, 1831.
William S. Dyer, BM.
David Beeler to Mary Dyer, Oct. 18, 1831.
James McCubbin, BM.
Jacob Beeler to Nancy Cleveland, Jan. 10, 1831.
Isaac Beeler, BM.
Peter Beeler to Anna Vance, Dec. 21, 1831.
Joseph Bunch, BM.
Giles I. Bledsoe to Mary Perrin, Feb. 25, 1831.
Nelson Jarnagin, BM.
Elijah Boatman to Elizabeth Flora, Jan. 5, 1831.
Edward Wilson, BM.
Samuel Brown to Elizabeth Hightower. Feb. 24, 1831.
Thomas Hawley, BM.
Hasting Butcher to Margaret Oaks, Jan. 26, 1831.
Richard Oaks, BM.
John Camron to Mary Pollard, Sept. 15, 1831.
James Pollard, BM.
William Carruthers to Rachel Moore, Nov. 27, 1831.
Stephen Moore, BM.
John Childs to Ann Arm, July 7, 1831.
Claibourn Haley, BM. (July 7, 1831).
Pierce Cody to Delmah Floyd, Sept. 1, 1831.
Robert Floyd, BM.
Rhinehart Coffman to Sarah Beeler, Jan. 22, 1831.
Leanard Coffman, BM.
Lewis Collins to Catherine Baughman, Aug. 25, 1831.
Samuel Widner, BM.
George Cupp to Celia Purkepile, April 25, 1831.
John Estes, Jr., BM. (April 28, 1831).
Isaac Daniel to Phebe Mayes, Feb. 5, 1831.
James McCarty, BM.
Stephen Daniel to Abigal Clounch, Jan. 27, 1831.
David Clounch, BM.
Elnathan Davis to Jane Harris, Dec. 28, 1831.
George B. Burns, BM.
John Dennis to Catherine Starnes, Aug. 8, 1831.
Eli Clark, BM. (Aug. 11, 1831).
David Evans to Rachel Davis, Dec. 13, 1831.
Hugh Jones, BM.
Henry Frost to Susan Hickle, June 11, 1831.
William Hickle, BM.
Bales E. Gains to Mary Ann Beard, Feb. 21, 1831.
John Davis, BM.
Henry Gambill to Sarah Watson, July 6, 1831.
John Easley, BM.

James Gilmore to Mary Cates, Jan. 17, 1831.
James Wilson, BM.
Pryer Goan to Martha Moore, March 2, 1831.
David Goans, BM.
Jacob Graybeal to Catharine Graham, Nov. 26, 1831.
Bolis E. Gaines, BM.
Jacob Griffin to Mary McBride, Feb. 12, 1831.
Martin Griffin, BM.
Ienola B. Hall to Susan B. Howell, Oct. 10, 1831.
Thos. R. Howell, BM.
William Hammers to Rachel Acuff, Oct. 26, 1831.
Claiborn Acuff, BM.
Singleton Hancock to Linsy Lamb, Oct. 9, 1831.
James Hancock, BM.
Evan Harris, Jr. to Mary Low, Feb. 9, 1831.
William Jarnagin, BM.
James Helton to Nancy Jones, Aug. 23, 1831.
Alexander Helton, BM.
Stephen Henderson to Elizabeth Long, Oct. 10, 1831.
John Harris, BM. (Oct. 18, 1831).
Jese Hill to Mahala Moyers, Jan. 11, 1831.
George Semore, BM.
James Hodge, Jr. to Elza Pollard, Feb. 6, 1831.
James Pollard, BM.
William Hollinsworth to Martha Baker, Dec. 3, 1831.
William Watson, BM.
Isaac Holston to Nancy Mallicoat, May 7, 1831.
William Mallicoat, BM.
Thomas Hunt to Louisa B. Kline, Jan. 27, 1831.
Benj. R. Bittle, BM. (Jan. 27, 1831).
Benjamin Ivy, Jr. to Mary Kidwell, Nov. 3, 1831.
William Hodge, BM.
Jacob Jackson to Rebecca Sellars, March 10, 1831.
Ruben Dodson, BM.
Ambrose Johnson to Lucinda Farmer, Dec. 13, 1831.
John Rucker, BM.
Alexander Joice to Delila Kirk, Sept. 24, 1831.
James McCarty, BM. (Sept. 26, 1831).
Lewis Jones to Sarah Brown, Oct. 24, 1831.
Benjamin Ivy, BM. (Oct. 27, 1831).
Charles M. Lea to Rebecca Hightower, Feb. 2, 1831.
Samuel Brown, BM.
Abraham Livungston to Lucinda D. Rich, Dec. 31, 1831.
Hugh Houston, BM.
Andrew May to Mary Boseman, Dec. 27, 1831.
Hiram Pierce, BM.
William Mays to Cynthia Lynn, Aug. 20, 1831.
Fredric Mayes, BM.
Edward Mayse to Jane Jones, Sept. 7, 1831.
James McCarty, BM.
George McAnally to Anne Cain, Jan. 30, 1831.
John McAnally, BM.

James F. McCarty to Carolina Letha May, Oct. 18, 1831.
    Isaac McCarty, BM.
James McCubbin to Mariah Dyer, Aug. 18, 1831.
    James Strange, BM.
Solomon Miller to Nancy Bowman, Feb. 11, 1831.
    Lewis Beets, BM. (Feb. 11, 1831).
Isaac Mitchell to Catharine H. Kirkham, Nov. 22, 1831.
    James Yates, BM.
Preston Mitchell to Rachel Churchman, Nov. 10, 1831.
    William Moody, BM.
William M. Moody to Elizabeth Lowe, April 20, 1831.
    Richard Granthouse, BM.
John Ollevin, Jr. to Lavina Bunch, Aug. 15, 1831.
    John Ollevin, BM.
Enoch Petit to Elizabeth Newton, Jan. 22, 1831.
    Henry Boatman, BM.
Major Pollard to Elizabeth Smith, Oct. 25, 1831.
    James Hodge, BM.
Ralph Purkepile to Nancy Pierce, Dec. 1, 1831.
    Abraham Spoon, BM.
William Rogers to Melesa Briant, March 2, 1831.
    James Rogers, BM.
George W. Rose to Mary Jennings, Nov. 28, 1831.
    Roel Jennings, BM.
John Rucker to Mahala Thomas, Dec. 13, 1831.
    Ambrose Johnson, BM.
Rufus W. Scruggs to Mary Jarnagin, Jan. 5, 1831.
    John B. Grigsby, BM.
Joseph T. Sevier to Matilda Thomas, April 17, 1831.
    Hugh Horton, BM.
James Simmons to Clarsa Davis, Sept. 28, 1831.
    David Barton, BM.
David Smith to Anna Trogdan, Jan. 20, 1831.
    John Smith, BM. (Jan. 20, 1831).
William Smith to Harriet Leffew, Sept. 15, 1831.
    James James, BM.
William Smith to Nancy Powle, Aug. 3, 1831.
    William Sharp, BM.
George Sparkman to Polly January, Oct. 6, 1831.
    Edmund Chesher, BM.
Elijah Stansberry to Sophia Ford, Sept. 19, 1831.
    Benjamin M. Cravy, BM.
James H. Starns to Catherin Kinder, Aug. 1, 1831.
    William Hollingsworth, BM. (Aug. 1, 1831).
William Thomason to Cassandra Crain, Jan. 16, 1831.
    Edmund Cheshire, BM.
James Wringler (or Swingler) to Sally Churchman,
    Oct. 6, 1831. James Mallicoat, BM.

1832

Alfred Acuff to Rebecca Dyer, Aug. 2, 1832.
    Richard Acuff, BM.

GRAINGER COUNTY MARRIAGES

Stephen Atkin to Milly Rectar, Jan. 2, 1832.
James H. Starnes, BM.
James Barton to Nancy Flora, Feb. 25, 1832.
Pleasant M. Senter, BM.
John Bird to Rachael Hixon, June 7, 1832.
John Hixon, BM.
John A. Blackburn to Anna Colvin, Oct. 12, 1832.
Hugh Jones, BM. (Oct. 12, 1832).
John Boatright to Sarah Morgan, Jan. 16, 1832.
Ahab Bowen, BM.
James Bragg to Cinda Clanch, July 24, 1832.
William Brookers to Elizabeth Ramsey, March 15, 1832.
Jeremiah Lovell, BM.
Armstead Bunch to Pricilla Teague, Jan. 5, 1832.
Stephen Routh, BM.
William Carroll to Mary Rush, Sept. 4, 1832.
Jacob Woods, BM. (Sept. 4, 1832).
John Chandler to Catherine Nicely, Dec. 31, 1832.
Jonas Nicely, BM.
William Chase to Jane Campbell, Dec. 20, 1832.
James Kennon, BM.
Martin Cleveland to An McPheters, Oct. 9, 1832.
Joseph Clark, BM.
David Counte to Sarah Spoon, Jan. 26, 1832.
Abraham Spoon, BM.
Davis Crain to Sarah Beckham, Nov. 21, 1832.
John Crain, BM.
John Crouse to Elizabeth Hynds, April 24, 1832.
William Walker, BM. (April 24, 1832).
Lea Dire to Caroline Ore, April 12, 1832.
Henry Alsup, BM. (April 18, 1832).
John Farmer to Phebe Leffew, May 19, 1832.
Hugh Farmer, BM. (May 20, 1832).
John Gillmore to Lucinda Collison, Oct. 17, 1832.
James Gillmore, BM.
Fountain Harris to Elizabeth Elliott, April 10, 1832.
William Jones, BM.
Miles Harris to Rebecca Ellet, June 18, 1832.
George Harris, BM.
Henry Hawkins to Betsey Mitchell, Nov. 9, 1832.
William Brown, BM. (Nov. 11, 1832).
Colbert Hayes to Mary Pane, Feb. 3, 1832.
Jacob Hipshire, BM. (Feb. 3, 1832).
Jacob Heneger to Margaret A. Grimes, Jan. 2, 1832.
John Dennis, Jr., BM.
William Hill to Rebecca Hammock, July 16, 1832.
John Phipps, BM.
Colbert Hipshere to Jinney Hayes, Nov. 14, 1832.
Elijah Hipshire, BM.
Bartholomew Hodge to Nelly Mitchell, Feb. 2, 1832.
John Holt, BM.
A. Bigal P. Holt to Martha Evans, March 24, 1832.
Archibald Green, BM.

GRAINGER COUNTY MARRIAGES

John Holt to Elizabeth Brooks, May 23, 1832.
  John Ivy, BM. (May 27, 1832).
Elijah Hopper to Nancy Jones, Oct. 8, 1832.
  John Daniel, BM.
James G. C. Hoskins to Charlotte Moody, Aug. 11, 1832.
  Thomas Hoskin, BM.
John F. Huddleston to Mary Smith, May 2, 1832.
  John Easley, BM. (May 8, 1832).
Fielden S. Hunt to Nancy Nanney, April 24, 1832.
John Ivy, Jr. to Nancy Williford, April 7, 1832.
  Berry Mayse, BM. (April 10, 1832).
John January to Nancy Sparkman, Sept. 5, 1832.
  Hardy Sparkman, BM.
John Kinder to Jane Cockram, Aug. 18, 1832.
  Jacob Kinder, BM.
David Kits to Innece Willis, Sept. 12, 1832.
Elijah Leffew to Biddy Teague, July 21, 1832.
  Robert W. Watson, BM.
Peter Legges to Rebecca Walker, Jan. 24, 1832.
  John Crawley, BM.
George W. May to Frances Hightower, Jan. 16, 1832.
  Elijah Harrell, BM.
John Mayes, Jr. to Sarah McGee, March 14, 1832.
  James Eaton, BM.
James R. McAnally to Elizabeth I. Grove, Feb. 1, 1832.
  Henry Grove, BM. (Feb. 4, 1832).
Jonathan L. McCarty to Syntha Kirk, March 26, 1832.
  Nues O. Rennon, BM.
Thomas McGolrick to Minerva Stratton, May 3, 1832.
  Parthena Long, BM.
James Miller to Jenetta Rogers, June 14, 1832.
  Dennis Roberts, BM.
John Mitchel to Delila Churchman, Feb. 29, 1832.
  Jefferson Nance, BM.
Elijah Mitchell (Jr. ?) to Sarah Davis, Oct. 30, 1832.
  Isaac Mitchell, BM. (Oct. 30, 1832).
John Moore to Catherine Branson, July 14, 1832.
  Valentine Molder, BM.
Robert Mullins to Catherine Dennis, Sept. 22, 1832.
  James H. Starns, BM.
Jefferson Nance to Jane Churchman, Feb. 29, 1832.
  John Mitchell, BM.
John Nance to Celia Vineyard, Feb. 17, 1832.
  John Mitchell, BM. (Feb. 19, 1832).
Claibourn Nash to Nancy Dodson, Sept. 27, 1832.
  Dedman Nash, BM.
John Olliver to Mahala Mayes, Feb. 15, 1832.
  Frederic May, BM.
John Ousley to Caroline Hinchey, July 18, 1832.
  Samuel Gilmore, BM. (Aug. 12, 1832)
Gilbert Patterson to Mary Chesher, Feb. 11, 1832.
  Presley S. Chesher, BM. (Feb. 16, 1832).
James Phipps to Martha Routh, Aug. 9, 1832.
  High Routh, BM.

GRAINGER COUNTY MARRIAGES

James Ray to Sarah Cox, Oct. 24, 1832.
  Robert Ray, BM.
Cox Renfro to May McKinney, May 20, 1832.
  Alexander Blain, BM.
Samuel Rite to Charity Rector, Jan. 12, 1832.
  Hiram Yates, BM.
Thomas Rush to Minerva Carroll, June 23, 1832.
  Jacob Woods, BM.
John Simmons to Betsy Smith, June 2, 1832.
  David Crain, BM. (June 3, 1832).
Russell C. Smallwood to Phebe Martin, Aug. 9, 1832.
  Noah Willis, BM.
John Smith to Oney Spencer, May 31, 1832.
  John Davis, BM.
William Sparkman to Lucinda Ray, Jan. 14, 1832.
  Mitchell Sparkman, BM.
William Sparkman to Prescia Nichols, Sept. 14, 1832.
  Aquilla Todd, BM. (Sept. 19, 1832).
Adam Starns to Phebe Cockram, Oct. 30, 1832.
  Eli Rector, BM.
Peter Thacker to Emeline Ford, July 21, 1832.
  Nathaniel Thacker, BM.
Robert W. Walker to Susan A. Curl, Sept. 5, 1832.
  William Hightower, BM. (Sept. 5, 1832).
Thomas Walker to Margarite Crouse, Aug. 8, 1832.
  Pascal J. Jarnagin, BM.
Edward West to Elizabeth Gillmore, Feb. 27, 1832.
  Thomas Chamberlain, BM. (March 1, 1832).
Samuel West to Parthena Gilmore, Sept. 28, 1832.
  Edward West, BM.
James Whitlock to Catherine Daniel, Dec. 18, 1832.
  William Mitchell, BM.
Coleman M. Witt to Rachael Taylor, Dec. 15, 1832.
  Hughs W. Taylor, BM. (Dec. 18, 1832).

1833

John Ailor to Levena Harrell, Sept. 30, 1833.
  Hugh Jones, BM. (Oct. 1, 1833).
Hiram Baker to Lucinda Monroe, Aug. 17, 1833.
  Wm. Hollingsworth, BM. (Aug. 17, 1833).
George Boatman to Sarah Cox, Nov. 20, 1833.
  John Evans, BM.
Henry Boatman to Edy Cox, May 20, 1833.
  James Riggs, BM.
James B. Boyd to Julia Y. Yates, Jan. 24, 1833.
  Wm. Moody, BM.
Joel Bradshaw to Mary Coffee, Sept. 24, 1833.
  Thos. Clevenger, BM.
Moses Brock to Mahala Dyer, Sept. 20, 1833.
  Thomas Brock, BM.
John Brooks to Elizabeth Pierson, Feb. 18, 1833.
  (Feb. 19, 1833).

GRAINGER COUNTY MARRIAGES

Amstead Bunch to Priscilla Teague, Jan. 5, 1833.
(Jan. 6, 1833).
Hardin Cameron to Elizabeth Ray, Oct. 17, 1833.
Samuel West, BM.
Lewis Campbell to Elizabeth Samson (or Lawson),
April 17, 1833. John Campbell, BM.
Robert Cardwell to Leigh Ore, Dec. 17, 1833.
John Cox, BM.
Rowling Chiles to Elizabeth Greer, Feb. 4, 1833.
Hardin Willis, BM. (Feb. 8, 1833).
Joseph Clark to Martha Grove, Jan. 10, 1833.
Archibald P. Greer, BM.
John Cluck to Jane Robinson, Aug. 10, 1833.
James Daniel, BM.
John Cox to Eliza Rule, Dec. 11, 1833.
Jonathan Noe, BM.
Carter J. Dalton to Mary Coffee, Sept. 2, 1833.
Timothy Daulton, BM.
James Daniel to Martha Kennon, Aug. 12, 1833.
John Kennon, BM.
Colby Daulton to Elizabeth McGinnis, Dec. 20, 1833.
David McCoy, BM. (Dec. 22, 1833).
Enoch Daulton to Jane Harrell, Sept. 2, 1833.
Timothy Daulton, BM.
Elza Davis to Mildred Gaines, Aug. 2, 1833.
Bales E. Gaines, BM. (Aug. 8, 1833).
John Dennis, Jr. to Matilda Harrelson, Sept. 28, 1833.
Levi Dennis, BM. (Sept. 29, 1833).
James Dennison to Emeline Milliken, June 29, 1833.
Samuel Dotson, Jr. to Nancy Hopson, Dec. 17, 1833.
Hugh W. Farmer, BM.
John Dyer to Polona Whitlock, March 28, 1833.
Lea Dyer, BM.
William A. Dyer to Margaret Brigman, March 11, 1833.
William Dyer, BM.
James Eaton to Lucy Johnson, Nov. 11, 1833.
John Meek, BM. (Nov. 13, 1833).
John W. Eaton to Margaret Williams, Dec. 5, 1833.
Robert Masengill, BM.
Hugh Farmer to Susan Stone, Jan. 30, 1833.
Pleasant Watson, BM. (Jan. 31, 1833).
Addison Fry to Elizabeth Lewis, Sept. 6, 1833.
Isaac Butler, BM.
Wilson Gilmore to Martha Cates, Dec. 18, 1833.
James Gillmore, BM.
James Greer to Elizabeth Wiles, Feb. 22, 1833.
Robert Daniel, BM. (Feb. 26, 1833).
Nathan Greer to Elizabeth Ferguson, April 13, 1833.
James Greer, BM. (April 14, 1833).
John Grigsby to Carolina H. Jarnagin, Jan. 10, 1833.
Joseph H. Davis, BM.
Henry Grove to Nancy Satterfield, Nov. 11, 1833.
Joseph Clark, BM.
Aaron Hamilton to Abby Dennis, March 22, 1833.
George Seamore, BM.

Daniel Hixon to Mary Leffew, May 30, 1833.
William Smith, BM.

James D. Hodge to Mary Riggs, April 17, 1833.
Jese Williams, BM.

David Holt to Delpha Miles, Jan. 2, 1833.
(Jan. 2, 1833).

Thomas C. Hoskin to Lucinda Meek, Aug. 20, 1833.
Charles Hoskins, BM. (Aug. 22, 1833).

James Howeth to Elizabeth Lively, May 29, 1833.
Andrew Bowen, BM. (May 30, 1833).

William Idol to Margaret Cabbage, April 26, 1833.
William Nicely, BM.

Wiley D. Jones to Sarah C. Copeland, July 6, 1833.
James Cheek, BM.

Sallomon Kitts to Lety Bailey, March 16, 1833.
Joseph Kitts, BM. (March 18, 1833).

George Lemmons to Lucinda Smith, July 10, 1833.
Lea Dyer, BM.

Lawson Long to Susan Bentley, April 8, 1833.
Ruben Long, BM. (April 11, 1833).

Francis Lyons to Mary M. Hightower, Sept. 14, 1833.
Thomas Hawley, BM.

Sterling Malicoat to Elizabeth Roach, Feb. 12, 1833.
Jacob Long, BM.

Wm. C. Mallicoat to Margaret Dotson, Nov. 16, 1833.
Mallicoat J. Claibourn, BM. (Nov. 19, 1833).

John Maxfield to Malinda Bowlind, April 9, 1833.
John Harris, BM. (April 11, 1833).

James R. McAnally to Nancy Minerva Curry, Aug. 14, 1833.
(Aug. 14, 1833).

Robert McBee to Elizabeth Dyer, Nov. 9, 1833.
Wm. K. Latham, BM.

Eli McDaniel to Elsena Roach, Jan. 1, 1833.

George W. McNees to Elizabeth Smith, Oct. 11, 1833.
Jonathan L. McCarty, BM.

George Moore to Jincy Collins, June 1, 1833.
Jacob Row, BM.

Richard Moore to Elizabeth Mays, Feb. 16, 1833.
(Feb. 16, 1833).

Nicholas Nicely to Betsy Strange, Jan. 2, 1833.
Stephen Petre, BM. (Jan. 3, 1833).

William Nichols to Biddye Teague, April 20, 1833.
Levin Routh, BM.

Nicholas Noe to Harrett Darnell, Oct. 8, 1833.
Joseph Noe, BM. (Oct. 10, 1833).

Benjamin Peck to Mary Moyers, Aug. 20, 1833.
William Williamson, BM.

Nathan Perry to Mary Collins, March 5, 1833.
(March 5, 1833).

John Ramsey to Mary Ann Clarkson, May 18, 1833.

Felps Reed to Mary Thompson, March 29, 1833.
Wyatt Saterfield, BM.

Henry Rice to Elizabeth K. Senter, July 15, 1833.
Saml. B. Tate, BM.

Joel Rice to Mary Powell, Nov. 23, 1833.
  Edward Chesher, BM.
Alfred Roach to Jane McDaniel, Aug. 28, 1833.
  John Collison, BM.
John Robinson to Ann Bentley, Jan. 2, 1833.
  Charles Reed, BM.
Coleman Rush to Lucy Easter, July 6, 1833.
  Johnson Lacy, BM.
John Satterfield to Elizabeth Ruckard, Feb. 2, 1833.
  William Ruckard, BM.
George W. Seamore to Sarah Vitatoe, Jan. 20, 1833.
  James Vitetoe, BM.
Gabriel Shelton to Nancey Simmons, Sept. 12, 1833.
  Benjamin Craighead, BM. (Sept. 23, 1833).
Nathaniel Shipley to Margaret Taylor, Jan. 1, 1833.
  Russell Riggs, BM. (Jan. 1, 1833).
William Taylor to Liddy Donner, Dec. 27, 1833.
  John Donner, BM.
Ezekiel Trogdon, Sr. to Drucilla Whitehead, Feb. 11,
  1833. John Crain, BM.
James Tuttle to Judith Smith, Jan. 26, 1833.
  James Smith, BM.
George Vandergriff to Elizabeth Nicely, March 15,
  1833. Woolry Nicely, BM.
Haden Warwick to Catherine Sharp, March 16, 1833.
  James Sharp, BM.
Stephen Woolsey to Liddy Ann Hubbs, Dec. 16, 1833.
John Zachary to Elizabeth Devault, Aug. 7, 1833.
  William Hightower, BM.

1834

Simon Acuff to Susan Strange, Dec. 24, 1834.
  William Acuff, BM. (Dec. 25, 1834).
William Alexander to Levisy Smith, March 28, 1834.
  John Smith, BM.
Hiram Aytes to Rebecca Sparkman, Nov. 25, 1834.
  James Bise, BM.
John Aytes to Elizabeth Bunch, Sept. 7, 1834.
  James Boyd, J. P., BM.
Joseph Beeler to Anna Parker, Oct. 21, 1834.
  Benjm. McFarland, BM.
John Biggs to Adeline Rayl, March 11, 1834.
  George W. Rayl, BM. (March 13, 1834).
Redman Bird to Mary Daniel, Jan. 20, 1834.
  Hillard Bird, BM.
Ezechael Boatman to Mary Boatman, Jan. 23, 1834.
  John Cox, BM.
James Boatright to Elizabeth Taylor, June 14, 1834.
  Hugh McElhaney, BM.
John Brabson to Martha Smith, Oct. 22, 1834.
  Stephen Butler, BM.
George Brock to Sarah Elkins, Sept. 12, 1834.
  John Brock, BM.

Reynolds Brogan to Delpha Grady, July 3, 1834.
    Robert Mitchell, BM. (July 7, 1834).
William Bush to Jane Hammel, May 30, 1834.
    Henry Brown, BM.
John Carr to Nancy Perrin, March 29, 1834.
    Giles J. Bledsoe, BM.
James S. Churchman to Mary Young, July 25, 1834.
    Enos Hammer, BM.
Benjamin Coats to Hannah´Chandler, June 19, 1834.
    Claibourn Johnson, BM.
Mark Daniel to Martha May, Feb. 18, 1834.
    Frederic May, BM.
Hugh A. Duff to Sarah Brown, March 8, 1834.
    William G. Eaton, BM.
James Duff to Elizabeth Easley, Oct. 28, 1834.
    Joshua Curl, BM.
Martin Dunahoo to Cynthia Dyer, Feb. 19, 1834.
    William Dunahoo, BM.
Joseph Foster to Eliza Morris, Nov. 21, 1834.
    Asa Evans, BM. (Nov. 21, 1834).
John Gilmore to Martha Stalsworth, July 23, 1834.
    Samuel Gilmore, BM.
William Grant to Susan Coram, Dec. 23, 1834.
    George Grimes, BM. (Dec. 23, 1834).
Thomas Harvy to Mariah Lephew, Nov. 7, 1834.
    Enoch Mackey, BM. (Nov. 13, 1834).
Christopher Hitch to Catherine Jennings, Oct. 6, 1834.
    Jese Cleveland, BM.
John Hubbs to Rhoda Lane, Jan. 28, 1834.
    Levi Lane, BM. (Jan. 30, 1834).
Charles Inman to Nancy Stubblefield, Oct. 16, 1834.
    Raleigh Stubblefield, BM.
William Johnson to Louisa Easterly, Sept. 10, 1834.
    John Easterly, BM.
Hughes O. Kennon to Caty Kirk, Nov. 4, 1834.
    James Yerby, BM.
Preston H. Lea to Mary H. Peck, March 25, 1834.
    George S. Eckell, BM.
Eli McDaniel to Elvira Roach, Jan. 1, 1834.
    Charles Cates, BM.
James McGee to Rachael Mayes, Jan. 2, 1834.
    Wiley B. McGee, BM.
Charles McGinnis to Pegga Rucker, Feb. 4, 1834.
    Archibald McGinnis, BM.
Joseph McGinnis to Susan Nash, Feb. 5, 1834.
    John Nash, BM.
James R. McGolrick to Savannia Jarnagin, March 15,
    1834. Samuel H. Copeland, BM. (April 1, 1834).
Daniel McKinney to Hannah West, Oct. 11, 1834.
    Thomas West, BM.
Lea A. Monroe to Nancy Atkins, May 17, 1834.
    William Sharp, BM.
Stephen Moore to Anice Nance, Aug. 23, 1834.
    Pryor Goans, BM.

William D. Morgan to Dicy Martain, Nov. 10, 1834.
Martin Bridgman, BM.
Dodson P. Mynatt to Lucinda Corum, Aug. 7, 1834.
Hardin Willis, BM. (Aug. 10, 1834).
Mathias Norris to Julian Minett, April 15, 1834.
William Dennis, BM.
John Perrin to Louisa Vinyard, Feb. 22, 1834.
John Nance, BM. (Feb. 23, 1834).
Joseph Petre to Lavena Jane Watson, Dec. 21, 1834.
Thomas Pierson to Mary Piatt, Jan. 10, 1834.
Hiram Pierson, BM.
Samuel Rhea to Elza Right, June 28, 1834.
Green Simmons, BM.
Isaac Sampsel to Sarah Hightower, July 27, 1834.
George M. May, BM.
Isaac Simpson to Callie Smith, Aug. 18, 1834.
James Flanagan, BM.
Henry Sharp to Mary Cavender, Aug. 23, 1834.
Pryor Goans, BM.
Henderson Sparkman to Eliza Coffee, Feb. 16, 1834.
John Crain, BM.
William Sparkman, Senr. to Martha F. Findley, May 13,
1834. John Easley, BM.
Philip Snyder to Nancy Hubbs, Jan. 7, 1834.
William Crawford, BM.
James Vittetoe to Pharaba Dennis, Jan. 20, 1834.
George W. Vittetoe, BM.
Godwin T. Watson to Sarah Piatt, Nov. 2, 1834.
Thomas Watson, BM.
Wiley R. Watson to Columbia Burnett, Oct. 16, 1834.
John Campbell, BM.
Pleasant Williams to Jane Gray, Sept. 25, 1834.
James Meek, BM.
Richard Williams to Sarah Kennon, Dec. 3, 1834.
John Easley, BM.
Calet Witt to Margaret R. Demarcus, March 15, 1834.
William K. Latham, BM.
Peter Wolfenbarger to Lucinda Williams, Nov. 12, 1834.
Sandy Wolfenbarger, BM. (Nov. 18, 1834).
John Wyrick to Anna Morgan, March 6, 1834.
John S. Fry, BM.

1835

William Acuff to Lucinda Vitetoe, Feb. 12, 1835.
Thomas Acuff, BM.
Emmanuel Adkins to Polena McNely, Nov. 1, 1835.
Joel Mallicoat, BM.
Stephen Adkins to Rebecca Vandagriff, Jan. 6, 1835.
James Brock, BM.
Helyard Bird to Catherine Noe, Feb. 5, 1835.
John Easley, BM.

Ahab Bowen to Mary L. Easley, March 21, 1835.
William K. Latham, BM.
Vincent B. Brabston to Sarah Smith, Jan. 28, 1835.
Henry Counts, BM.
James Branson to Flora Watson, July 18, 1835.
Benjamin Branson, BM.
Lewis Campbell to Barthena Lefever, Jan. 1, 1835.
John Campbell, BM.
Lewis Campbell to Peggy Washman, April 30, 1835.
John Campbell, BM.
Thomas Car to Nancy Williams, Nov. 14, 1835.
Henry Car, BM.
Goldman B. Carden to Rosanah Monroe, Dec. 22, 1835.
Samuel Gill, BM.
Daniel H. Cates to Rachael Smith, Oct. 1, 1835.
John Chesney to Ruthy Lain, Jan. 9, 1835.
Wortham Easley, BM.
Alfred Christian to Eliza Jarnagin, May 5, 1835.
Samuel Goan, BM.
William M. Cocke to Sarah F. Cocke, Jan. 9, 1835.
David Barton, BM.
Tandy Dalton to Matilda Coffee, Aug. 27, 1835.
Carter Dalton, BM.
Edward Daniel to Melvina Trogan, March 24, 1835.
Isaac Dyer to Catherine Norris, May 18, 1835.
William Dennis, BM.
John Dyer to Susan Branson, Sept. 19, 1835.
Benjamin Branson, BM.
Richard E. Farley to Susan Ann Farley, July 23, 1835.
John Edwards, BM.
Julian Frazier to Martha Morris, Dec. 17, 1835.
James M. Frazier, BM. (Dec. 20, 1835).
William Freeman to Sarah Churchman, March 21, 1835.
Daniel Eaton, BM.
Lorenza Frost to Mary Hickle, Feb. 3, 1835.
Henry Frost, BM.
Benjamin Fry to Eliza Fisher, July 7, 1835.
Andrew J. Mitchell, BM.
Robert E. Gaines to Celia Coram, Jan. 13, 1835.
John Davis, BM. (Feb. 1, 1835).
William G. Grove to Sarah Corum, Dec. 14, 1835.
William Davis, BM.
Abraham Hamers to Louisa McMillan, April 11, 1835.
William Hamers, BM.
Enos Hammers to Eliza Coffman, March 7, 1835.
William Hammers, BM.
John Haney to Anna Daniel, Feb. 11, 1835.
P. Holstine, BM.
Abel Hawkins to Jane Booker, Feb. 16, 1835.
John Large, BM.
William Hayworth to Sarah Daniel, June 7, 1835.
Lawner Bradshaw, BM. (June 11, 1835).
Edward Hodge to Pheby Mays, Feb. 25, 1835.
William Hodge, BM.

GRAINGER COUNTY MARRIAGES

Philamon Hodges to Ann Bridgeman, Jan. 17, 1835.
John Hodges, BM.
Gabriel Holdis to Martha Manes, Feb. 16, 1835.
Ile McAnally, BM.
Charles C. Hoskins to Mary Meek, April 28, 1835.
Thos. Hoskin, BM.
Julian Ivy to Cinthia Mathis, Feb. 24, 1835.
John Mathias, BM.
Payton J. Jeffries to Mary Davis, Feb. 16, 1835.
John Ivy, BM.
James Johnston to Minerva Wadkins, Oct. 26, 1835.
Reuben Clark, J. P., BM. (Oct. 26, 1835).
James Jones to Margarett Linn, Oct. 11, 1835.
Washington Jourdian to Louisa Frazier, July 29, 1835.
Enoch Macky, BM.
Jacob Kline to Martha Cardwell, Oct. 29, 1835.
John Easley, BM.
James Knight to Eliza Reece, Aug. 22, 1835.
William Baker, BM.
James Lay to Susanna Cox, March 14, 1835.
William Bledsoe, BM.
Williams Mays to Elizabeth Mays, Jan. 30, 1835.
Eamoria Pemberton, BM.
Benjamin McFarland to Sarah Lebo, Sept. 12, 1835.
John R. Kiliken, BM.
Selburn Mefford to Netty Rice, March 2, 1835.
Martin Miller to Nancy Davis, Nov. 8, 1835.
Richson Ray, BM.
Jese Minsy to Martha Boyd, Aug. 5, 1835.
Jacob Godwin, BM. (Aug. 5, 1835).
John Morgan to Agnes Branson, Nov. 25, 1835.
Nelson Dyer, BM. (Feb. 12, 1835).
Valentine Moulder to Anna Yeaden, Feb. 6, 1835.
Wm. C. Mackey, BM.
Preston P. Nance to May Vinyard, July 25, 1835.
Ruben Grove, BM.
Samuel Newman to Sarah Johnson, Sept. 8, 1835.
Levi Long, BM.
Joseph Noe to Sarah Rich, Aug. 8, 1835.
James Carmichael, BM.
Abner Norris to Elsena Norris, Oct. 18, 1835.
Isaac Dyer, BM. (Feb. 26, 1835).
John Payne to Nancy McGinnis, May 23, 1835.
Edward McGinnis, BM.
William Popjoy to Winney Baker, Jan. 17, 1835.
Jno. Easley, BM. (Jan. 19, 1835).
David Ray to Polly Craig, Oct. 31, 1835.
Amon Ray, BM.
Joseph R. Ray to Polly Ray, Feb. 4, 1835.
Mack Sparkman, BM.
Martin Right to Patsy Sparkman, Jan. 18, 1835.
Robert Ray, BM.
Absolam Roach to Vicey Janeway, Dec. 10, 1835.
John Roberts to May Hixon, Jan. 5, 1835.
Dennis Roberts, BM.

83

Greenberry Satterfield to Lucinda Norris, Aug. 12,
  1835. Samuel Parker, BM.
Coleman Seamore to Laveesa Smith, Jan. 15, 1835.
  Caswell Dennis, BM.
William Sharp to Fereby Starnes, Jan. 5, 1835.
  Edward Tate, BM. (Feb. 6, 1835).
Green Simmons to Anney Wilson, Sept. 23, 1835,
  Chesley Trogan, BM. (Sept. 23, 1835).
Robert Smith to Roday Corum, July 18, 1835.
  Martin Beeler, BM.
Samuel Smith to Sarah Dyer, Jan. 19, 1835.
  Thomas S. Cocke, BM.
Godwin Solomon to Ann Mays, Jan. 14, 1835.
  Robert Mitchel, BM.
Samuel Stalsworth to Elizabeth Brochers, Sept. 29,
  1835. David Brochers, BM.
Solomon Stout to Eliza Hynds, Nov. 6, 1835.
  Levi Satterfield, BM.
James Stroud to Nancy Bird, Feb. 17, 1835.
  Amos Stroud, BM.
David N. Tate to Mary Chamberland, March 5, 1835.
  Henry Boyd, BM.
John Vaughan to Phebe A. Francisco, Dec. 15, 1835.
  Daniel Green, BM.
Refus Wiatt to Jane Blair, Feb. 16, 1835.
  Nathan Gray, BM.
William Williams to Catherine Wolfenbarger, Jan. 15,
  1835. Peter Wolfenbarger, BM.
Reuben Wolfenbarger to Nancy Strange, Nov. 21, 1835.

1836

Alfred W. Armstrong to Margaret Faulkner, Nov. 15,
  1836. Wm. E. Cocke, BM.
John Barron to Sarah Millar, Nov. 23, 1836.
  Jesse Williams, BM.
Jacob Beeler to Lucinda Hollingsworth, Feb. 1, 1836.
  Joseph Beeler, BM.
Benjamin Branson to Ann Acuff, Jan. 11, 1836.
  Simeon Acuff, BM.
William Booker to Barbary Devault, Jan. 14, 1836.
  James Booker, BM.
William Brown to Elizabeth Brown, George Brown, BM.
  (Dec. 6, 1836).
Charles Bunch to May Coffman, Oct. 2, 1836.
  James Bunch, BM.
David Burnet to Anna Mayes, Sept. 16, 1836.
  Wm. G. McDaniel, BM.
John Burnett to Mary Adkins, Oct. 29, 1836.
  John Branson, BM. (Nov. 6, 1836).
James Butler to Unity Whitehead, Aug. 21, 1836.
  James Simmons, BM.

Perrin Cardwell to Eliza Norris, Nov. 26, 1835.
Andrew P. Mitchell, BM.
William Clark to Eliza Mallicoat, May 19, 1836.
Jackson Churchman, BM.
Loyd Cockrum to Sarah Kinder, Aug. 10, 1836.
Jackson Churchman, BM.
Andrew P. Coffman to Elizabeth Clark, Feb. 1, 1836.
Enos Hammers, BM.
Alexander Collins to Emely Gressom, Aug. 8, 1836.
Moses Collins, BM.
John Collison to Nancy Grove, Sept. 1, 1836.
James McFarland, BM.
William Counts to Elizabeth Forkner, Feb. 17, 1836.
Andrew Forkner, BM.
William Daniel to Justice Claunch, Oct. 25, 1836.
Wenright Atkins, BM.
John B. Elledge to Elizabeth Edwards, May 24, 1836.
Anderson Hopper, BM.
Daniel Flora to Hannah Blair, July 23, 1836.
Isaac Flora, BM.
Stephen Frost to Nancy Kitts, Jan. 25, 1836.
(Feb. 4, 1836).
Ezekiel Goforth to Lucy Burnet, March 11, 1836.
Elias Lickliter, BM. (March 12, 1836).
Martin Greenlee to Nancy Solomon, Oct. 6, 1836.
Marcus Daniel, BM.
James Guy to Catherine Hamers, Feb. 15, 1836.
Benj. Ford, BM.
Hiram Hayes to Leurana Farmer, July 12, 1836.
Ruben Coffee, BM.
Colby Hays to Sarah Pain, Dec. 31, 1836.
Colbert Hayes, BM.
John Holt to Anna Price, Sept. 28, 1836.
James F. Carmichael, J. P., BM.
Anderson Hopper to Susan Pollard, June 10, 1836.
John Oakly, BM.
Charles C. Hoskin to Mary Meek, April 28, 1836.
Calvin Huddleston to Darcus Smith, April 19, 1836.
Thomas M. Brown, BM. (May 12, 1836).
Hamilton Ivy to Elizabeth Williams, Dec. 19, 1836.
John Ivy, BM. (Dec. 25, 1836).
John Joice to Nancy Mayes, Dec. 27, 1836.
Thomas Joice, BM.
Samuel Jones to Jane Willis, July 23, 1836.
John Hixon, BM.
Robert Joyce to Dinnah Hodge, Nov. 5, 1836.
Thomas Joyce, BM. (Nov. 10, 1836).
Hiram Lain to Eleanor Heart, Aug. 25, 1836.
Abner Dail, BM.
John Lain to Margaret James, July 21, 1836.
Peter Spoon, BM.
Isaac Lowe to Elizabeth Ferguson, Nov. 30, 1836.
Wm. M. Moody, BM.

Clements C. Mallicoat to Eliza Cardwell, July 23, 1836.
John Cardwell, BM.
Absolom Manley to Winney C. Dyer, Dec. 27, 1836.
(Dec. 29, 1836).
John McAnally to Louisa Mann, Sept. 14, 1836.
J. P. Holder, BM.
William McGill to Jane Denever, Dec. 6, 1836.
David Counts, BM.
James D. Mitchell to Narcissa Mynatt, Sept. 21, 1836.
John Mitchell, BM.
Robert Mitchell to Elizabeth Carpenter, Feb. 18, 1836.
Hugh Jones, BM.
William Moore to Polly Demarcus, Sept. 19, 1836.
William Moffett, BM.
Daniel P. Morris to Francis Sparkman, Aug. 18, 1836.
George Sparkman, BM.
Joseph Newman to Elizabeth Blane, May 26, 1836.
Andrew J. Mitchell, BM.
Jonas Nicely to Catherine Chandler, Jan. 1, 1836.
John Chandler, BM.
Edward Pemberton to Martha Hodge, Jan. 8, 1836.
Welcomb Hodge, BM.
Chesley Ray to Jane Ray, Feb. 15, 1836.
Samuel Right, BM.
George Seamore to Amy Brock, July 26, 1836.
Caswell Dennis, BM.
Overton Sexton to Eda Satterfield, July 21, 1836.
James Brawley, BM. (July 29, 1836).
Thomas Smith to Mary Corum, May 21, 1836.
Robert Smith, BM.
Thomas Stroud to Nancy Bird, Feb. 17, 1836.
Montgomery Thornburg to Ann Dyer, April 20, 1836.
William Toliver to Mary Moore, April 27, 1836.
Thomas Harvey, BM. (May 22, 1836).
Thomas Townsley to Elizabeth Ann Shelly, Nov. 23, 1836.
James R. Frazier, Nov. 24, 1836.
Chesley Trogden to Serena Mitchell, May 20, 1836.
John Bailes, BM.
William Turner to Permelia Walker, Aug. 15, 1836.
Thos. K. Howell, BM. (May 1, 1836).
Jacob Vandergriff to Mary Watson, Oct. 4, 1836.
John Branson, BM.
James G. Walker to Elza Harris, Nov. 19, 1836.
John C. Helm, BM. (Nov. 24, 1836).
Hardin Watson to Martha Lathim, Feb. 6, 1836.
Samuel Watson, BM.
James Willeford to Sarah Stone, Sept. 12, 1836.
Wm. Holston, BM.
James William to Racheal Noe, Jan. 7, 1836.
John Noe, BM.
William Williams to Matilda Mitchel, Sept. 5, 1836.
John Bird, BM. (Sept. 8, 1836).

John Baker to Emaline Howerton, Nov. 28, 1837.
William Hollingsworth, BM. (Nov. 28, 1837).
David Ballinger to Sarah Willson, March 6, 1837.
James Willson, BM. (March 6, 1837).
William Box to Elizabeth Green, Aug. 4, 1837.
Robert Cardwell, BM. (Aug. 4, 1837).
John Branson to Martha Watson, Jan. 16, 1837.
Stokley Vititoe, BM. (Jan. 16, 1837).
Shadrack Bunder to Nancy Brownlow, July 3, 1837.
Thos. S. Cocke, BM. (July 5, 1837).
Vardiman Burnet to Susana Mayes, June 23, 1837.
David Burnet, BM. (June 23, 1837).
Robert Cardwell to Nancy Mayes, Oct. 23, 1837.
James Cardwell, BM. (Oct. 23, 1837).
Alexander E. Case to Lucender Ray, Aug. 26, 1837.
Jackson Churchman to Rachel Kindar, Sept. 21, 1837.
James B. Boyd, BM. (Sept. 21, 1837).
William Collins to Mary Ann Carter, July 2, 1837.
Enos Dalton, BM. (July 2, 1837).
Lewis Daniel to Betsey Hilton, Feb. 4, 1837.
Daniel Noe, BM.
Edmund Davis to Jane Jones, Dec. 16, 1837.
William Bunch, BM. (Dec. 16, 1837).
Joseph H. Davis to Amanda M. Jarnagin, Dec. 7, 1837.
James H. Jones, BM. (Dec. 7, 1837).
William H. Davis to Susanna Mitchell, Aug. 17, 1837.
Elija Davis, BM. (Aug. 17, 1837).
Drury Elkins to Sarah Hill, July 29, 1837.
Robert Hill, BM. (July 29, 1837).
Hamilton Elledge to Nancy Holt, Feb. 15, 1837.
Pharoa Price, BM. (Feb. 15, 1837).
Bailes E. Gaines to Rhoda Cowen, Aug. 7, 1837.
Robert C. Gains, BM. (Aug. 7, 1837).
James Gibbons to Martha Smith, Jan. 10, 1837.
Corneleus Gowforth, BM. (Jan. 10, 1837).
Nicholas Gibbs to Vicey Hamilton, Nov. 1, 1837.
Caleb Putman, BM. (Nov. 1, 1837).
William Godwin to Louisa H. Henderson, Dec. 30, 1837.
Millar W. Easley, BM.
Peter Gowan to Katherine Petty, Dec. 4, 1837.
Prior Beeler, BM. (Dec. 4, 1837).
George W. Graham to Harriet Hickle, Sept. 4, 1837.
Martin Greenlee to Nancy Solomon, Oct. 17, 1837.
Enos Hammer to Eliza Coffman, March 9, 1837.
Roodman Harrell to Martha Cardwell, Oct. 12, 1837.
John Harrell, BM.
Maddison Hawey to Anna Bunch, April 12, 1837.
Thomas Howey, BM. (April 12, 1837).
Jacob Haynes to Nancey Shelton, July 1, 1837.
Thomas S. Cocke, BM. (July 1, 1837).
Shadarick Inman to Eliza Jane Riggs, June 26, 1837.
Felps Riggs, BM. (June 26, 1837).

GRAINGER COUNTY MARRIAGES

William James to Elizabeth Robinson, Sept. 14, 1837.
George Robinson, BM. (Sept. 14, 1837).
Aquilla P. Jones to Juliann McCollum, Oct. 6, 1837.
Thos. James, BM.
Elijah Jones to Susanna Harvey, April 12, 1837.
Thomas Harvey, BM. (April 12, 1837).
Abraham Lallis to Mary Purkey, Dec. 2, 1837.
Hutson Robertson, BM.
John Lamden to Mary Warick, Aug. 16, 1837.
Levi Harrell, BM.
Wilson Manly to Tamer Watson, Dec. 27, 1837.
James Cardwell, BM. (Dec. 27, 1837).
John Mathis to Mary Noe, Jan. 19, 1837.
Neelin J. Cox, BM. (Jan. 19, 1837).
George Mayes to Pricila Godwin, Dec. 18, 1837.
George Lacy, BM. (Dec. 18, 1837).
Henry Mayes to Nancy McGinnis, Nov. 21, 1837.
John Lafferty, BM. (Nov. 21, 1837).
James Mayes to Louisa Gray, Jan. 2, 1837.
Isaac Daniel, BM. (Jan. 2, 1837).
Jackson McAnally to Nancy Moore, Oct. 28, 1837.
William Lay, BM.
Reuben McDall to Margaret Donahoo, July 26, 1837.
Abner Dale, BM.
William McGill to Jane Denson, Dec. 19, 1837.
George P. Moody to Jane Countz, March 8, 1837.
James Lacey, BM. (March 8, 1837).
Calvin L. Mynatt to Elizabeth William, Jan. 28, 1837.
James D. Mitchell, BM. (Jan. 28, 1837).
Ira Needham to Anny Seamore, Dec. 2, 1837.
Aaron Hamilton, BM. (Sept. 6, 1837).
Wm. Norris to Leanner Norris, April 3, 1837.
George Norris, BM. (April 3, 1837).
Charles I. Owens to Nancy Ivy, July 23, 1837.
William Pain to Ann M. Thomas, Jan. 2, 1837.
James Rucker, BM.
Nathaniel Patterson to Jane Conn, May 27, 1837.
Thomas Patterson, BM. (May 27, 1837).
Nathan I. Philips to Katherine Pulse, Sept. 20, 1837.
William McAlhany, BM. (Sept. 20, 1837).
Robert Philips to Elizabeth Hill, June 9, 1837.
Ahab Miller, BM. (June 9, 1837).
Samuel Pollard to Elizabeth Smith, Oct. 25, 1837.
David Ray to Anna Roach, Jan. 3, 1837.
Charley Ray, BM. (Jan. 3, 1837).
O. H. P. Reed to Maria Jane Bull, Jan. 21, 1837.
Daniel Reed, BM.
James Reeder to Mary Jackson, March 13, 1837.
Thomas Reeder & Jas. Kinnon, BM. (March 13, 1837).
Josiah Rhoton to M. C. Fort, Sept. 14, 1837.
T. D. Knight, BM. (Sept. 14, 1837).
James Roach to Nancy Ray, Dec. 22, 1837.
James Daniel, BM.

Elijah Rock to Nancy Bunch, Oct. 21, 1837.
    Elijah Rook & Newton Cannon, BM.
Samuel Rucker to Elizabeth Acuff, Dec. 4, 1837.
    John Dotson, BM.
David Rush to Polly Reed, Dec. 3, 1837.
Wilburn Russel to Jane Paschal, May 1, 1837.
    Levi Satterfield, BM. (May 1, 1837).
John Ruth to Sarah Leach, Aug. 23, 1837.
    Stephen Ruth, BM. (Aug. 23, 1837).
Joseph Sallins to Jane McPhetridge, Jan. 2, 1837.
    James Sallings, BM. (Jan. 2, 1837).
Samuel Shockley to Polly Hollandsworth, Aug. 1, 1837.
    (Aug. 6, 1837).
Lewis Shoemaker to Susanna Norris, May 27, 1837.
    Thomas Norris, BM.
Boby Smith to Elizabeth Dafrow, June 26, 1837.
    Wm. W. Cocke, BM. (June 26, 1837).
Edward L. Tate to Mary Ann Gray, Sept. 21, 1837.
    Thomas Tate, BM. (Sept. 21, 1837).
George W. Tate to Margaret C. Tate, Aug. 10, 1837.
    John L. Moffett, BM. (Aug. 10, 1837).
Franklin W. Taylor to Eliza Jane Graham, Nov. 16,
    1837. Thomas J. Lea, BM. (Nov. 16, 1837).
John F. Thompson to Jane Adaline West, Oct. 30, 1837.
    Alexander West, BM.
Isaac F. Vititoe to Elizabeth Needham, Sept. 5, 1837.
    James Vititoe, BM. (Sept. 5, 1837).
Samuel Watters to Elizabeth Oaks, March 29, 1837.
    Solomon Wyrick, BM. (March 29, 1837).
James Williams to Rachel Noe, Jan. 4, 1837.
Isaac Wright to Milinda Shipley, July 29, 1837.
Solomon Wyrick to Glac Donehoo, April 11, 1837.
    William Donehoo, BM. (April 11, 1837).

(?), Eles 9
(?)-gges, Thomas 32
Abbott, Elizabeth 39
Acuff, Alfred 68, 73
  Ann 84
  Benjamin 13
  Cain 8
  Catherine 9
  Charles 65
  Clabourn 68
  Claiborn 72
  Claiborne 58
  David 42
  Elizabeth 87
  Frances 50
  Franky 9, 60
  Henry 19, 21
  James 23, 68
  Jeremiah 58
  John 15, 34, 36, 42, 45, 71
  John, Jr. 71
  Kain 1
  Nancey 12
  Patsy 64
  Polly 12
  Rachel 72
  Rebecka 13
  Richard 8, 12, 23, 68, 73
  Sally 26
  Sarah 49
  Simeon 84
  Simon 79
  Thomas 23, 45, 68, 81
  Thos. 58
  William 12, 19, 79, 81
Adams, Mary 69
  Sally 33
  Susannah 69
Adkins, Amey 13, 14
  Anderson 22
  Barnabas 71
  Cassy 51
  Caty 33
  Elizabeth 16
  Emmanuel 81
  George 65
  James 16
  Lewis 12
  Mary 24, 84
  Richard 13, 40
  Stephen 81
Agy, Isaac 65
Ailor, John 76
Akins, Willis 36
Albert, Martin 23
Aldridge, Joel 52
  Sarah 58, 61

Aldridge (cont.)
  William 63
Alexander, William 79
Alford, John 25
Allsop, Randolph 8
  Robert 8
Allstall, Robert 30
Allsup, Henry 46
  James 1
  James R. 71
  Thomas 23
Alsop, Agnes 11
  Ann 9
  Henry 47
  Nancy 37
  Randolph 9
Alstot, Robert 32
Alsup, Henry 36, 66, 70, 74
Anderson, Amanda 43
  John 12, 28, 65
  Rebecca 26
  Salley 18
  Thomas 30
  William 30
  William J. 45
Andrican, Sally 37
Anglea, William 48
Annett, Jacob 51
Archer, Carnelious 10
  Cornelious 13
  John 65
Archey, John 15
Arm, Ann 71
Armstrong, Alfred W. 84
  Benjamin 45, 53, 54
Arnet, Jacob 41
Arnett, Jacob 45
  Mary 33
Arnold, Peggy 22
  Thomas D. 44
Arnwin, John 8
Arnwine, Albartis 23
  Catharin 64
  Daniel 23
  John 5
Arter, Sarah 2
Arthor, John 2
Artis, Joyes 5
Arwine, Alburtis 45
  Cloe 65
  Elizabeth 32, 34
  James 45, 64
  John 32, 34
Ashart, Elizabeth 16
  Peggy 2
Ashburn, Martin 1
  Polley 18
Asher, Agey 13
Ashert, Jenney 3
Astin, Zachariah 17

Atkin, Eli 67
  George 67
  Stephen 74
Atkins, Catherine 37
  Elizabeth 37
  Fanny 51
  John 50
  Moses 65
  Nancy 80
  Nathan 68
  Richard 23
  Wenright 85
  William 60
  Winright 63
Atkinson, William L. 45
Austin, Steven 2
  William 2
Aytes, Elizabeth 42
  Hiram 79
  James 38
  John 79
  Sarah 40
Bailes, Daniel 6
  Elizabeth 2
  John 8, 86
  Ruth 3
  Susannah 19
Bailey, John 22
  Lety 78
Baker, Deliah 34
  Elizabeth 42
  Hiram 76
  John 87
  Martha 72
  Mary 33
  William 13, 83
  Winney 83
Balard, William 36
Ball, Elender 64
  Elizabeth 43
  James 43, 45
  John 41, 45
  Merine 8
  Osbourne 10
  Peggy 58
  William 28, 31
  Winney 38
Ballard, Mary 21
  Nathan 28, 31
  Richard 26, 38
  Sally 28
Ballenger, Henry 12
Ballinger, Aron 68
  David 87
Barber, Artemis 26
Barby, Elza 42
Barnard, James 58
Barnett, Jaramiah 48
  William 39
Barney, Pearson 25
Barr, John 2

Barret, Presley 55
Barrett, Jasuetha 56
Barron, John 84
Barrow, Julian 61
Barton, David 73, 82
  James 70, 74
  Jas. 8
  Parthena 61
  Wesley 50
  William 8
Bason, Abner 21
Bass, John 2
Bassett, Spencer 30
Bates, Alexander 58
  Allen 58
  Phebe 29
Batis, Elizabeth K. 46
Baughman, Catherine 71
Bayles, Samuel 23
Beadwell, Jesse 13, 16
Bealor, Ann 2
  Caty 46
Bean, Aaron 65
  Anney 3, 5
  Elizabeth 7
  Fetney 15
  George 2, 5, 6
  George, Jr. 2
  Hazard 13
  Jesse 2
  Joel 7
  Lida 40
  Robert 36, 47
  Ruthey 6
  Ruthy 8
  Washington 6, 8
  William 19
Beans, Nicholas 30
Beard, Mary Ann 71
Bearden, Alexander 45
  Marcus D. 42
Beason, Ruth 26
Beatas, Ann 2
Beavers, Sally 12
Beck, (?) 8
Beckham, Eliza Jane 70
  Sarah 74
Bedsaul, George 39
Beeler, Abraham 34
  Anna 10
  Daniel 55
  David 57, 71
  Easter 29, 63
  Elizabeth 36
  George, Jr. 23
  George, Sr. 23
  Isaac 58, 71
  Jacob 58, 71, 84
  John 8, 50, 68
  Joseph 24, 34, 45,
    79, 84
  Martin 84
  Mary 24
  Peter 29, 71
  Prior 87
  Sarah 71
Beelor, Daniel 35
  John 18
  Joseph 44
  Peggy 44
Been, Emond 37
Beets, Lewis 73
Belton, Dudley 53, 59
Benney, William 56
Benson, Martin H. 61
Bentley, Ann 79
  Polly 57
  Susan 78

Berry, Elizabeth 25
Bethrem, Isaac 30
Bettis, Mary 64
Beverly, Nancy 66
Biba, Pryor 68
Bibbins, Elijah 45
Bidwell, Phereby 18
Biggs, Elizabeth 30
  John 79
Bingham, Polley 23
  William 23
Bird, Abraham 13
  Amy 27
  Helyard 81
  Hillard 79
  John 74, 86
  Nancy 84, 86
  Redman 79
Bise, James 79
Bishop, William 10
Bittle, Benj. R. 72
  Charles R. 55
  Mary Ann G. 65
Black, Mathew 2
  Nancey 5
Blackburn, John 13, 21
  John A. 74
  Lathim 60
  Thomas 60
Blackley, Ruth 28
Blackman, Moses 39
Blain, Alexander 76
  Margery 69
  Mary 63
  Robert 13
Blair, Elizabeth 29
  Hannah 85
  James 35
  James, Jr. 30
  James, Sr. 30
  Jane 84
  Joseph 55
  Mary 7, 29
  Nancy 57
  Polly 35
  Richard 47
  Samuel 3
  Robert 3
  Sarah 1
Blake, Joab 53
  John W. 39, 51
  Willby 25
Blane, Elizabeth 86
Blanset, William 48
Bledsoe, Giles I. 71
  Giles J. 48, 80
  Sally 44
  William 83
Blevens, Richard 8
Blige, Jonathan 1
Boatman, Elijah 71
  Elizabeth 27
  Ezechael 79
  George 76
  Henry 35, 73, 76
  Mary 79
  Richard 60
  Sarah 35
  William 17, 60
Boatright, Chasley H.
    39
  James 19, 79
  John 74
  Samuel 19
  Susan 59
  William 19, 45, 64
Boling, Alexander 55
  Edmund 53

Boling (cont.)
  Joseph 7
  Linda 56
  Lucy 7
Bolinger, Caty 40
Bolton, Danial 42
  Elizabeth 30
  Frances 39
  Peter 39
  Susannah 15
  Thomas 17, 21, 24
Boman, Frances 47
  Martha 57, 58
Bomar, Robert 25
Bond, America 40
  Benjamin 14, 30
  Betsy 49
  Charity 30
  Polly 43
  Sally 48
Booker, George 48
  Henry T. 63
  James 84
  Jane 82
  William 84
Booths, Patsey 46
Boseman, Mary 72
Boulter, Jemima 13
Boulton, David 51
  John 14
  Peter 39, 41, 55
Bounds, Hannah 65
Bowan, James 13
Bowdown, Enoch 53
Bowen, Ahab 74, 82
  Andrew 34, 78
  Ann 5
  David 55
  Elizabeth 59
  Evi 42
  George 53
  Henry 9, 10, 15, 50
  Henry, Jr. 13
  Henry, Sr. 14
  James 2, 4, 10, 11, 14
  Jamima 19
  John 50
  Mary 33
  Nancey 4
  Nicholas 48, 50
  Polly 30
  Rase 56
  Rebecca 34
  Reese 50
  William B. 32, 36, 60
Bowers, Andrew 65
  David 63
  John 65
  Reece 55
Bowing, Mary 11
Bowlind, Malinda 78
Bowling, David 12
  Ezekiel 53
  Teney 49
Bowman, (?) 42
  Elizabeth 14
  Martha 53
  Nancy 73
  William 53
Box, Jonathan 41
  Robert 41
  Samuel 31, 39
  William 87
Boyd, Elizabeth 51
  Henry 84
  James 79
  James B. 76, 87
  Martha 83

Boza, Robert 69
Brabson, John 79
Brabston, Vincent B. 82
Braden, Nancy 43
  Richard 34
Bradford, Benj. 3
  Benjamin 6
  Elizabeth 3
  John 5
  Mary 6
Bradley, Isaac 51
  John 60, 65
  William 68
Bradshaw, Joel 76
  Nancy 31
  Pierce 65
  W. 63
Brady, Willis J. 62
Braem, John 39
Bragg, Anna 37
  James 74
  Nancey 15
  Richard 31, 34
Braint, Eliza Ruth 19
  James 19
Brannum, Beaverage 12
  Beverage 12
  James 12
  Sally 12
Branson, Agnes 83
  Benjamin 82, 84
  Catherine 75
  David 15, 19
  James 82
  John 84, 86, 87
  Johnathan 17
  Lemuel 60
  Myra 60
  Nathaniel 26
  Samuel 13, 15
  Sarah 62
  Solomon 64
  Susan 82
Branston, Elizabeth 64
Brason, Isaac 11
Brastly, Sally 56
Bratwell, Nancy 53
Brawley, James 86
Bray, Benjamin 60
  Fanney 14
  Hagner 31
  Henry 31
  Nancey 23
  Sarah 24
  Stagner 23
Breaden, Polly 48
  Susanah 33
  William 33
Breeden, Edward 63
  Thomas 29
Breeding, Susan 59
Brevare, Sarah 48
Briant, Delia 55
  Elizabeth 62
  James 61, 66
  Melesa 73
  Patsy 61
  Rachel 38
  William 62
Bridgeman, Ann 83
  Jane 50
  Malvina 69
  Martin 68
Bridges, Elizabeth 4
  James 2, 3
  Squire 53
  Susanna 5
Bridgman, Martin 81

Bright, George 53, 58
  John 22
  Moses 50
Brightwell, Sarah 54
Brigman, Margaret 77
Brigs, John 21
Bristo, Polly 34
Bristow, Samuel 18
  Thomas 21
Britian, Elizabeth 21
Britt, Joseph 9
  Rebecca 9
Brochers, David 84
  Elizabeth 84
Brock, Allen 10
  Amy 86
  Anna 41
  Betsey 44
  Dicy 26
  Edward 48
  Elender 49
  Elizabeth 7, 38
  George 26, 38, 79
  James 36, 81
  Jesse 10
  John 42, 79
  Joseph 10
  Lenard 34
  Lenord 36, 38, 39
  Leonard 23
  Lora 5
  Moses 48, 76
  Obediah 32
  Polly 27
  Sarah 7
  Thomas 76
  Winny 35
  Theana W. 32
Brocker, Jerry 48
  Larvos 53
Brockers, John 28
  Thomas 36
Brocks, Thomas 36
Brockus, Nancy 67
  William 41
Brocus, Thomas 31
Brogan, Raynolds 5
  Reynolds 80
Brookers, William 74
Brooks, Charles 28
  Elizabeth 28, 75
  John 28, 76
Brown, Amelia 67
  David 10
  Edward 8, 11
  Elizabeth 15, 84
  George 84
  Henry 32, 80
  Hepsia 62
  Hezekiah 32
  Isaac 8
  James 28
  John 32, 33, 36, 40,
    46, 47, 48, 49, 53
  Joseph 42
  Mary 7, 70
  Polly 32, 51
  Samuel 15, 71, 72
  Sarah 72, 80
  Shedrick 18
  Thomas 37
  Thomas M. 85
  W. M. 58
  William 8, 15, 18, 31,
    42, 69, 74, 84
Brownlow, Nancy 87
Brumfield, Humphrey 58
Brummet, Elijah 43

Brummet (cont.)
  Elizabeth 43
Brunt, Abraham 15
Bruvinton, John 23
Bryan, Elizabeth 42
  John 21
  Joseph 21, 28, 43
  Josiah 17
  Thomas 28
Bryant, James 25, 42
  Jenny 25
  John 42
Brye, James 62
Bucher, Jane 35
Buckacre, William 44
Buckner, Ezra 46
  Henry 5
Buggs, Elizabeth 8
Bull, George 8
  John 5, 8, 15, 37
  John, Sr. 5
  Joseph 23, 45
  Maria Jane 88
  Polly 30
  Richard 14
  Sarah 48
Bullin, Isaac 65
  Joseph 65
Bullock, Agens 69
  Elijah 21
Bumpower, Betty 35
Bunch, Amstead 77
  Anderson 21
  Anna 87
  Armstead 74
  Bechman 61
  Charles 84
  David W. 36
  Delilah 21
  Elizabeth 79
  Elsa 38
  James 84
  Jesse 15
  John 4, 10, 21, 36, 43
  John, Jr. 17, 18
  Joseph 71
  Joseph C. 60
  Josiah 62
  Josiah C. 65
  Lavina 73
  Mary 29
  Nancy 89
  Orlena P. 63
  Patsey 33
  Polley 10
  Pryor P. 53
  Sally 21, 50
  Samuel 27, 43
  Samuel C. 63
  Serenia 4
  Suckey 5
  Susanah 28
  Thomas 10, 21
  William 8, 21, 29, 49,
    87
  Winslow W. 53
Bunde, David 10
Bunder, Shadrack 87
Burch, Rosannah 30
Burge, William 57
Burk, Betsey 14
  Rilaw 14
Burke, Richard 14
  Ryland 14
Burket, Sarah 41
Burnet, David 84, 87
  Eliza 19
  Frances 36

93

Burnet (cont.)
James 21, 27
John 34, 36
Lucy 85
Presley 62
Sally 62
Vardiman 87
Burnett, Benard 50
Claiborne 21
Columbia 81
Elizabeth 46
James 21, 28, 41
Jeremiah 52
John 84
Patsey 28
Richard 21
Sarah 65
William 28
Burnham, Joshua 17
Mary 14
Burns, George B. 71
Burton, John 2, 4, 11
William 10, 32
Busby, Mary 6
William 61
Bush, William 80
Bushong, Joseph 50
Butcher, Barnabas 12
Ezekiel 58
Hasting 71
Holston 67
Isaac 58, 63
John 21
Polly 63
Sarah 67
Buther, James 28, 30
Butler, Isaac 77
James 84
Mary 58
Stephen 65, 79
Buzby, John 3
Byrd, Henry 37
John 6
Cabbage, Adam 41
Betsey 45
Jacob 39
John 26
Patsy 51
Caffey, Winney 17
Cain, Anne 72
Hugh 60
Louisa 60
Caits, Barry 55
Rebeccah 58
Caldwell, St. Clair F. 37
Callison, Polley 22
Samuel 21
Callum, Mary 2
Callume, Sarah 13
Calvin, John 12
Cameron, Abraham 26
Hardin 77
Campbell, Alexander 12
Charles 41
David 10
Davis 45
Easter 53
Elizabeth 17, 47
George 60
Jain 20
James 12, 22, 31, 60, 62, 69
James S. 69
Jane 74
John 65, 77, 81, 82
Lewis 77, 82
Mary 53

Campbell (cont.)
Nancy 60
Sarah 35, 62
Usley 12
Camron, John 71
Canhill, Frankey 18
Cannon, Elizabeth 59
Hughes 53
James 34
John 66
Kesiah 66
Nancey 27
Newton 89
Polly 39
Cantrell, Stephen 21
Capps, Benjamin 28
David 41
Elizabeth 3
Jacob 60
Mary 53
Rachael 17, 52
Rebecca 47
Sarah 29
Caps, David 39
Jacob 39
Car, Henry 82
Thomas 82
Carathers, Anna 49
Carback, Mariah 63
Mariah Ann 65
Thomas 63
Carden, Goldman B. 82
John 60
William T. 63
Carder, William 55
Cardin, William T. 43
Cardivile, Alice 69
Cardwell, Anthony 46, 48
Daniel 39, 40, 45, 50, 53, 54
Eliza 86
James 87, 88
John 43, 69, 86
Martha 83, 87
Mary 69
Perrin 85
Robert 77, 87
Thomas G. 50
William 43, 63
William L. 63
Wm. L. 63, 65
Carmack, Edward 4
Carmical, Daniel 58
Samuel 59
Carmichael, Duncan 2
James 83
James F. 85
Carmichal, Abigal 1
William B. 65
Carney, John 45
Nancy 45
Carnut, Wm. 60
Carnutt, David 66
Fanny 35
Frances 50
William 35, 36, 57, 66
Carole, Alfred 49
Carpenter, Elizabeth 34, 86
Carr, Henry 61
John 80
Carrigan, Hugh 1
Carrol, James 43
John 43
Carroll, Minerva 76
Prudence 69
Rebecca 67

Carroll (cont.)
William 74
Carruthers, Rebecca 60
William 71
Carson, John 6
Carter, Mary Ann 87
William 6
Wm. 8
Carthers, Betsy 42
Carwiles, Catherine 65
Casady, Frances 62
Case, Alexander E. 87
Benjamin 27
Eleakin 26
Casey, Anney 18
John 2
Letty 61
Samuel 2, 49
Cass, Elizabeth 3
Cassady, Elizabeth 50
James 50, 65
Nancy 47
Casy, Joshua 32
Cates, Anderson 50
Charles 58, 80
Daniel H. 82
Martha 77
Mary 72
Samuel 39, 45
Stephen 50
Cavender, Mary 81
Caveriden, Sally 56
Cawley, Elizabeth 69
Cayton, Elijah 28
Certain, Rachel 24
Chais, Charles 48
Chamber, Hanah 29
Chamberlaim, Ninion 22
Chamberlain, Andrew 69
Janet 22
Jeremiah 7
Mary 17
Thomas 76
Chamberlan, Thompson 39
Chamberland, Mary 84
Chamberlian, Elizabeth 23
Chamberlin, Margaret 47
Ninian 29
Peggy 16
Polley 20
Chamberling, Elizabeth 45
Chambers, Anny 22
Daniel 36
Rhoda 22
Sally 28
Chammes, Asbury 41
Chandler, Betsy 33
Catherine 86
Daniel 33
Hannah 80
John 67, 70, 71, 74, 86
Nancy 67
Polly 62
Thomas 39
Chandlers, Asbury 21
Chaney, James 48
Channey, Rebecca 49
Chapman, Joseph 53
Chase, Jacob P. 65
John 60
William 74
Cheek, James 61, 78
Jas. 70
Jesse 16
Milton 55
Sally 16
William 36

94

Chersher, Thomas 32
Chesher, Anny 46
  Edmund 73
  Edward 79
  Mary 75
  Presley S. 75
  Sytha 23
  Thornton 21, 23
Cheshir, Thornton 19
Cheshire, Edmund 73
Chesney, John 82
Chesser, Edward 47
Chetty, Elizabeth 25
Childres, Elizabeth 70
  Susanah 47
Childs, John 71
Chiles, Rowling 77
Chillis, Jane 70
Chisum, Elisabeth 1
Christian, Alfred 82
  Allen 7
  Oney 7
Churchman, Delila 75
  Edward 48
  Hannah 65
  Jackson 85, 87
  James S. 80
  Jane 75
  Melinda 51
  Nancy 29
  Polly 38
  Rachel 56, 73
  Rebecca 23, 52
  Reubin 8
  Roda 40
  Rubin 8
  Sally 73
  Sarah 82
  Thomas 23, 29, 34
Chusher, Elizabeth 33
Claibourn, Mallicoat
  J. 78
Clanch, Cinda 74
Clapp, Delia 61
Claridge, Hayman 48
Clark, Armstead 69
  Edward 59
  Eli 28, 34, 71
  Elisabeth 10
  Elizabeth 3, 85
  Fanney 8
  George 19
  Isham 5
  James 23, 53
  John 26, 27, 50
  Joseph 50, 51, 74,
    77
  Levi 28, 31
  Patsy 51
  Poley 6
  Polly 58
  Reuben 83
  Tressie 11
  William 30, 32, 44,
    50, 85
Clarkson, Mary Ann 78
Clasop, William 15, 16
Classop, Jenny 16
Classton, Daniel 14
Claunch, Justice 85
  Milley 5
  Peggy 21
  Sally 63
Clauson, Peter 3
Claxton, Anney 5
  Sarah 15
Clay, Cynthia 39
  Eleazar 8

Clay (cont.)
  Eliazer 9
  Macah 56
  Margret 17
  Nancy 9, 33
  Sabrine 9
  William 8
Clayton, Clay 24
  Daniel 9, 11
  John 35
  Lindy 35
Clear, Peter 21
Clemmons, Richard 15
Clerk, Elizabeth 3
  Joseph 5
  Margaret 4
Cleveland, Abey 61
  Jese 69, 80
  Martin 74
  Nancy 71
Clevenger, Thos. 76
Clifton, Anney 14
  Fanny 3
  Francis 3
Cline, Sarah 32
Clipper, Joseph 66
Cloud, Betsy 44
  Samuel 15
Clounch, Abigal 71
  David 71
  Elizabeth 18
Clowen, Daniel 21
Clower, Anney 17
Clowers, James 49, 52
  Sally 28
Clowes, James 32
Clown, Anney 15
Cluck, Daniel 36, 39
  Henry 39
  John 77
Clurk, John 3
Coats, Benjamin 7, 80
  David 41, 55
  Jesee 55
  Kinsey 17, 21
  Lewis 60
Cobb, Barsheba 65
  Eliza 45
  Franky 25, 27
  Harrold 27
  Jesse 45
  Joseph 1
  Mary 59
  Patsy 24
  Pharoah B. 68
  Thomas 24
Cobby, Coffee 69
Cocke, Anny E. 42
  James 1
  James C. 66
  James R. 67
  John 9, 10, 14, 22,
    25, 28, 33, 36, 37,
    39
  Mary Jane 31
  Rebeckah 32
  Sarah F. 82
  Stephen 39, 40
  Sterling 23, 26, 33,
    43
  Thomas 66
  Thomas C. 62
  Thomas S. 84, 87
  Thos. S. 87
  William E. 32, 38, 46,
    51
  William F. 36
  William M. 82

Cocke (cont.)
  Wm. 55
  Wm. E. 49, 55, 62, 84
  Wm. W. 89
Cockram, Jane 75
  Massey 56
  Phebe 76
Cockrim, Nancy 37
Cockrum, Loyd 85
  Luise 46
  Margat 8
Cody, Pierce 71
Coffee, Dilpha 63
  Eliza 81
  James 56, 68
  Jenney 16
  Joel 66
  John 56
  Mary 76, 77
  Matilda 82
  Meredith 16
  Merriel 9
  Mira 62
  Ruben 85
  Sally 9
Coffer, Meredith 46
Coffey, John 45
Coffiman, William 41
Coffman, Andrew 41
  Andrew P. 85
  Barton 63
  Betsey 47
  David 28
  Eliza 82, 87
  Leanard 71
  May 84
  Michael 28
  Nancy 20
  Rhinehart 71
  Rinhart 18
  Salomy 41
  Thomas 41
  William 39, 65
Coffy, Ann 41
  John 41
  Mirideth 15
Coke, Sterling 31
  Wm. E. 59
Colby, Coffee 69
  Sarah 37
Cole, Elisha 5
Coleman, William 50
Colinsworth, Louisa 67
Collingsworth, Addison 56
Collins, Alexander 85
  Allen 60
  Biddy 60
  Conley 63
  David 7, 8
  Dowell 15
  George 63
  Griffin 15, 45
  Isaiah 14
  James 56
  Jincy 78
  John 45
  Lewis 71
  Mary 66, 78
  Moses 60, 85
  Nelley 5
  Peggy 8
  William 87
Collinsworth, Addison 70
  Mary 70
Collison, John 79, 85
  John, Sr. 5
  Lucinda 74
Collissen, James, Jr. 5

Colson, Elizabeth 67
  Sarah 28
Colvin, Anna 74
  Elijah 48
  James' 58
Combs, Elizabeth 50
  Francis 56
  Geo. M. 47
  George 3
  John 17, 45, 58
  Joseph 69
  L. B. 59
  Lewis 10, 17
  Nancy 27
  Phillip 18
  Pleasant 69
Condray, Mathius 26
Condrey, Peggy 46
  Pherney 46
Condry, Dennis 30
  Elizabeth 51
  Henry 50
  Homar 60
  Isaac 56
  James 23
  Nancey 30
  Pherncy 43
  Saudel 30
  William 12
Conley, Betsey 19
  Jeminah 7
Conn, James 20, 23, 25
  Jane 88
Connel, Abraham 56
Conner, John 22
  John 51
Conway, Dennie 12
Coody, Nancy 46
Cook, Hezekiah 15
  Isaac 53
  John 43
  Nancy 24
  Patsy 4
  Rebecca 34
  Rosanna 18
  William 24
Cooke, Barberry 7
  Sinthia 4
Coom, Michael 12
Coons, Sarah 14
Cooper, Isaac 4, 7
  John 1, 3
  Patsey 14
  William 4, 7, 14, 28
Cope, Prudence 5
Copeland, Jacinthea 39
  John 69
  Mary 22
  Samuel H. 80
  Sarah C. 78
Copland, Anna K. 38
  John 3
  Thomas 17
Coram, Celia 82
  Polly 58
  Rushey 69
  Susan 80
  Thornton 60
Cordell, Nancy 20
Cornut, John 60
Cornwell, Elijah 31
Corothers, Elizabeth
  20
Correthers, John 10
Corrithers, Elizabeth
  20
Corum, Dolly 67
  Lucinda 81

Corum (cont.)
  Martin 60
  Mary 86
  Polly 43
  Roday 84
  Sarah 82
  Thornton 60
  William 54
Cothern, Mary 65
Cothill, Rubin 14
Cotner, Barbara 30
  Catherine 62
  Martin 28
  Rosana 36
Cotrill, Ralien 15
Cotton, James 26
  Polley 19
Coulter, J. 6
Counce, Aaron 33
  Henry 44
  Nicholas 39
Counte, David 74
Counts, Aaron 46, 52,
  57, 67
  David 51, 53, 59, 63,
  64, 86
  Henry 50, 53, 59, 82
  James 66
  Jese 52, 66
  Jessee 53
  Nancy 56
  Phillip 1
  Susan 53
  William 85
Countz, Arron 36
  Caty 25
  David 15, 20
  Isaac 10
  Jane 88
  Jesse 47
  John 3, 10, 11, 13
  Nicholas 28
  Peggy 20
  Susanna 13
  William 3
Covender, Benjamin 60
Cowen, Rhoda 87
Cox, Abraham 32
  Anny 26
  Benjamin 36
  Bremas 48
  Brewis 46
  Charles 11
  Daniel Clay 9
  Dorcus 58
  Dudley 20
  Edmond 23
  Edy 76
  Elisha 26
  Elizabeth 46
  Hannah 11, 47
  Harmon 43
  Harmond 28
  Herman 49
  Hopkins 34
  Jean 10
  Jeramiah 15
  Jeremiah 19
  Jese 69
  John 32, 77, 79
  Lucy 14
  Margrett 19
  Neelin J. 88
  Patsey 15
  Sarah 76
  Solomon 43
  Susanna 83
  William 4

Coxe, Sally 40
Crabb, Elizabeth 11
  John 18
  Stephen 3
Craig, Polly 83
  Thomas 41
Craighead, Benj. 59, 63
  Benjamin 53, 57, 63, 79
Crain, Cassandra 73
  Charles 32
  Charles, Sr. 32
  David 76
  Davis 74
  John 74, 79, 81
  John, Jr. 60
  Prudence 50
  Sally 16
Craves, Precilla 29
Cravs, Pricilla 25
Cravy, Benjamin M. 73
Crawford, Mary 18
  Moses 51
  Polly 46
  William 81
Crawley, Henry 24
  John 75
Crawly, Polly 24
Creech, Jesse 41
  John 66
Creely, Polly 56
Crewe, Mary 11
Crews, Henry 53
  Howell 56
Creyton, John 32
Criner, John 7
Crisby, John 19
Cristol, Ritchard 1
Cross, Gibbons 19
  Patsey 15
Crouce, Henry 14
Crouse, Elizabeth 52
  John 63, 74
  Margarite 76
  Mary 14
  Mathias 14
  Nemoe 69
Crow, John 18
  Rebecka 18
  William 48
Crows, Anna 27
Cruise, John B. 53
Culvahouse, Betsy 54
  John 58
Culvehouse, Edward 46
  Lewis 63
Culverhouse, John 61
Culvyhouse, Nancy 48
Cunningham, Anna 53
  Darkis 5
  Ezabella 19
  Olevey 6
Cupp, George 71
Curl, Elizabeth 61
  Elleanor M. 56
  Joshua 80
  Susan A. 76
  William H. 63
Curry, Nancy Minerva 78
Cutter, Seth 19
Cutts, Paschal 54
  Robert 55
Cyrus, Nancy 32
  Nimrod 34
  Enock 34
Dafrow, Elizabeth 89
Dail, Abner 44, 85
  Elizabeth 44
  Jonathan 47

Dail (cont.)
Ruth 30
Dale, Abner 88
Barbara 14
Ebben 53
Elizabeth 61
Isabella 4
Jonathan 19, 41
Nancy 69
Dalten, Carter 48
Dalton, Aggy 32
Agnes 32
Carter 45, 82
Carter J. 77
David 36
Enos 87
Haniah 42
Hannah 45
Mary 26
Meredith 63
Meridia 28
Reubin, Jr. 19
Reubin, Sr. 19
Rubin 28
Tandy 82
Timothy 63, 69
William 69
Damewood, Isaac 56, 66
James 53, 56
Peggy 21
Daniel, Anna 82
Catherine 76
Delila 3
Dinah 67
Edward 25, 31, 82
Elizabeth 16, 23
Isaac 71, 88
Jacob 56
James 51, 77, 88
John 31, 75
Joseph 16, 43
Lewis 87
Marcus 85
Mark 80
Mary 66, 79
Micheal O. 13
Mima 70
Rachel 55
Rebecca 28
Robert 63, 77
Sarah 35, 82
Stephen 11
William 46, 53, 85
Dannel, Mary 29
Danner, Jacob 32
Danniel, Elizabeth O. 8
Dannil, Liddy 7
Darnell, Harrett 78
Darnold, Sidney 60
Daughty, William 58
Daulton, Colby 77
Enoch 77
Timothy 77
David, Elias 8, 40
Davidson, Abner 8
Alexander 9, 10
Allin 34
Briant 34
Jacob 31
James 43
John 34
Joseph 8
William 12, 31, 43
Davis, Benjamin 20, 23, 40
Catherine 44
Charlotte 22
Clarenda 70

Davis (cont.)
Clarsa 73
Edmund 87
Elnathan 71
Elza 67, 77, 87
Enoch 3
Isaac 8
James 10, 18, 46, 56, 64
James, Jr. 63
John 2, 36, 46, 56, 66, 67, 71, 76, 82
Joseph H. 77, 87
Margaret 2
Mary 83
Mary Ann 46
Moses 4
Nancy 83
Nathanile 8
Polley 18
Polly 23
Rachel 71
Rebecca 43, 48
Robert 46
Sally 53
Samuel 43
Sarah 75
Temperance 26
Thomas 17
William 53, 82
William H. 87
Davison, Bleir 5
James 5
Deakins, John 17
Debord, William 8
Deer, James 69
Defoe, Polley 18
Delosure, Sally 12
Demarcus, Margaret R. 81
Polly 86
Denerant, Wilson C. 51
Denever, Jane 86
Denham, Philip 26
Dennis, Abby 77
Betsey 13
Caswell 84, 86
Catherine 75
Easter 49
Edward 23, 26, 27, 28
John 26, 39, 71
John, Jr. 74, 77
Joseph 20, 46, 51, 53
Joseph, Jr. 63
Letty 68
Levi 38, 49, 69, 77
Mahala 53
Mary 51
Nancy 69
Pharaba 81
Rachel 9, 27
Salley 54
Sarah 34
Thomas 9
William 29, 39, 52, 66, 81, 82
Zephrona 48
Dennison, James 77
Denniston, Robertson 31
Dennon, John 46
Denny, John 12
Densar, Katherine 66
Denson, Catherine 70
Jane 88
Dent, Elizabeth 47, 52, 55
Jeney 28
John 51, 54

Dent (cont.)
Lucindia 36
Polly 38
Sarah 54
Temple M. 57
Derham, Mahaly 52
Nancy 39
Derur, Nannie 3
Devault, Barbary 84
Elizabeth 79
Thomas 48
Deveaul, David 5
Dever, Nance 3
Dial, Abel 30
Dickerson, Judith 14, 15
Dickiner, Ailcey 11
Dickson, Nancy 56
William 44
Dinckin, Nancy 43
Dire, Lea 74
Dixon, Hartin 1
Jeremiah 16
Dobb, Alexander 46
Dobbin, Sarah 68
Dobbins, Griffin 54
Dobston, John 12
Dockery, Greenville 53
James 25
Dodson, Elisha 10
James 36, 38
Jesse 19
John 4, 5, 12
Martin 12
Mary 7
Nancy 75
Nimrod 1
Ruben 72
Ruth 33
Samuel 5, 18, 19, 33, 43
Sarah 5
Solomon 8
William 24, 40
Doghead, Mary 4
Dolson, Betsy 45
Donah, John 6
Donahoo, Margaret 88
Donahugh, Henry 58
Donathan, Elijah 6, 8
Donehoo, Glac 89
William 89
Donelson, Alexander 10
Joel 26
John 25
Donner, John 79
Liddy 79
Dora, John 5
Dossett, Willis 20
Dotson, Clabourn 56
Elish 41
James 53
John 14, 89
Margaret 78
Mary 65
Rolly 44, 48
Ruben 66
Saml. 56
Samuel 55
Samuel, Jr. 66, 77
Stephen 48, 61
William 22, 63
Douglas, Hetty 51
John 61
Douglass, Berryman 19
Polley 21
Dove, William 61
Drake, Charles 12
Elizabeth 35

97

Drake (cont.)
Lucy 27
Draper, Thena 40
Dresser, Henry 14
Duff, Hugh A. 80
James 80
Duglass, Catherine 19
Duke, John 10
Nancy 11
Richard 3
Susey 19
Dumbille, Ellender 11
Dumbelle, Mary 8
Dunahoo, Martin 80
William 80
Duncan, Abner 29
Joel 69
Duncomb, Benjamin 46,
54
Philip 46
Dunevan, Wilson 56
Dunham, Philip 46
Dunhaw, Dicy 44
Dunkin, Joseph 4
Polly 43
Theny 16
Dunlap, Jenny 2
Dunlop, Jenney 2
Dunn, Thomas 8, 18, 20
Timothy 1
Dunnahew, Delila 69
Dunning, William 37,
39
Durham, Elizabeth 14
Durharam, William 14
Duyless, Mary 8
Dyche, Michael 23
Dyer, Agnes 7, 70
Ann 8, 86
Anna 68
Charleston 32
Charlton 26, 32, 48
Cynthia 80
Elizabeth 19, 37, 65,
78
Ellender 14
Franky 11
George 34, 46, 54
Hannah 66
Isaac 26, 28, 33, 36,
63, 82, 83
Isaac B. 39
James 8, 19, 31, 46,
62
James, Jr. 8, 63
Jenny 10
Joel 14, 24
John 77, 82
Joseph 16, 38, 49,
53
Joshua 32
Lea 70, 77, 78
Lucinda 36
Mahala 76
Mariah 73
Mary 71
Mary Ann 18
Nancy 26, 34, 67
Nelson 83
Owen 43, 47, 51
Polly 36, 62
Rebecca 73
Sarah 47, 84
Spilsby 19
Thomas 39, 41, 49
Wenney 49
William 14, 18, 27,
54, 66, 69, 77

Dyer (cont.)
William A. 77
William S. 27, 71
Wilson 66
Winford 43
Winney C. 86
Winny 32
Dyke, Catherine 61
Jacob 61
Easeley, Miller W. 11
Easely, Susannah 10, 11
Easley, Caroline H. 66
Elizabeth 19, 80
Francis 36
Jno. 83
John 67, 71, 75, 81,
83
Martha 45
Mary L. 82
Millar W. 87
Miller W. 11
Sarah 50
Warham 55
William 56, 61
Worsham 25, 39
Wortham 82
Easly, Miller 22
Easter, Lucy 79
Easterly, John 49, 80
Louisa 80
Eastise, Mary 42
Eastridge, James 7
Eaton, Andrew C. 56,
65, 67, 68, 69, 70
Andy E. 65
Daniel 82
Elisha 54
James 75, 77
Jas. 8
John W. 77
Joseph 8, 25, 29
Margaret 56
Marget 8
Mary 4
Robert D. 16
William 29
William G. 80
Eckell, George S. 80
Edger, Mary 29
Edington, John 46
Edmons, Delia 57
Edward, John 36
Edwards, Brown 29
Elizabeth 85
John 82
Lewis 17, 18
Edyman, Kimbles 1
Elder, Andrew 16
Elkin, James 32
Elkins, Drury 87
Elizabeth 55
James 12, 23
Joseph 44
Mary 24
Patsey 28, 32
Patsy 44
Sarah 40, 79
Stacy 63
William 46
Elledge, Hamilton 87
John B. 85
Ellet, Rebecca 74
Elliot, Matthew 9
William 9
Elliott, Abner 17
Elizabeth 17, 74
Ellis, Grace 16
Lewis N. 61

Ellis (cont.)
Mary 55
William 36
Elmore, David 7
Elsey, John 7
Ely, Mary 2
Emmery, Benjamin 32
England, James 58
English, Matthew 5
Ennis, Mary 15
Epps, Edward 11
William 36
Erby, Charles 49
Erly, Elizabeth 49, 51
Eress, Elizabeth 1
Ernwine, John 9
Ertic, America 59
Estes, Ceale 16
John 6, 51
John, Jr. 71
Sally 6
Sarah 57
Estis, Nancy 47
W. 43
William 61
Ethons, David 19
Etter, Samuel 30
Eustice, Anney 35
Washington 35
Evans, Acy 61
Ambrose 66, 70
Andrew 4
Andrew C. 26
Anney 8
Asa 80
David 4, 5, 71
Elijah 17
George 43
Harmon 4
Jesee 56
John 76
Lewis 48
Martha 74
Mary 29, 53
Sarah 58
Seney 60
Walter 41
William 43
Everet, Susanah 6
Evins, Joel 4
Ezel, Solomon 34
Ezell, James 31, 34
Jesse 34, 38
Fain, Catey 60
Fargerson, Elizabeth 33
Polly 21, 43
Farley, Richard E. 82
Susan Ann 82
Farmer, Hugh 74, 77
Hugh W. 77
James 34
John 74
Lucinda 72
Farr, Nancy 20
Faulkner, Margaret 84
Fears, Jack 26
James 19, 21, 33
Sarah 4
William 21
Fergeson, James 10
Ferguson, Alice 57
Andrew 48, 62
Benjamin 1
Edward 56
Elizabeth 77, 85
Mimey 15
Richard 63
Thomas 43, 48, 69

Fielding, Elizabeth 69
  James 61
  Jane 62
  Sally 56
  William 61
Fields, Disey 68
  Joel 36, 51
  Joseph 29
  Letty 39
  Mary 29
  Robert 21, 27
  Susannah 34
Fiers, Mary 3
  William 3
Fincher, John 39
Findley, Martha 64
  Martha F. 81
  Samuel A. 46
Finley, Archibald 54
Fisher, Eliza 82
Flanagan, James 81
Fletcher, Elizabeth 70
  Hannah 39
  William 54
Flora, Daniel 85
  Elizabeth 71
  Isaac 69, 85
  Nancy 74
Floyd, Delmah 71
  Hiram 66, 68
  Johnathan 66
  Lemuel 48
  Polly B. 36, 60
  Robert 71
Ford, Benj. 85
  Betsy 65
  Elizabeth 10
  Emeline 76
  John 58
  Matilda 58
  Sophia 73
Forkner, Andrew 85
  Elizabeth 85
Forrest, Richard 10
Fort, Jacob H. 39
  M. C. 88
Fortner, Mahala 54
  Visa 54
Foster, Fanny 5
  Joseph 80
  Vita 46
Fowler, James 23
Fox, George 44
  Sally 44
Francis, Elizabeth 54
Francisco, Phebe F. 84
Franklin, Robert 57, 63
Frazier, James M. 82
  James R. 86
  Julian 82
  Louisa 83
Free, Lucritia 60
  Philip 16, 28
Freeman, William 82
Frost, Henry 71, 82
  John 48, 66
  Lorenza 82
  Stephen 85
Fry, Addison 77
  Benjamin 45, 82
  Henry 59
  John 32
  John S. 81
  Martha 24
  Robert 36
Frye, Benjamin 46
  Margaret 69
Gain, Joseph 24

Gaines, Anna 60
  Bailes E. 87
  Bales E. 77
  Bolis E. 72
  David 9
  Mildred 77
  Nicholas 54
  Robert 21
  Robert E. 82
Gains, Bales E. 71
  Martha 1
  Robert C. 87
  Sarah 7
  William 32
  William H. 19
Galian, James 38
  John 37
Gallant, James 29
  Polley 12
Gallian, Betsey 26
  Jacob 15
  John 39
Gallion, Elizabeth 11
  James 41
  Joshua 5
  Mary 37
  Precia 43
  Sarah 21
  William 36, 37
Galyon, Elizabeth 18
  Jacob 14
  John 27
  Josiah 18
  Thomas 14
Gambill, Henry 71
Gamewell, Thomas 66
Garison, Fracom 61
Garland, Susanah 41
Garner, Maser 60
Garratt, John 18
  William 18
Garret, John 18, 48
  Polley 18
Garrett, Gray 68
Garrison, John 54
Garroth, Elizabeth 8
Gassage, Elizabeth 40
Gaults, Joseph 41
Gentry, Nancy 35
George, Henry 16
  William 34
Gibbons, James 87
  Robert 56
  Thomas 4
Gibbs, John 7
  Nicholas 87
Gibson, Abyram 21
  Archebus 5
  Barnabas 5
  Caleb 41, 49
  Garret 31
  Lindsy 36
  Linsey 42
  Lizy 41
  Memey 19
  Polley 11
  Valentine 5
  William 16
Giffin, Thomas 31
Gilbert, Thomas 9
Gilbraith, Elizabeth 5
Gill, Eliza 49
  Martha 56
  Mary 52
  Samuel 82
  Sarah 58
Gillmore, Elizabeth 76
  James 74, 77

Gillmore (cont.)
  John 74
  Nancy 22
  Samuel 21
Gilmore, Anny 29
  Elizabeth 9
  Hugh 14, 21, 28, 36, 39
  Isbel 14
  James 72
  Jno. 1
  John 9, 80
  Mary 55
  Parthena 76
  Samuel 75, 80
  William 43
  Wilson 77
Ginnins, Obediah 4
Gipson, Mary 7
  Valentine 7
Glasgow, Dicy 43
  John 39
  Polley 18
Glassop, Charlotte 42
  William 23, 26
Glassup, Zachariah 56
Glossupp, Jonathan 61
Glosupp, Jonathan 58
Goan, Polly 28
  Pryer 72
  Samuel 82
Goans, David 72
  Drury 37
  Levi 4
  Mary 37
  Pryor 80, 81
Godwin, Betsy 47
  Claiborn 68
  Jacob 66, 70, 83
  John 61, 62
  Mahala 49
  Margaret 62
  Peter 48
  Pricila 88
  William 87
Goforth, Cornelius 69
  Ezekiel 85
Goin, Jeremiah R. 66
  Rebecca 26
Going, Levi 56
  Sally 53
  Shadrach 53
Goins, Elizabeth 66
  Isabella 29
Golden, Elizabeth 44
Golder, Polly 49
Goldin, Anna 33
  Jacob 45
  Joseph 23
Gorden, Robert 5
Gordon, Nancey 5
Goulden, Milly 52
Goulding, Anney 6
Gowan, Peter 87
Gowen, Drury 9
  Nancy 9
Gowforth, Corneleus 87
Gowin, Betsy 66
  Drury 58
  Henry 69
  Nathan 66
  Preston 66
Gowing, Caleb 43
  Claborn 43
  David 43
  Nancy 53
Gowins, Martha 58
Gradley, Anney 16
Grady, Barbary 64

Grady (cont.)
  Delpha 80
  Douglas 61
Graham, Catharine 72
  David 43
  Eliza Jane 89
  George W. 87
Granlee, John 48
Grant, Elizabeth 63
  Jinsey 63
  Mariah 61
  Rebecca 53
  William 80
Grantham, Abitha 35
  Alice 52
  Anney 20
  Rachel 36
  Rheda 37
  Willis 61
Granthouse, Richard 73
Grasly, Jonah 41
Grason, Elizabeth 38
Grasty, Josiah 41
Graves, John 22
Gray, Catherine 29
  Elizabeth 51
  James 66
  Jane 81
  John 12, 25, 31, 50
  Louisa 88
  Mary Ann 89
  Moses 25
  Nathan 84
  Sarah 62
  William 23, 25, 29,
    43
Graybeal, Jacob 72
Grayham, William 16
Grayson, Elizabeth 8
  Francis 38
  Nancy 26
Grean, John 61
Grear, Anny 65
  Nathan 63
Green, Archibald 74
  Austin H. 56
  Daniel 84
  Elizabeth 87
Greenlea, Eli 66
Greenlee, Elizabeth 27,
    55
  James 21, 41
  Martin 85, 87
  Mary 54
  Nancy 33
  Nanie 31
Greer, Archibald P. 77
  Elizabeth 77
  James 77
  Nathan 77
  Polly 14
  Stephen 16, 40
  William 41
Gregory, John 41
Gressom, Emely 85
Gresson, Thomas 18
Grey, John 43
Griffin, Jacob 63, 72
  James 51
  John 42
  Madison 63
  Martin 72
  Richard F. 54
  Sally 42
  Samuel 56
  Spencer 11
  Thomas 32, 40
  William 31

Griffits, Griffy 19
  Jane 49
  Thomas 33
  William 32
Griffitts, John 21
  Margaret 36
Grigsby, John 77
  John B. 73
Grimes, George 80
  Margaret A. 74
  Nancy 26
Grisham, Agneys 40
Grisom, Betsy 9
Grison, Eliner 19
Griss, Michael 15
Grove, Benjamin 9
  Elizabeth I. 75
  Henry 75, 77
  Martha 77
  Nancy 85
  Ruben 83
  William G. 82
Groves, Nancey 9
  Reubin 12
  Rubin 16
  Teamour 12
Grub, Henry 56
Grubb, Elizabeth 66
  Jacob 66
Guest, John 1
  Joseph 1
  Susanna 5
Guinn, Elijah 43
Guy, James 85
Guynn, William 1
Gyton, Patsey 31
Hacker, John 24
  Valentine 39
Hagerty, John 19
Haggard, James R. 56
Hail, James 49, 52
Hailey, Edward 14
  John 4, 10
  Patey 8
  Tabitha 10
Haines, Elizabeth 11
  Rachael 13
  Sarah 9
Hains, William 18
Haley, Claibourn 71
  Philips R. 58
Hall, A. 58
  Allman 45
  Allmand 43
  Charlotte 41
  David T. 33
  Elisha 31
  Ienola B. 72
  Jesse 18
  Joel 21
  John 8, 10, 13
  John, Jr. 9, 12
  John, Sr. 9
  Joseph 28
  Lamken 7
  Magdaline 12
  Marion 24
  Rachel 39
  W. 17
  William 12, 21, 68
Hallford, Jacob 32
  Lucy 32
Hamelton, Alexander 14
Hamers, Abraham 82
  Catherine 85
  Enos 26
  William 82
Hamil, John 16

Hamilton, Aaron 77, 88
  Anna 39
  Anney 2
  Nancy 30
  Peggy 38
  Rebeccah 59
  Vicey 87
  William 37
Hammac, John 43
Hammack, Elizabeth 17
  John 14
  John, Jr. 18
  John, Sr. 18
  Peter 5, 10
  Susanna 15
  Susannah 19
  William 7
Hammel, Jane 80
  Rebecca 66
Hammer, Enos 51, 80, 87
  Magdaline 52
  Enos 39, 82, 85
  Ezra 66
  Joel 39
  Martha 68
  Patsey 28
  Ruth 36
  Sarah 41
  William 72, 82
Hammock, Daniel 39, 47,
    52
  Ephraim 43
  Ephriam 57
  John 43
  Martin 43
  Mary 23
  Nancy 55
  Polley 23
  Rebecca 74
  William 39, 44
Hamock, Elizabeth 13, 25
Hanah, John 6
Hancock, Benjamin 58
  James 63, 72
  Jas. 58
  Singleton 72
  William 7
Hancocke, James 61
Hancoke, Edwin 61
Hand, John 43
Handcock, Nancy 51
Hanes, Robert 40
Haney, George 66
  John 82
Hankin, Edward 69
Hankins, Abel 7
  Edward 5
  Eli 16
  Elizabeth 10, 16
  James 48
  Jane 53
  Jinny 22
  John 10
  Merchant 69
  Rachel 29
  Rhoda 55
  Richard 7
  Susanna 46
  Thomas 5, 22, 33
  William 29, 34, 69
Harbert, David 2
Harbin, Edward 33
  John 56
  Samuel P. 33
Harbison, Aaron 26
Hardin, Bohamas 63
  Charles 36
Harlon, Squire 14

100

Harlon (cont.)
William 14
Harlowand, William 20
Harman, Viney 13
Harmon, James 4
Levina 15
Nancy 36
Polly 30, 31
Samuel 64
William 14
Harny, Isaac 35
Harper, Calia 43
Harpole, Henry 56
Harrel, Larkin L. 54
William 54
Harrell, Coalman 34
Elijah 75
Elijah S. 61, 68
Jane 77
John 87
Levena 76
Levi 88
Lewis 51
Roodman 87
Sarah E. 68
Harrelson, Matilda 77
Harris, Alley 32
Elizabeth 30, 38
Eliziah 45
Elza 86
Evan, Jr. 72
Fountain 74
Gallant 46
George 74
Isaac 23, 49
James 10, 11, 20, 57
James G. 59
Jane 56, 71
Jesse 45
John 16, 32, 39, 59,
72, 77
John C. 64
Kesizah 64
Malon 41
Mary 21, 36, 41
Matilda 68
Miles 74
Nancy 32, 62
Nehemiah 14
Parthena 71
Peter 10, 13, 14, 20,
54
Polly 12
Rhody 68
Richard 22, 30
Rubin 46
Samuel 4
Sarah 2
Susannah 22
William 23
Harrison, John C. 64
Richard 69
Sally 29
Harriss, Thomas 29
Hart, Handse 3
Thos. 3
William 26
Harvey, John C. 40
Joseph 42
Mary 67
Pryor 60, 66
Sally 18
Susanna 88
Thomas 86, 88
Harvy, Thomas 80
Haskins, William 7
Hathcoat, John 23
Hauk, George 12

Haukins, John 12
Thomas 12
William 6
Haulston, Rebecca 50
Haumack, William 5
Haun, George W. 54
Jacob 43
Jno. 54
Sally 43
Havely, Thomas 52
Hawey, Maddison 87
Hawith, Catherine 34
Hawkins, Abel 82
Catherine 57
Elizabeth 6, 31
Henry 6, 8, 23, 74
John 7
Matilda 42
Richard 37
Sally 58
Sarah 8, 58
Susan 67
Susanah 23
Valentine 5
Hawley, Thomas 53, 64,
71, 78
Haworth, James 9
Joel 22
Hayes, Colbert 74, 85
Hiram 85
Jinney 74
Nancy 64
Haygood, Tapley 3
Haymore, Mary A. 67
Haynes, Ebby 24
Jacob 87
Rebeccah 56
Sarah 66
Sterling 23
Zelphy 28
Hayns, Starling 29
Hays, Colby 85
Frankey 18
Matilda 61
Nancey 17
Neomi 6
Thomas 61
Hayse, Lucinda 12
Haywood, Tapley 16
Hayworth, Mary 69
William 82
Headrick, Catherine 41
Heart, Eleanor 85
Heavins, Joseph 34
Hedrick, John 43, 61
Heins, Zepheniah 46
Hellums, Rachel 6
Helm, John C. 86
Helms, John 7
Jonathan 7
Helton, Alexander 72
Hannah 56
James 36, 46, 72
John 31
Mary 58
Meseander 26
Susannah 36
Hencily, Benjamin 37
Henderson, Alta Mincy
65
Carter 43
Catherine 70
George 23, 70
Hiram 48
Jain 23
John 51
Louisa 46
Louisa H. 87

Henderson (cont.)
Polly 28
Rowland 46
Sarah 29
Stephen 72
Susannah 51
Thomas 1, 4, 29
William 9, 10, 23
Wm. 1
Heneate, Alexander 23
Heneger, Jacob 74
Henry, Robert 14
Henshaw, Jonathan 61
Joshua 61
Herril, John 22
Hickey, Joshua 10, 58,
64
Joshua 58
Hickle, Harriet 87
Mary 82
Susan 71
William 71
Hickman, John 22
Peggy 64
Hicks, John 37
Hickson, John 51
Polly 29
Hicky, Joshua 47
Higgs, Alexander 64, 66
Luda 41
Highlander, Nancey 24
Hightower, Abner 61
Elizabeth 71
Epaphroditus 39
Epephroditus 33
Eph. 56
Frances 75
Mary M. 78
Rebecca 72
Sarah 81
Susan 61
William 76, 79
Hill, Abel 37, 54
Abraham 25
Betsey 24
Branham 54
Elizabeth 43, 88
James 9, 37
Jenney 19
Jenny 20
Jese 72
Joab 3, 4
John 18, 20, 49, 69
Joseph 26, 37
Katherine 49
Mary 26, 29
Nancy 49
Peggy 42
Pheby 36
Polly 4
Robert 87
Sarah 25, 87
Tempey 37
William 5, 51, 74
Hillinsworth, Josiah 50
Hilton, Betsey 87
Sally 42
William 37
Hinchey, Caroline 75
John 46
Hinds, Mary K. 68
Noel B. 56
Zachariah 56
Hines, James 50
Malkjah 40
Mary 41
Patsy 54
William 40

Hinghs, Nancy 55
Hinshaw, George 33
  Mary 21, 41
Hipshear, Elijah 61
  Jacob 61
  Lucinda 61
Hipshere, Colbert 74
  Henry 66
Hipshire, Elijah 74
  Jacob 74
  William 41
Hipshur, Henry 2
  Matthew 1
Hitch, Christopher 80
Hits, Richard 7
Hix, James 33
Hixon, Daniel 78
  John 74, 85
  May 83
  Rachael 74
Hobs, Caty 17
Hock, Jane 34
Hodge, Bartholomew 74
  Deedama 47
  Dinnah 85
  Edmond 44
  Edward 66, 67, 82
  Frazer 51
  Frazier 59
  Henry I. 69
  James 64, 73
  James, Jr. 72
  James D. 78
  Jesse 31
  John 43
  Lifty 46
  Lucy 9
  Martha 86
  Mary 64
  Philip 31
  Phillip 1
  Rebecka 3
  Temple 48
  Welcomb 86
  Welcome 42
  William 66, 72, 82
Hodges, Betsey 25
  Betsy 38
  Edmon 34
  Eli 23
  James 14, 20
  John 10, 83
  Moses 1, 7, 14
  Philamon 83
  Rebecca 16
  Welcome 1, 19, 20
  William 18
Hoffar, Henry 59
Hogg, Neomi 6
  Reubin 4
Hogge, Obediah 4
Holdis, Gabriel 83
Holder, J. P. 86
Holestan, Elizabeth 23
Holinsworth, Joseph 42
Holland, Mary 41
Hollandsworth, Polly 89
Hollingsworth, Lucinda
  84
  William 73, 87
  Wm. 76
Hollinsworth, Anna 55
  Joseph 27
  Josiah 55
  Polly 28
  William 72
Hollis, Zacharias 69
Holly, Caleb 69

Holly (cont.)
  Mariah 69
Holstine, P. 82
Holston, Henry 60
  Hugh 62
  Isaac 72
  Lucinda 60
  Peter 66
  Samuel 63
  William 61
  Wm. 86
Holt, A. Bigal P. 74
  Alsey 26
  David 78
  Franky 1
  Henry 14, 58
  James 9
  John 9, 66, 74, 75,
    85
  Lucinda 46
  Michall 22
  Nancy 87
  Polly 64
  Ruthey 17
  William 5
Homeall, Jno. 9
Hommel, Mary 53
Hones, William B. 22
Hooper, James F. 68
Hooser, Mary 9
Hopper, Anderson 85
  Archabald 31
  Charles 31, 33, 41
  Elijah 75
  Susan 52
  Thomas 59
  Vaney 17
Hopson, Elizabeth 22
  Nancy 77
Horn, John 51
Hornback, Elijah 18
  James 14
Horner, John 7
Horton, Hugh 73
  Nelson 19
Hoskin, Charles C. 85
  Thomas 75
  Thomas C. 78
  Thos. 83
Hoskins, Charles 78
  Charles C. 83
  James G. C. 75
Houlston, Polly 38
  Sally 54
Housely, Amy 21
Housley, Elizabeth 25
Houston, Hugh 63, 72
Howard, Abraham 7, 13
  Elizabeth 9
  Lucy 12
  Nancy 13
  Richard 12
  Robert 57
  William 9
Howel, Benjamin 6
  Caleb 25
  Cintha 32
  Polly 27
  Susanna 3
  Welcom 39
Howell, Benjamin 14,
  17, 40, 48
  Caleb 24
  Candis 1
  Condis 31
  Dicey 39
  Elizabeth 15, 17
  Henry 1, 4, 5, 19, 24

Howell, Jenney 25
  Jesse 44, 47
  John 20, 25, 31, 40,
    44
  Keziah 49
  Prudance 58
  Susan B. 72
  Susanna 1
  Susannah 30
  Thos. K. 86
  Thos. R. 72
  William 29
Howerton, Emaline 87
  William 18
Howeth, James 78
Howey, Thomas 87
Howorth, William 5
Hubbard, Hanna 6
  James 69
Hubberd, Jacob 48
  Samuel 48
Hubbs, John 29, 49, 66,
  80
  Liddy Ann 79
  Nancy 81
Huckeyby, Sarah 14
Huddleston, Calvin 85
  David 16, 20, 23, 27
  Jeany 28
  Jinny 12
  John F. 60, 75
  Robert 16, 28
  Thomas 7
Hudson, Benjamin 17
  Ezekiel 7
  James 10
  Mary 10
  Susanna 14
Hughes, Hardeman 4
  James 28
  Milly 52
  Sarah 59
Hughs, Delilah 53
  Robert 7
Hugings, Margret 3
Hulstine, Peter 66
Humbard, Jacob 1
  May 60
  Samuel 46
  Sarah 44
  William 44, 60
  William P. 56
Humbert, Catharn 25
Hume, Charles 49, 61
Humes, Nancy 22
Humphrey, Nathan 26, 27
  Solman 33
Humphreys, Henry 33
Hundley, James 61
  Margret 68
Hunley, T. P. 68
  Thomas 66
  William 14
Hunnycut, Jinny 9
Hunt, Fielden S. 75
  Thomas 72
Hunter, Aly 55
  Francis 31, 37, 46
  John 13, 27
  Mathew 13
  Nancey 13
  Nancy 31
  Peggy 42
  Polly 22
  Tempy 59
  Thomas 35
  William 13, 37, 42
Hurcheson, Charles 16

Hurd, Elizabeth 21
Hurst, Hiram 23
Hurt, Susanah 36
Husk, James 28
Hust, James 29
Huston, Hugh 38
Hutchenson, William 22
Hutcherson, Nancy 23
Hutcheson, Jesse 5
  John 16
  Mary 5
  Paul 5
Hutchinson, Charles 15
  Colman 14
  Nancy 15
  William 14
Hutchison, Lewis 20
  Lucy 24
  Nancy 20
  Spencer 24
Hutton, John 4, 8
Hynds, Eliza 84
  Elizabeth 74
  Parthena 60
  Sarah 64, 66
Idol, William 78
Idols, Mary 52
Inclebarger, William 35, 40
Inglebarger, William 38, 40
Inklebarger, Sally 52
Inman, Charles 80
  Shadarick 87
Irby, James 59, 70
  John 64
  Margaret 53
  Milton 64
Irvine, Anna 46
  John 46
Irwin, Margaret 44
  Nancy 14
Isreal, Silas 26
Issell, Jesse 22
Ivey, Benjamin 18
  David 31
  Delila 1
  John 24, 64
  Thomas 14
  Vardaman 2
Ivie, Baxter 26
Ivy, Baxter 40
  Benjamin 72
  Benjamin, Jr. 72
  Hamilton 85
  James 49
  Jane 69
  Jeney 25
  John 75, 83, 85
  John, Jr. 75
  Julian 83
  Nancy 56, 67, 88
  Patsey 45
  Phillip 7
  William 51
Jack, Betsy 57
  Feby 26
  James 49
  John F. 10
  Mary 34
  Samuel 58, 69
  William 27
Jackett, John 15
Jackson, David 5, 9
  Jacob 34, 72
  James 64
  Jinney 17
  Mary 34, 88

Jackson (cont.)
  Robert 9
James, Abraham 11, 29
  Barbara 28
  Clarisa 12
  Delany 11
  Elijah 33
  Elizabeth 21, 38
  James 61, 73 .
  Jesse 12
  John 40, 42, 45
  Laban 5
  Margaret 85
  Mary 29
  Nancy 37
  Newberry 9, 21, 22
  Patsey 45
  Peter 41
  Polly 21
  Rachel 42
  Tandy 44
  Thomas 9, 10, 33
  Thos. 88
  William 9, 14, 29, 44, 88
  William, Jr. 9
Janes, Sarah 34
  Thomas 31, 35
Janeway, Isaac 61
  Vicey 83
January, Isaac 61
  John 75
  Polly 73
  Thomas 61
Jarnagin, Amanda M. 87
  Anna 63
  Carolina H. 77
  Caswel 59
  Caswell 33
  Cazwill 40
  Charlotte 44
  Chesley 56
  Drury 9
  Eliza 82
  Francis E. 56
  George 25
  Holly 9
  James 67
  Jeremiah 33
  John 48
  Lewis 29
  Mahaly 55
  Mary 52, 73
  Minny 22
  Nelson 71
  Parthena P. 63
  Pascal J. 76
  Polly 8
  Rody 48
  Savannia 80
  Thomas 40, 49
  William 67, 72
Jarnigan, Isaac 6
  Polly 6
Jeffers, Isbell 5
  Polley 6
Jeffies, Thomas 33
Jeffries, Payton J. 83
Jenings, Edward 3
Jennings, Catherine 80
  Elizabeth 50
  John 49, 55
  Mary 73
  Pleasant 61
  Rachel 8
  Roel 73
  Sally 61
  Wm. D. 49

Jennkings, Nancy 49
Jentry, Jesse 18
Jimon, Rachell 2
Jinings, Thomas 7
Jinnings, Jesse 11
  Nancy 51
Johns, Henry 53
  John 54
  Samuel 56
Johnson, Ambrose 72, 73
  Barbary 53
  Benjamin 44
  Claibourn 80
  David 64
  John 56
  Joshua 54
  Lucy 77
  Marth. 48
  Martin 58
  Mary 50, 55
  Mourming 55
  Sanford 41
  Sarah 83
  Thomas 41
  Viney 57
  William 80
Johnston, Drucilla 66
  Elizabeth 24
  James 3, 35, 83
  Jaramiah 48
  Mary 6, 7
  Pleasant 3, 4
  Thomas 44
Joice, Alexander 72
  James 59
  John 85
  Mary 66
  Thomas 67, 85
  Wortham 67
Jonas, Mary 55
  Sarah 69
Jones, Aquilla 7
  Aquilla P. 88
  Charles 37
  Debby 34
  Elijah 88
  Elizabeth 29
  Happy 61
  Hugh 47, 48, 52, 57, 59, 65, 67, 71, 74, 76, 86
  Isabella 70
  James 54, 63, 83, 87
  Jane 72, 87
  Lewis 72
  Lucindia 38
  Mary 60
  Mary Sturdivent 13
  Nancy 21, 72, 75
  Patsey 20
  Polly 33
  Sally 37
  Samuel 85
  Stephen 70
  Susanah 37
  William 15, 74
  Wm. 70
Jonson, Betsy 44
Jonston, William 27
Jordan, Ewel 64
Jourdian, Washington 83
Jourdon, Ceily 25
Joyce, Robert 85
  Thomas 85
Karling, Thomas D. 43
Kearns, Alvina 43
  Lavina 22
  Michael, Jr. 11

Kearns (cont.)
  Nicholas 22-
Keeling, Hartwell 16
Keen, William 59
Kein, Anderson 45
  Malinda 45
Keith, William 14, 22,
  23
  Zachariah 28
  Zacheriah 20
Keller, John 22
Kelley, Wm. 3
Kellums, Rachel 6
Kelly, Nathan 36
  Thomas 16
Kelso, Mary 30
Kemp, James 16
Kendrick, Wm. P. 56
Kenedy, John 44
Kennedy, Sarah 4
  William 31, 44
Kenney, Nancey 4
Kennon, Hughes O. 80
  James 70, 74
  John 77
  Martha 77
  Nancy 70
  Sarah 81
  William 54
  Wm. 59
Kerdith, John 16
Ketch, James 61
Kidwell, Anna 26
  Betsey 24
  Charles 24
  David 36, 51
  Hannah 39
  Isaiah 5
  James 26
  Jane 36
  John 44
  Joshua 64, 67
  Josiah 15
  Margaret B. 39
  Mary 51, 72
  Nancy 30
  Sarah 59
Kile, Polly 3
Kiliken, John R. 83
Killer, Sarah 66
Kills, Peter 27
Kimbrow, Thomas 46
Kindar, Rachel 87
Kinder, Catherin 73
  Jacob 75
  John 75
  Sarah 85
King, Betty 39
  Ezekial 16
  Hanna 3
  Hillsman 11
  James 3, 31
  Jane 36
  John 24
  Mary 20
  Mary Ann 58
  Matilda 54
Kinnon, Jas. 88
Kirby, Richard 22
  William 22
Kirk, Ailsey 20
  Alexander 40
  Armsted 48
  Arnsted 20, 30
  Barbary 41
  Caty 80
  Delila 72
  Ezekiel 24

Kirk (cont.)
  Madison 66
  Malinda 62, 65
  Margaret 40
  Nancy 19
  Syntha 75
  William 19
Kirkham, Catharine H.
  73
  Elizabeth 50
  John 60
  Mary 18
  Sarah O. 56
  Wm. 1
Kirkhim, John 35
Kirkingdall, Stephen 14
Kirkpatrick, Anny 41
  William 57
Kirley, John 22
Kitchen, George 14
  John 30
  Patsey 1
  Thomas 18
Kitchens, Jesse 9
Kits, David 75
  Sally 62
Kitts, Catherine 65
  John 24
  Joseph 69, 78
  Mary 37
  Nancy 85
  Peter 69
  Sallomon 78
  Winney 71
Kline, Isaac 40, 66
  Jacob 61, 83
  Louisa B. 72
Kneedham, Henry 41
Knight, James 83
  T. D. 45, 53, 88
  Trestron D. 56
  Tristram D. 49
Knox, David 20
  John 20
Kyle, Wm. 4
Lacey, James 88
Lacy, David 37
  George 88
  Johnson 79
  Mark 29
  Pheby 36
  William 31
Lafferty, John 65, 88
Lafin, Betsey 19
Lain, Hiram 85
  John 85
  Ruthy 82
Lallis, Abraham 88
Lamb, Linsy 72
Lambdin, Patsy 51
Lamden, John 88
Lamon, Thomas 64
  William 64
Landrum, Robert M. 53
Lane, Dolly 63
  Elizabeth 13, 65
  James 6
  John 24, 54
  Levi 80
  Margret 6
  Patsy 48
  Polley 4
  Polly 50
  Rhoda 80
  Samuel 31
  Tempy 47
  William 28
  Wm. 9

Large, John 34, 69, 82
  Mary 69
  Mary Ann 64
  Thomas 42
  William 42
Larimore, Nancey 23
Lasey, James 52
Latham, Clabourn W. 62
  Clabourne 60
  Claiborne 55
  Susan 50
  William K. 81, 82
  Wm. K. 78
Lathim, Elizabeth 39
  Louisa 59
  Martha 86
Lathum, Matilda 43
Lawry, William 37
Lawson, Elizabeth 77
Lay, Hess 4
  James 83
  Jess 4
  John 24
  Littleberry 14
  Lucey 23
  Thomas 24
  William 29, 88
Lea, Charles M. 72
  David 9
  John 9, 10, 11
  Preston H. 80
  Thomas J. 89
  Zacheriah 9
Leabo, Daniel 23
Leabow, Isaac 42
  John 24
  Joseph 24
Leach, Sarah 89
Lebo, Louise 41
  Sarah 83
Lebow, Daniel 18
  Febly 30
  Isaac 62
  Jacob 46
  John 1
  Martha 47
  Polly 25
Ledbetter, Nancey 14
Lefever, Barthena 82
Lefew, Joseph 33
  Pleasant H. 57
Leffew, Eligha 35
  Elijah 75
  Harriet 73
  Joseph 49
  Mary 78
  Phebe 74
Leford, Robert 12
Legges, Peter 75
Lemar, Yancey 2
Lemmons, Elizabeth 60
  George 78
  Jese 57
  Patience 38
  Robert 60
  William 54
Lephew, Mariah 80
  William 64
Lerimere, Catherian 35
Levi, Nathaniel 27
Levington, Catharine 61
Lewis, Benj. 62
  Caty 17
  Elizabeth 77
  James 49, 51, 53, 59
  Nancey 48
  Samuel 30
  Seth 62

Lewis (cont.)
William 46, 68
Lickliter, Elias 85
Lide, John W. 44
Lilley, John 49
Linch, John 20
Line, William 27
Linn, Margarett 83
Lipscomb, Ann Virginia 64
Nancy 61
Lipscombe, Mary E. P. 44
Little, Merrey 17
Littleton, Marques 25
Littrell, John 18
Lively, David 64
Elizabeth 78
Nancy 45
Liveston, Jese 51
Livingston, Jesse 52
Nancy 60
Livungston, Abraham 72
Lix, John 9
Lloid, Anny 47
Lockhart, Samuel 37
Lockwood, Margaret 6
Long, Anthon 67
Barbary 39
Catherin 62
Catherine 41
Elijah 16
Elizabeth 49, 52, 59, 65, 72
Hannah 32
Jacob 24, 69, 78
James 57
Jane 43, 59
Jemima 39
Jno. 53
John 18, 37, 39, 42, 46, 49, 52, 53, 55
Joseph 16, 24
Lauren 57
Lawson 59, 78
Lefer 61
Levi 83
Mary 43, 59
May 34
Partemon 67
Parthena 75
Perlemore 59
Rachel 33
Reuben 68
Ruben 78
Sally 30, 68
Young L. 64
Longacre, Ruth 27
Longmire, Anny 37
Lord, Sarah 35
Love, Samuel 59
William 7
Lovel, Delila 53
Elizabeth 24
George 22
Jermiah 44
John 54
Polly 31
Loveles, Thomas 49
Lovell, Jeremiah 41, 74
Low, Mary 72
Samuel 52
Thomas 67
Lowe, Addison 54
Debitha 53
Elizabeth 73
Isaac 85
Saml. 52

Lowe (cont.)
Samuel 57
Loyd, Elizabeth 58
Jane 56
Joseph 53
Robert 56, 58, 63
Lyde, John W. 64
Lyne, Elizabeth 53
Lynhart, Elizabeth 1
Lynn, Cynthia 72
Lyons, Francis 78
Macby, George H. 44
Silas 44
Mack, Ruthy 66
Mackey, Enoch 67, 80
Wm. C. 83
Macky, Enoch 83
Maddon, Thomas 42
Madlock, Sarah 31
Magby, Sam'l 2
Magee, Louisa 66
Zara 12
Magic, Nehemiah 62
Maize, John 14
Nancey 14
Majors, David 54
Dicey 54
Malicoat, Dedman 51
Faney 42
James 22, 41, 51
John 51
Mary 62
Sabra 45
Sterling 78
Mallicoat, Clements C. 86
Eliza 85
Ellen 56
James 51, 60, 73
James K. 64
Joel 81
John 63
Judith 21
Mary 70
Nancy 72
Philip 27
W. M. 64
William 72
Wm. C. 78
Malson, John 5
Mandinghall, Elsay 11
Manes, Martha 83
Manis, James 64
Manley, Absolom 86
Mary Ann 66
Delilah 48
Manly, Wilson 88
Mann, Catharun 44
James 9
Katherine 42
Louisa 86
Matilda 63
Sarah 70
Thomas 16
Thomas (Captain) 9
Manning, Vilet 40
Mansfield, Elizabeth 32
Isaac 49
Maples, Edward 44
John 40, 51
Polly 42
Sally 22
William 69
Wilson 51
Marcheall, Mary 12
Mardock, John 14
Margian, Henry 20
Margran, John 7

Margrave, Thomas 17
Margrove, John 13
Marsall, Bartlett 8
Marshal, Bartlett 6
Jno. 57
Marshall, Bartley 15
Martain, Dicy 81
Martin, Cintha 51
Elizabeth 56, 63
James 64
Jane 54
Joel 13, 16, 51
Jonathan 64
Mary 2
Nancy 64
Peggy 3
Phebe 76
Robert 14, 19, 24, 51, 57, 67
Robert, Jr. 67
William 14, 57, 67
Winefred 11
Masengill, Robert 77
Robt. 65
Masingale, Solomon 20
Mason, Betsy 14
Nancy 13
Massengill, Mary 35
Mary J. 68
Robert 21
Massingill, Eliza 31
James 33
Robert 27
Mathias, John 83
Mathis, Cinthia 83
John 88
Matlock, Charles 33
Henry 19
John 4
Maulsly, John 9
Maxfield, Benjamin 44
John 78
Maxwell, Benjamin 25
Elizabeth 9
John 20
Nimrod 12
May, Andrew 72
Carolina Letha 73
Charity 37
Frederic 67, 75, 80
George M. 81
George W. 75
Isabal 4
Martha 80
Polly 48, 50
Mayers, Frederick 19
Mayes, Anna 84
Dudley 16
Elizabeth 27, 70, 83
Fredric 72
George 88
Henry 88
Isaac 45
James 46, 88
Jane 64
John 29
John, Jr. 75
Mahala 75
Nancy 85, 87
Phebe 71
Rachael 80
Susana 87
Thomas 4
Mayples, Edmund 15
Josiah 18
Mays, Ann 84
Betsey 26
Dudley 16

Mays (cont.)
Edward 41
Elizabeth 5, 67, 78
Gardner 11
Gooding 20
Goodwin 22
James 25
Jenney 18
John 18
Nancy 16
Phebe 31
Pheby 41, 82
Precilla 25
Susannah 2
Susanner 3
Thomas 35
William 5, 18, 72
Williams 83
Mayse, Berry 67, 75
Edward 31, 33, 54, 72
Henry 54
James 31
Martha 46
Polly 48
Rachel 50
Mayses, E. 48
Mayson, Sally 10
McAlhany, William 88
McAnally, David 14, 34
David, Jr. 13, 49
George 72
Ile 83
Jackson 88
James R. 75, 78
John 72, 86
Matilda 63
Telitha 53
McBee, John 33
Robert 78
Samuel 7, 30
Silas 47
Tabitha 7
William 67
William P. 52, 67
McBride, Mary 72
Rebcah 5
Synthia 63
McBroom, John 23, 29
Stephen 29
Thomas 7, 49
McCallum, William 60
McCarroll, Patsy 55
McCarrur, Campbell 18
McCarrus, Mary 12
McCartey, James 3
McCarty, Enoch 11
Isaac 73
Isaac F. 57
James 2, 71, 72
James F. 73
John 16, 20, 25
Jonathan L. 75, 78
Nancey 11
McCarver, Joshua 20
McCinny, Carolina 40
McClinsy, Anney 35
McCloud, Thomas 40
McCombs, George 8
McConnel, Abraham 49
Hugh 53
Jacob 47
Mary E. C. 64
McCouster, David 42
McCoy, Carnelous 11
David 37, 62, 77
Elizabeth 64
Joel 37

McCoy (cont.)
Neal 6
Polly 6, 41
William 44
McCrary, Nancy 54
McCristian, Robert 33
McCubbin, James 71, 73
John 9
McDall, Reuben 88
McDaniel, Eli 78, 80
James 42, 64
Jane 79
John 69
Wm. G. 84
McDannel, Susan 50
McDonald, Lewis 12
Thomas 5, 9
McDowell, John 47
McElhaney, Hugh 59, 79
Linsey 52
Nelly 50
Ruthey 59
Sally 57
McElhany, Alxr. 44
Hugh 59
Moses 69
McElhatten, Jeney 25
McElheney, John 10
McElhemy, John 13
McElheny, Jenney 20
John 2, 10, 19, 20
Polley 19
McElhiney, Racheal 14
McEnelley, Charles 4, 16
Ruth 6
McEnelly, Berry 5
Charles 7
Ruth 8
McFarland, Benjamin 83
Benjm. 79
James 85
McFarlin, Alexander 59
McFerron, Bartin 8
McFerson, Barton 9
McFetridge, Rachel 52
McGee, Alfred 70
James 80
Sarah 75
Wiley B. 80
Winfry 70
Zera 38
McGill, Rollin 25
William 34, 43, 44, 46, 86, 88
McGinnigats, Barbery 32
McGinnis, Andrew 62
Archibald 80
Charles 80
Edward 83
Elizabeth 77
Joseph 80
Mary Ann 62
Nancy 83, 88
Polly 2
William 4
McGolrick, James R. 80
Thomas 75
McHaffie, John 37
McKahan, Nancy 53
McKee, Mathew 6
McKennon, John 70
Roderick 70
McKinney, Daniel 80
Jane 47
May 76
McKinny, Eliza 64
McMillan, Louisa 82

McMillan (cont.)
Robert 39
McMillen, Robert 33
Thomas 27
McNamee, Isaac 4
McNees, George W. 78
McNely, Polena 81
McNess, John I. 22
McNey, Isabel 42
McNiece, Jane 41
McPeters, John 12
McPheeters, Andrew 13
McPherson, Henry 4
McPheters, An 74
Andrew 49, 57
Andrew S. 48, 64
Dan 49
Jesse 64
McPhetridge, Daniel 59
Jane 89
John 44
Sally 60
William 7
Wm. 9, 11
McVay, Eli 7
Fellis 1
Mary 15
Susana 31
McVey, James 70
Medlock, Elizabeth 4, 5
Sarah 10
Meek, James 81
John 77
Lucinda 78
Mary 83, 85
Mefford, Anna 50
Elizabeth 62
Selburn 83
Meltin, David 47
Memo, Elizabeth 49
Mendingall, Hanna 6
Mendinghall, Elsey 9
Mercer, Rebecker 2
Merchant, Sinthey 17
Wm. S. 33
Merit, Samuel 31
Merritt, John 51
Messer, Rebecker 2
Metter, Nancey 16
Mickings, Rebecca 22
Midall, William 25
Midkiff, Almira 47
Armerilla 40
Heister 36
Isaiah 1, 2, 3, 21, 22, 25, 29, 40, 64
Jeremiah 5
John 2, 3
Manuel 49
Marget 22
Marrel M. 48
Mary 25
Nancy 4, 9
Sarah 3
Temprence 25
Thomas 40, 45, 47
Midlock, Moses 18
Polley 10
Miles, Delpha 78
Milhanks, Anna 69
Milikin, George 47
Millakin, Alexander 29
Millekin, Alexander 36
Millar, Sarah 84
Miller, Absalom 67
Agnes 7
Ahab 88
Augdon 27

106

Miller (cont.)
  Barthena 38
  Betsy 51
  Caty 2, 49
  Charity 13
  Cristina 36
  Daniel 42
  David 44
  Frederick 3
  George 31
  Harmon 5
  James 67, 75
  Jane 38
  John 15, 59
  Julius 6
  Levi 16, 54
  Martin 49, 83
  Mary 42
  Nelson 35
  Noah 67
  Obediah 59
  Peter 4
  Polly 49, 59
  Solomon 73
  Stephen 35, 44
Millican, Alexander 30
Milligan, Alexander 20
  Hannah 31
  Samuel 27, 31
  Solomon 12
Millikan, Elinor 44
Milliken, David 11
  Emeline 77
Millins, John 6
  Julius 6
Mills, Charity 13
  Elizabeth 56
  John 42, 58
  Zachariah 6
Mincey, Sarah 67
Minett, Dacy 46
  Julian 81
Minice, Elizabeth 34
Minsy, Jese 83
Minter, Hannah 42
Miriate, John 62
Mitchel, Anny 1
  Aquilla 33
  Brick 27
  Greenberry 16
  John 75
  Jubel 67
  Matilda 86
  Polly 16
  Robert 59, 84
Mitchell, Amy 62
  Andrew J. 82, 86
  Andrew P. 85
  Aquilla 62
  Benjamin 45, 47
  Berry 26
  Betsey 74
  Cily 22
  Diedima 54
  Elijah 24, 28, 33,
    54, 75
  Elijah, Jr. 75
  Elizabeth 2
  Green 67
  Greenberry 15
  Isaac 73, 75
  James 12
  James D. 86, 88
  John 75, 86
  Mary 61
  Merry 29
  Nancy 45
  Nelly 74

Mitchell (cont.)
  Preston 73
  Rhoda 39
  Robert 57, 80, 86
  Robt. 56, 65
  Ruth 54
  Serena 86
  Susanna 87
  William 29, 47, 54,
    62, 76
  Mittan, Alice 57
  Mobly, Letita 52
  Moffet, Samuel 25
  Moffett, John L. 89
    William 86
  Moffit, Elinor 38
    John 16
  Molder, Absolem 68
    John 37
    Valentine 75
  Monroe, Elizabeth 12
    Lea A. 80
    Lucinda 76
    Margaret 24
    Polley 13
    Robert 62
    Rosanah 82
    Sullavan Loyd (Genl.)
      32
  Monrow, George 12, 27
    John 27
  Moody, Amelia 59
    Charlotte 75
    Elizabeth 18
    George P. 88
    John 27
    Lucy 22
    Mary 55
    Nancy 37
    Sarah 62
    William 73
    William M. 73
    Wm. 56, 76
    Wm. M. 85
  Mooney, Charles 18
    William 12
  Moore, Benjamin 22
    Cardwell C. 37
    Elizabeth 20, 44
    George 78
    Isabella 27
    James 1, 13, 37
    James S. 35, 37
    Jane 55
    John 11, 13, 17, 19,
      20, 22, 75
    John (Captain) 20
    Levi 13
    Lidy C. 37
    Margaret 23
    Martha 72
    Mary 7, 86
    Nancy 10, 21, 88
    Rachel 71
    Richard 78
    Robert 37
    Sally 54
    Samuel 9, 11, 13, 20
    Sarah 40
    Stephen 71, 88
    Susan 31
    William 24, 37, 43,
      86
  Moran, Peggy 20
  More, Betsey 28
  Morgan, Able 20
    Allen Dodson 40
    Anna 81

Morgan (cont.)
  Catharine 14
  Chesley 24
  Dodson 37
  Dotson 51
  Elley 21
  John 37, 83
  Lucinda 7
  Naney 12, 45
  Nathan 15
  Polley 3
  Rebecca 66
  Rebecka 20
  Sally 12
  Sarah 74
  Thomas 13, 35
  William 20, 21
  William D. 81
  Morris, Daniel P. 86
    Dorothy 60
    Eliza 80
    Elizabeth 9
    G. 18
    Girland 35
    Gideon 13
    Harmon 33
    Martain 11
    Martha 82
    Nancey 19
    Sarah 32
    Shadrick 13
    Thomas 22, 49
    William 33
  Morrison, Samuel 37
    William 34, 37
  Morriss, Shadrick 20
  Morrow, James 20
  Morse, Nancy 59
  Mortan, Thomas D. 55
  Moser, Savary 60
  Moses, Nancy 1
    Peter 31
    Rebecker 2
  Mosey, Jonathan 12
  Moss, Elizabeth 5
    Malinda 38
  Moulder, G. W. L. 43
    George 46
    Henry 32, 37
    Polly 60
    Sarah 37, 43
    Susan 48
    Valentine 83
  Moyer, Michael 13
  Moyers, Catherine 26
    Frederick 8, 24
    Henry 24
    John 26
    Mahala 72
    Mary 78
    Rachael 13
  Muchelberry, George 29
  Mulky, Elizabeth 8
  Mullins, Flora 57
    John 16, 22, 44, 67
    Mary 58
    Nancy 40, 45
    Robert 75
    Thomas R. 27
    Thomas Richardson 25
  Mumpower, Anna 66
    Benjamin 30
    Nancy 42
  Murfy, Jenny 22
  Murphey, Wm. 6
  Murphy, Catharine 60
    Jimima 31
    Liddy 43

107

Murphy (cont.)
  Randolph 59
  William 11, 59
Murray, William 46
Murrey, Thomas 6
Murry, Ann 2
  Patsey M. 10
  Sebinna 52
Musgrove, Catherina 2
Musteen, Elizabeth 23
Myers, Delila 70
  Mitchell 54
Mynate, Thos. 54
Mynatt, Calvin L. 88
  Dodson P. 81
  Joseph 62
  Martin S. 44
  Narcissa 86
  Sally 49
  Syntha 68
  William 54
  William C. 31
Mynett, John 23
Nall, James 16
  Larkin 12
  Nancy 20
  Polley 12
  William 24
Nance, Anice 80
  Clement C. 62
  Huch 51
  Jane 57
  Jefferson 75
  John 27, 75, 81
  Preston P. 83
  Rubin 40
  Sally 60
  Susan 55
Nanney, Nancy 75
Nash, Claibourn 75
  Deadman 62
  Dedman 75
  John 80
  Nancy 66
  Susan 80
  Susanna 54
  Thomas 62
Nations, Laban 16
Nau, John 7, 15
Neadham, Alfred 62
Neal, Nancy 6
  Rana 1
  William 6, 59
Nealy, Benjamin 44, 67
Needham, Anna 68
  Elizabeth 89
  Ira 88
  John 27, 67
  Milley 46
  Rebeccah 21
Neegin, Thomas 56
Neil, Isaac 57
Neill, Mary 46
Nelson, Susana 68
Nemoe, Nancy 51
Nemore, Hiram M. 57
Netherland, James W.
  64
Neugin, Thomas 29
Newberry, Thomas 24
Newgen, Thomas 22
Newman, Elizabeth 22
  Isaac 2
  John 46
  Joseph 86
  Pricilla 55
  Samuel 83
  William 54

Newton, Elizabeth 73
Nicely, Catherine 74
  David 24, 51
  Elizabeth 79
  James 47
  John 24, 51
  Jonas 74, 86
  Nicholas 78
  Ragina 47
  Susan 45
  William 42, 45
  Woolry 79
Nicholas, Mathias 51
  Polly 1
Nichols, Archibald 54
  Isaac 54
  Mathias 57
  Prescia 76
  William 78
Nickels, Mathias 62
Nickelson, William 67
Nickles, Abraham 65
  Comfort 63
  Polly 65
Nicley, John 47
Nipp, Mary 28
Nipper, James 35
  Jordan 35
Noah, Honar 51
Noe, Catherine 9, 81
  Daniel 70, 87
  David 25, 39, 52, 70
  George 10, 11, 19
  Jacob 22, 52, 57
  John 26, 59, 70, 86
  Jonathan 65, 70, 77
  Joseph 44, 57, 78, 83
  Mary 88
  Nicholas 78
  Racheal 86
  Rachel 89
  Sally 36
  Sary 44
  Solomon 57
Nole, William H. 70
Noles, William 40
Nolson, Nicholas 42
Nor, George 9
Norman, Larkin 33
  Mahaly 57
  Pleasant 33
Norris, Abner 83
  Anny 59
  Betsy 52
  Catherine 82
  Doris 24
  Eliza 85
  Elsena 83
  Gallent 37
  Garland 48
  Garrot 18, 45
  George 15, 54, 59, 88
  James 27, 59
  Jarred 53
  Jeremiah 21
  Joan 29
  Leanner 88
  Lewis 24
  Lucinda 84
  Mathias 81
  Nancy 30, 36, 40
  Polley 21
  Pricilla 51
  Susan 47
  Susanna 89
  Thomas 24, 37, 42, 89
  W. M., Sr. 54

Norris (cont.)
  William 15, 24, 27, 29,
    36, 37, 42
  Wm. 88
Norton, Nathan 3
  Wm. 7
Null, John J. 37
  John Justice 22
  Justice 21
Nunn, John 29
Oakes, Fanney 20
Oakly, John 52, 85
Oaks, Betsey 30
  Elizabeth 89
  Hannah 12
  John 27
  Margaret 71
  Mary 27
  Richard 27, 37, 61, 67,
    71
O'Connor, Michael 37
Oday, Fanny 19
  Levy 19
Odle, William 44
  William H. 46
Ody, Levi 15
O'Eilly, Joseph 8
Ogan, Catherine 60
  John 14, 15
Ogle, Herculus 11, 13
  John 10
  Thomas 13, 28
Ogles, Sally 22
O'Hara, (?) 35
  Martin 35
O'Harror, Martin 35
OHarror, Nancy 35
Ollevin, John 73
  John, Jr. 73
Olliver, John 75
Ore, Caroline 74
  Eliza 28, 34
  Elizabeth 11
  James 5
  Jas. 6
  Leigh 77
  Mary 63
  Rebecca T. 1
  Robert 38
  Sally 27
  William C. 44
Orm, John 49
Orr, Elizabeth 52
  William 52, 67
Ousley, John 75
  Samuel 19
Overton, Arthur 15
  Benjamin 16
  Jane 34
Owen, Agnes 7
  Agness 8
  Fair 20, 41
  Isaac 2
  James 16
  Jno. 3
  John 2, 29
  Lettie 4
  Sally 16
  Thomas 9
Owens, Benjamin 54
  Charles I. 88
  David 29
  Elizabeth 50
  Fare 29
  John 2
Page, Archilles 36
Pain, Charles 61

Pain (cont.)
Isaac 27
Moses 27
Sarah 85
William 88
Paint, John 69
Painter, Winston 63
Panel, Mary 2
Thomas 2
Parcker, Robert 11
Parker, Anna 79
Elisabeth 10
James 13, 47, 54
Nancy 48
Phebe 54
Rachel 56
Samuel 84
William 55
Parkeypile, George 16
Parkison, William 18
Parks, Robert 11
Parsley, Jese 59
Parson, Robert 6, 7
Partin, Elum 35
Talifaro 32
Winston 13
Paschal, Jane 89
Pastle, Sarah 1
Pate, Nancey 48
Patterson, Andrew 52
Gilbert 75
James 40
Jesse 31
Margaret 65
Mary 34
Nathaniel 88
Thomas 29, 65, 88
William 24
Patton, William 13
Paul, Elizabeth 27
Payn, Aquila 42
Charles 44
Polly 44
Payne, John 83
Peary, Samuel 13
Peck, Benjamin 78
Charles L. 59
Charles N. 56
Mary H. 80
Peeters, Joseph 15
Peetres, Sue 15
Pemberton, Eamoria 83
Edward 86
Pendexter, Morgan 35
Rachel 35
Penjour, James 7
Penn, Susannah 31
Percapile, Mary 59
Percyfield, Gilbert 47
Perin, John 30
Perkins, James 9, 17
Perkipile, Jacob 58
Perky, Betsy 43
Perle, Nelson 67
Perrimon, Mary 48
Perrin, Cloe 57
Joab 52
John 38, 42, 43, 47,
81
Joanna 3
Mary 71
Matthew 27
Nancy 80
Sarah 68
Perrion, (?) 7
Perry, (?) 7
Catherine 24
Elizabeth 27

Perry (cont.)
Gabarella 62
Gabnella 67
Hanna 17
James 24
John 64
Nathan 78
Robert 4
Sam'l 13
Thomas 70
Perryman, Charles 70
Charles M. 67
Sophy 50
Person, Jacob 6
Peter, Benton 33
Burton 25
Peters, Elizabeth 12
Hugh 57
Nancy 16
Joseph 16, 20
William 52
Petit, Enoch 73
Petre, Joseph 68, 81
Stephen 78
Petree, John 18, 49
Petterson, William 20
Pettit, Nehemiah 5
Petty, Katherine 87
Pevehouse, Abraham 6
Daniel 3
Jacob 6
Pew, Daniel 16
Easther 16
James Daniel 10
Jesse 10
Phane, Mary 74
Phara, (?) 35
Pharoh, Thomas 55
Philipa, William 59
Philipps, Elizabeth 62
Philips, Andrew 35, 48
Elizabeth 59
Isaac 70
Joel 50, 52
John 49, 58
Nancy 44
Nathan I. 88
Robert 88
Sarah 49
Violet 31
William 69
Phillips, Elizabeth 10
Nathan 11, 14
William 9
Phipps, Barcary 58
James 29, 58, 75
John 74
Polly 65
Rebeccah 61
Phips, Jacob 62
Piatt, Mary 81
Sarah 81
Pierce, Hiram 72
Nancy 73
Thomas 37
Pierson, Elizabeth 76
Hiram 81
Thomas 81
Pilant, James 29
Pilor, James 42
Pin, Elizabeth 69
Pinkston, Levinia 43
Poindexter, Elizabeth 31
Morgan 57
William 27
Pollard, (?) (Major) 73
Elza 72
James 71, 72

Pollard (cont.)
Lucy 29
Mary 71
Saml. 55
Samuel 29, 88
Sarah 51
Susan 85
Polley, John 49
Pope, Mary Ann 41
Popejoy, John 57
Nancy 66
Popjoy, William 83
Posey, Cynthia 64
Powel, Abraham 17
Elizabeth 53
Powell, John 29
Mary 79
Polly 68
Powle, Nancy 73
Prator, John 30
Pratt, John 16
Mary 57
Willis 57
Willis L. 70
Presman, Basil 4
Prewitt, Abraham 15
Price, Anna 85
Elizabeth 16
Nancy 46
Pharoa 87
Rebecca 16
William 64
Prigmore, Daniel 15, 35
Privett, Mathew 18
Proffett, Mary Ann 67
Proffit, David 38
John 38
Proffitt, Elizabeth 64
Gabriel 62
Joseph 61, 62, 64
Prophett, Caty 47
David 47
Pruit, Abraham 15
Pugh, Archibald 39
Pullen, Leroy 47
Purcifield, Thomas 24
Purkapile, John 57
Purkepile, Celia 71
Ralph 73
Purkey, Catherin 68
James 61
John 64
Joseph 62
Mary 88
Purkeyfield, Kitty 44
Purkipile, John 47
Pulse, Katherine 88
Putman, Caleb 87
Quinn, Kitty 45
Quinner, Sally 40
Rader, William 61
Ragsdale, Nansy 51
Ragsdel, Rebecah 45
Rail, Carry 46
Rolly 12
William 12
Raines, Lewis 64
Rains, Kiziah 5
Ramsey, Elizabeth 41, 74
John 30, 39, 44, 78
Randolph, James 9
Robert 13
Rankin, Alex. 45
Ray, Abner 25
Amon 83
Anny 25, 47
Caty 18
Charley 88

Ray (cont.)
Chesley 86
David 17, 59, 83, 88
Davis 13
Delilah 45
Elizabeth 77
Jacob 18
James 76
Jane 62, 86
Joseph 33
Joseph R. 83
Lucender 87
Lucinda 76
Nancy 88
Polly 59, 83
Richson 83
Robert 52, 59, 83
Samuel 25, 38
Tabitha 54
Talitha 59
Thomas 17, 18, 33, 38, 44
Thomas, Jr. 60
Raye, Jesse 48
Rayl, Adeline 79
Anne 4
Francis 67
George 67
George W. 79
Washington 49
Rayle, George 38
Jesse 38
Rayons, Elizabeth 42
Rays, Betsy 44
Read, Adeline 35
Jane 40
Readman, John 30
Rectar, Milly 74
Rector, Charity 76
Clacy 9
Clary 8
Eli 76
John 18
Polley 23
Richard 11
Redding, Mathew 17
Polley 17
Redus, Wm. 3
Reece, Caleb 17
Catharine 35
Christian 20
Daniel 9
David 35
Eliza 83
Elizabeth 35, 39
Hannah 15
Hisey 33
Isaiah 39, 42
Roger 35
Seamore 33
Thomas 18
Thomas, Jr. 15, 17
William 18, 42, 49
Yarnell 20
Reed, Catherine 68
Charles 79
Daniel 88
Felps 78
George G. 44
Jane 70
Jeremiah 70
O. H. P. 88
Polly 89
William 35
Willie 32
Reeder, Alexander 38
James 88
Thomas 88

Reeder (cont.)
William 38, 53
Reedy, Elizabeth 7
Shadrick 7
Reese, Elizabeth 17
William B. 47
Renfro, Cox 76
John 57
Joseph 54
Levenia 66
Stephen C. 66
Rennon, Nues O. 75
Rentfrow, David 52
Repas, Ephram 67
Reynolds, Lewis 64
William 55, 64
Rhea, Archibald Neal 22
Benjamin 9
Elizabeth 1
Fareby 7
Jarren 62
Jesse 67
John 2, 3
Joseph 1, 9
Mosses 7
Samuel 81
Thomas 9
Rhinehart, George 40
John 16
Rhineheart, John 40
Rhoton, Josiah 88
Rice, Clarine 45
Daniel 47
Elizabeth 7
Henry 7, 78
Joel 79
John 64
Levi 7
Netty 83
Rich, George 52
Joseph 9, 10, 31
Lucinda D. 72
Sarah 83
Richard, John 57
Richardison, Samuel 32
Richards, John 24
Joseph 57
Richard 24, 47, 51
Thomas 57
Richardson, Augustine 3
Betsey 29
James 27, 29
John 39
Martha 62
Mary 39
Milley 11
Samuel 25, 34
Suckey 25
Richerson, Jane 27
Ricketts, Catherine 39
Ridith, John 16
Riece, David 26
Riggs, Edward 37
Eliza Jane 87
Ellis 35, 54
Felps 87
Hannah 7
James 76
Jese 69
Levi 35
Lewis 46, 47
Lunis 35
Margit 17
Mary 20, 78
Nancy 13
Nineon 58
Ninion 27, 36
Polly 70

Riggs (cont.)
Russell 79
Right, Elizabeth 52
Elza 81
Lucinda 64
Martin 83
Samuel 86
Rite, Samuel 76
Roach, Absolam 83
Alfred 79
Anna 88
Aron 3
Aroon 8
Elizabeth 78
Elsena 78
Elvira 80
James 88
John 52
John W. 24
William 57, 65
Roak, Aron 10
Roane, Archibald 11
Roberson, James 44
Wiley B. 58
Roberts, Dennis 54, 57, 75, 83
Isabel 44
Jane 67
John 83
Martha 54
Nancy 52
Sally 13
Sarah 68
W. M. 57
William 11
Robertson, Abraham 4
Daniel 40
Elizabeth 54
Field 30
Hezekiah 20
Hutson 88
James 36, 41
John 38
Kiah 35
Nancey 11
Nancy 31
Rachel 12
Rody 29
Suanner 3
Thomas 12, 64
William 30
Winfrey 40
Winphrey 34, 36
Robinson, Elizabeth 88
George 59, 88
Jane 77
John 79
Rebecca 47
Wiley 47
William 10
Roch, Elizabeth W. 28
John W. 28
Rock, Aron 3, 30
Elijah 89
Roddy, Thomas 44
Rodgers, Cornelous 2
Mary 67
Nancy 10
William 15
Roe, Elizabeth 58
Roeolin, Elizabeth 14
Rogers, Elenor 70
James 73
Jenetta 75
John W. 64
Meriah 55
William 70, 73
Rolan, Janey 53

Rolings, Sarah 40
Rollins, William 24
Romans, Sally 52
Romine, Laten 35
Rook, Aaren 21
  Aron 15, 17
  Elijah 89
  Hezekiah 17, 67
  Nelly 21, 57
  Willis 67
Rookard, Ambrose B. 59
  Brown B. 40, 67
  William 67
Rooks, Aaron 24, 34
  Nancy 50
Rose, George W. 73
  Nancey 18
  Robert 42
Ross, Hannah R. R. 33
  Hugh 3
Routh, High 75
  Joseph 30
  Levin 78
  Martha 75
  Sarah 71
  Stephen 74
Row, Jacob 68, 78
  Sarah 66
Rubble, John 62
Ruckard, Elizabeth 79
  Polly 54
  William 79
Rucker, Dolphy 28
  Edmund 57
  James 88
  John 69, 72, 73
  Nancy 27
  Pegga 80
  Samuel 89
  William 33
Rule, Eliza 77
Rush, Coleman 79
  David 89
  Mary 74
  Thomas 68, 76
Russel, Elizabeth 20
  Wm. 4
Russell, Agnes 4
  Barthena 49
  Dice 2
  Elizabeth 6
  George 2
  James 3
  John 5, 6
  Mathew 30
Ruth, Isaac 41
  Jacob 57
  Jain 19
  John 89
  Stephen 89
Rutherford, Joseph 42
  James 70
  Simeon 70
Salling, Henry 64
Sallings, James 89
Sallins, Joseph 89
Sampsel, Isaac 81
Samsel, Hiram 66
Samson, Elizabeth 77
Sanderland, Ambrose 64
Sanders, Harmon 64
  John 6, 64
  Philip 10
  William 57
Sandery, Susanah 40
Sandress, Sarah 8
Sandris, Mary 19
Saney, William R. 32

Saterfield, Hosia 30
  Wyatt 78
Satterfield, Eda 86
  Greenberry 84
  John 56, 79
  Levi 84, 89
  Nancy 77
Saunders, Stanford L. 47
Savage, Roddy 68
  Rody 66
  Sally 61
Schaderick, Hardy 49
Scot, Nancy 15
Scott, John 45
  Powell 11
Scrogins, Bartin 1, 2
Scruggs, Rufus W. 73
Seabolt, Andrew 18
Seaman, Samy 38
Seamans, Allie 34
  Jonathan 33
Seamons, John 25
Seamore, Anny 88
  Coleman 84
  George 68, 77, 86
  George W. 79
  James 26
  John 38
  Micagah 20
  Mildred 56
  Rachel 53
Sears, William 47
Seat, Joseph 17
Seaver, Joseph 66
  Sarah S. 66
Seglar, Mary 16
Sellars, Rebecca 72
Sellers, James 38
  John 52
  Robert 52
  Syntha 66
Selvage, James 30, 31
  Jeremiah 19
  Mary B. 19
  Nancy 27
  Sarah 31
  William 18
Selvedge, Dicy 43
Semore, George 72
  Isaac 12
Senter, Caroline 65
  Elizabeth K. 78
  James 38
  Pleasant M. 74
  Stephen M. 11, 29
Sevard, Nancy 21
Severs, Joseph 67
Sevier, Chas. 3
  Joseph T. 73
  Nance 3
Sexton, Overton 86
Shannon, Joseph 38
Sharp, Amos 22
  Catherine 79
  David 22, 29, 42, 49
  Edy 31
  Elizabeth 23, 40
  Hannah 52
  Henry 81
  James 79
  John 15, 17, 30, 49,
    51
  Meredith 51, 52
  Nicholas 11, 13
  Polly 32
  Sally 43
  Sampson 49, 50
  Samuel 34

Sharp (cont.)
  Thomas 22
  William 37, 67, 73, 80,
    84
Shedrick, Joseph 38
Shelly, Elizabeth Ann 86
Shelton, Anna 68
  Chrispen 25
  Crispin E. 33
  David 3, 7, 10
  Ezekiel 2
  Gabriel 79
  James 34, 35
  Joel 10
  John 32, 34
  John, Jr. 6
  Miller 32, 35
  Nancey 1, 6, 87
  Patsey 33
  Polly 4
  Ralph 25
  Rebecca 10
  Richard 2, 6, 10, 17,
    31
  Samuel 34
  Susannah 30
  William 6
Sherley, Balser 65
Sherrel, Polly 31
  William 31
Shields, James 59
  John 52, 59, 63
Shipe, Joseph 7
Shipley, Aaron 30
  Adam 30, 42, 49
  Anney 65
  Milinda 89
  Nathan 48, 51
  Nathaniel 79
  Prudence 70
  Thomas 70
  Wm. C. 68
Shiply, Adam 42
Shirley, Balser 44
  Bolser 55
  Elizabeth G. 54
  Mary A. 65
Shoats, Jacob 69
Shockley, Betsey 34
  Booker 45
  Calib 17
  Nancy 19
  Nelley 21
  Richard 32
  Samuel 89
  Sarah 32
  Thomas 34
  William 24
Shockly, Booker 42
Shoemaker, Lewis 89
  Nancy 33
Short, James 1
  John 59, 62
  Sarah 3
  William 47
Showman, Jacob 18
Shropshear, David 68
  Sarah 67
Shropsheer, John 6
Shropshire, Polly 57
Sigler, Abinida 37
  Peggy 22
  Philip 22, 24
Simmons, Betsey 30
  Green 81, 84
  Isham 26, 27, 32
  James 32, 70, 73, 84
  Jane 7

Simmons (cont.)
  Jemimah 23
  John 7, 18, 26, 28,
    68, 76
  John, Jr. 30
  Joseph 62
  Joshua 11
  Nancey 79
  Nancy 36
  Richard 30
  Robert 70
  Sally 18
  Thomas 27
Simms, Alexander 30
Simpson, Dolly 24
  Isaac 81
Sims, William 11
Sisley, Polley 13
Six, John 5
Slults, Joseph 15
Smallwood, Russel C.
    55
  Russell C. 76
Smeddy, Sarah 45
Smiddy, Dicy 42
  Fielding 59
Smith, Aaron 1
  Allen 46
  Ann 9
  Annie 30
  Archlus 50
  Archy 68
  Aron 2
  Avia 41
  Barthena 48
  Bartholomew 6
  Betsy 20, 76
  Betty 34
  Boby 89
  Britan 13
  Callie 81
  Charles 6, 11, 12
  Daniel 57
  Darcus 85
  David 7, 36, 73
  Dickson 50
  Dixon 41, 47
  Edward 47, 56
  Elenar 70
  Elizabeth 6, 10, 68,
    73, 78, 88
  Evan 53
  Ezekiel 6
  Fanny 11
  Frances 58
  Francis 63
  Frederick 58
  Fredrick 32
  George S. 4
  Isam 38
  Isham 25
  Jackson 12, 13
  James 45, 46, 79
  Jane 61
  Jenny 11
  Jinny 10
  Joel 32, 36
  John 1, 2, 3, 6, 17,
    24, 45, 73, 76, 79
  Joseph 25, 46, 47, 55
  Josiah 30
  Judith 79
  Jurdon 31
  Laveesa 84
  Levisy 79
  Lucinda 78
  Margat 46
  Martha 46, 79, 87

Smith (cont.)
  Mary 28, 61, 75
  Masey 38
  Matilda 32
  Merriam 27
  Milla 56
  Milly 46
  Moses 40, 62
  Nancy 15
  Nathanel 40
  Nathanell 44
  Nathaniel 29, 30, 38
  Nathl. 34, 35
  Patsey 10
  Patsy 10
  Polley 4
  Rachael 82
  Rebecca 23
  Richard 6
  Robert 7, 84, 86
  Sally 18
  Samuel 65, 84
  Sarah 33, 35, 44, 69,
    82
  Sevier 15
  Sterling 22
  Thomas 2, 17, 25, 55,
    62, 65, 70, 86
  Vedy 39
  W. M. 48
  Wesley 62
  William 3, 11, 43, 73,
    78
  Yathe 52
Snider, Elizabeth 16
Snodgrass, Jane 35
Snyder, Philip 81
Sollomon, Daniel 25
Soloman, Franky 45
  John 45
Solomon, Abraham 25
  Drury 27
  Godwin 84
  Goodin 42
  Henry 7, 27, 42
  Nancy 85, 87
  Thomas 52
Southerland, Jane 38
  Mary 11
  Ruth 21
Southerlin, George 7
  Pateance 10
  Philip 17
Southern, Robert 6
Sowders, Martha 23
Sowers, Eve 63
Sparkman, Angy 38
  Anna M. 67
  Charles 50, 58
  Francis 86
  George 16, 73, 86
  Hardeman 62
  Hardiman 55
  Hardy 75
  Henderson 81
  John 62
  Levi 25
  Mack 83
  Micial 62
  Mitchell 76
  Nancy 20, 75
  Patsy 58, 83
  Polley 25
  Rebecca 79
  William 76
  William, Sr. 81
Sparksman, Elizabeth 33
  John 47

Sparksman (cont.)
  William 33
Spencer, Frances 55
  Green 62, 70
  Nathaniel 70
  Oney 76
  Samuel 47
Spikes, Martin 52
Spires, Elizabeth 39
  Nancey 24
  Polly 39
  Sally 47
Spoon, Abraham 65, 73, 74
  Dolly 58
  Eli 68
  John 52, 58, 59, 68
  Nancy 64
  Peter 85
  Saráh 74
Spoonard, William 55
Spoons, Nancy 32
Spradling, Rebecca 15
Sprecher, George 5
Spring, John 10
Sprucher, George 5
Stagner, John B. 43
Stalians, Elizabeth 4
Stallsley, Amos 60
Stalsworth, John 62
  Martha 80
  Polly 63
  Samuel 84
Stanley, Betsey 22
  Mancy 12
Stansberry, Elijah 73
  William 30
Starling, Thomas D. 42
Starnes, Catherine 71
  Fereby 84
  James H. 74
  Sarah 67
Starns, Adam 76
  James H. 73, 75
Stations, Elizabeth 4
  Thos. 4
Stearns, Samuel 55
Stephen, George 6
  James 26
  Joshua W. 60
Stephenson, Joseph 11
Sterling, James 22
Steward, Edys 58
Stewart, Dalila 3
  John 3, 57
  William 3
Stiffee, John 8
Stiffy, John 26, 41
Stinson, George 2
Stockton, W. H. 42
Stokley, Thos. 64
Stone, Eliza 50
  Elizabeth 30
  Michael W. 62
  Mitchel 50
  Odsey 33
  Robert 6
  Sarah 86
  Susan 77
  William 24
Story, Susanna 5
Stout, Solomon 84
Strange, Betsy 78
  James 65, 73
  Mary 65
  Nancy 84
  Susan 79
Stratton, Minerva 75
Street, Anthony 10

Street, (cont.)
Tennessee 2
William 4, 6, 19
Stroud, Amos 84
Andrew 60
Christopher 68
James 84
Thomas 86
Thos. 60
Strut, William 10
Stubblefield, Ann 13
Drucella 7
Elizabeth 37
George 6, 50
Jamimah 44
Jas. 7
John 38
Joseph 15, 40, 53
Kessire 61
Nancey 24
Nancy 46, 80
Patsey 33
Polly 53
R. Lackey 6
Raleigh 50, 80
Robert 37, 50
Sarah 14
Stephen 20
William 18
Winneyford 64
Wyet 33
Sturd, Elizabeth 21
Stutt, Goodin 40
Sullins, John 4
Wonna 4
Sullivan, Spencer 30
Sunderland, Abraham 28
James 28
Sutherland, Ambrose 68
Jane 48
Solomon 26
Swaggerty, Margaret 69
Sward, Philip 18
Sarah 18
Sweeten, Jane 9
Sweny, Edward 17
Swingler, James 73
Syrus, Rachel 37
Talbert, James 52
Talbot, John 58
Talbott, John 57, 65
Tallent, James 50
Talley, Mathew 12
Tanner, Henry 41
Tate, David 27, 29, 35
David, Jr. 22
David, Sr. 27
David N. 84
Edward 20, 22, 27,
  35, 45, 84
Edward L. 89
George W. 89
John H. 30
Margaret C. 89
Margarette 22
Penelope 25
Saml. B. 78
Samuel B. 50, 55, 65
Sarah 70
Thomas 89
William F. 50
William T. 44
Taylor, Daniel 38, 46
Desdemony 26
Eben 70
Elika A. 70
Elizabeth 79
Emmy 60

Taylor (cont.)
Franklin W. 89
Hardiman 10
Hugh 11, 59
Hugh O. 43
Hugh W. 52
Hughes 27
Hughs W. 76
Jane 57
John 19, 27
Kesiah 10
Kisiah 11
Louisa 39
Lydia 49
Margaret 61, 79
Moarning 23
Nancy 49
Pendleton 66
Rachael 76
Richard 65, 70
Robert 8, 11
Samuel 13
Sarah 27
William 57, 69, 79
Wm. 59
Teague, Biddy 75
Biddye 78
Pricilla 74
Priscilla 77
Terrey, Samuel 7
Terry, Abby 26
Mary 68
Richard L. 2
Thacker, Edward 3
Jane 24, 41, 64
Nathaniel 62, 76
Patties 40
Peter 60, 76
Thomas, Ann M. 88
Francis 39
John 14
Mahala 73
Matilda 73
Samuel 47, 57
William 54
Thomason, Berty 62
Elisha 52
Jane 54
John 65, 67
Martha 38
Patsey 10
Robert 48
William 47, 62, 73
Wm. 55
Thompson, Abraham 65
Adam 62
Elizabeth 13, 40
Fanna 41
Isaac 13, 33
Isham 50
Jacob 42
Jane 57
John 6
John F. 89
Lezabeth 2
Lucinda 67
Mary 23, 78
Sally 18
Thomson, James 40
Patsey 17
Thornberry, Martin 26
Thornburg, Martin 40
Montgomery 86
Thornburgh, Samuel 62
Thornbury, Richard 13
Tindall, Henry 63
Todd, Aquilla 76
Toliver, William 86

Tomison, Robert 50
William 50
Tomlinson, James 64
Toner, Lydia 45
Toping, Margret 17
Townsley, Thomas 86
Traverse, Philip 38
Triston, Robert 52
Trogan, Chesley 84
Melvina 82
Trogdan, Abraham 66
Anna 73
Trogden, Abner 38
Chesley 86
Trogdon, Abner 54
Ezekiel, Sr. 79
Margret 32
Solomon 34
Trotman, John 19
Trout, James 65
Troutman, Thomas 26
Turley, Elizabeth 7
Thomas 19, 25, 26, 67
Turly, Thomas 46
Turner, George 20
John 17
Mahaly 52
Mary 57
Pascal 68
William 86
Tuttle, James 79
Peter 10
Underhill, Daniel 38, 41
Ruth 9
Underwood, Anthony 19, 40
Vance, Anna 71
Hugh 54
James 47
Vandagriff, Rebecca 81
Vandagrift, Gilbert 32
Vandegriff, Jacob 35
Vandergriff, George 79
Gilbert 26
Hannah 8
Jacob 32, 86
Leonard 13
Nancy 32
Rebeccka 4
Sally 22
Sarah 9
Vandogriff, Gilbert 30
Vaughan, John 84
Vetito, Thomas 19
Viditoe, Polly 48
Vineyard, Andrew 28
Celia 75
Chatharine 11
David 61
Elizabeth 24
Jacob 55
John 11, 28
Martin 55, 57, 60
Mathias 58
Polly 16
Susann 16
Vinyard, Andrew 31
Daniel 38
Dorthy 45
John 16, 38
Louisa 81
Martin 51, 60
Mathas 45
Mathias 45
May 83
Milley 31
Nicholas 38
Vitatoe, Sarah 79
Vitetoe, Elizabeth 70

Vitetoe (cont.)
George W. 70
James 79
Lucinda 81
Margaret 68
Vitito, Nancy 36
Thomas 36
Vititoe, Isaac F. 89
James 89
Stokley 87
Vittetoe, George W. 81
James 81
Vittito, William 42
Vittitoe, Sarah 51
Waddell, Saley 56
Waddle, David 64
Polly 51
Sally 64
Wade, John 69
Wadkins, Minerva 83
Waggenor, Elizabeth 16
Waggoner, Jesse 24
Samuel 19, 52
Thomas 30, 41, 44
Walker, Betsey 38
Caswell 40, 47
Caswell L. 38
David P. 47
Elisha 55
Elizabeth 53
James G. 86
John 11
Joseph 25
Mary 25, 49
Nancy 70
Permelia 86
Rebecca 75
Robert W. 76
Thomas 76
William 49, 52, 74
Wall, John 8
Wallen, Winefred 4
Walsey, James 14
Walters, Elendor 59
Nancy 47
Thomas 47
Ward, John 1, 4
Thomas 4, 8
Warden, William 57
Warick, Frederick 26
Mary 88
Warren, James L. 57
Warrick, John 4
Warricke, Elias 50
Patsy 50
Warwick, Haden 79
John P. 70
Warwrick, Wily 6
Washam, Joshua 36
Washburn, Joshua 32
Washman, Peggy 82
Waters, Baseton 35
Brackston 45
Jno. S. 67
John 47
Obediah 68
Sally 31
Watkins, Claiborn 68
Isaac J. 47
John 53, 55
Watson, (?) 32
David 15, 21, 22, 26,
60
Elizabeth 17
Flora 82
Godwin T. 81
Hardin 86
Henery 32

Watson (cont.)
Henry 34
James 70
John L. 57
June 15
Lavena Jane 81
Lucinda 15
Margaret 57
Martha 81
Mary 86
Pleasant 68, 77
Robert 17, 22, 23
Robert W. 75
Samuel 65, 70, 86
Sarah 71
Susanna 17
Tamer 88
Thomas 68, 81
Wiley R. 81
William 72
William C. 63
Watters, Samuel 89
Wealters, John 59
Weaver, John 45
Timnethy 45
Web, Solomon 2
Webb, Elizabeth 35
John 17, 24
John W. 24
Larkin 24
Polly 34
Webber, Seth 48
West, Alexander 89
Edward 76
Elizabeth 59
Hannah 80
James 59
James S. 63
Jane Adaline 89
Mary 39
Rachael 61
Samuel 2, 61, 76, 77
Thomas 52, 63, 80
Western, William 52
Weston, Pleasant 53, 60
Weyer, Jacob 8
Whalen, Mary 69
Richard 29
Whaling, James 22, 28
Jane 50
John 22
Rebecca 27
Richard 22, 27, 28
Wheeling, Rheda 37
White, Heziat 61
James 19
John Hailey 5
Polly 63
William 61
Whiteacre, Rice 13
Whitecotton, William 28,
32
Wm. 28
Whitehead, Drucilla 79
Unity 84
Whiteside, James A. 68
Thomas 25, 26, 52
Whitlock, James 35, 76
John 45
Mary 20
Polona 77
Whitlow, Pleasant 70
Wiatt, Refus 84
Wickliff, William 55
Widdows, Daniel 65
Widener, Elizabeth 57
Jacob 30
John 52

Widener (cont.)
Lewis 30
Widner, Margaret 28
Peter 50
Samuel 71
Wier, Thomas 61
Wiles, Betsy 37
Elizabeth 77
Willeford, James 86
Willet, Francis 13
Sally 13
William, David 9
James 86
Williams, Alexander 47
Edward 38
Elizabeth 57, 85, 88
Ellen M. 57
Etheldred 22
Ethelrid 39
Frances 65
Francis 47
Isaac 20, 22
Isham 24
James 34, 89
James B. 57
Jane 30, 57
Jese 78
Jesse 84
John 32, 34, 58
Jonathan 11, 26
Joseph 38, 58
Lucinda 81
Margaret 34, 77
Martha 26
Mary 43, 69
Nancy 82
Pleasant 81
Reas 36
Reece 62
Richard 56, 81
Samuel 11, 20, 22, 24
Sarah 25
Thomas 6, 22
William 84, 86
William F. 38
Williamson, David 65, 70
William 55, 78
Williford, Nancy 75
Willinton, Kitty 18
Willis, Elender 63
Hardin 77, 81
Innece 75
Jane 85
John 63
Lucy 33
Moses 32, 34
Noah 76
Patsy 44
Robert 15, 35
Sarah 33
Susanah 37
Susannah 70
Thomas 33
Weston 70
Wills, John F. 2
John S. 6, 8
Willson, Aelcey 13
Amos 28
David 20
James 13, 87
Robert 17
Sarah 87
Wilson, Abraham 17
Anney 84
Dorsey 54
Edward 71
James 22, 49, 62, 72
John 5, 22

Wilson (cont.)
  Margarite 54
  Ninse 2
  Rebeccah 27
Winder, Ennouch 11
Windes, Enoch 16
Windham, Jane 31, 35
  Nancy A. 9, 10
  Rachel 5
  Rody 3
  William 3, 23, 29
Winslow, Elizabeth 20
  Robert 20
Winstead, William 56
Winyeard, John 14
Wirack, Joseph 50
Wirick, Mitchell 50
  Nancy 40
  Polly 41
Wiseman, Nancy 40
Witcher, Amy 15
  Clabourn 70
  Lacey 70
  Mary 26
  Sarah 18
Witt, Calet 81
  Coleman M. 76
  George 60
  Joel 11
  Nancy 24
Wittson, Thomas 5
Woldridge, Daniel 42
Wolf, Carolin 62
  George 64
Wolfenbarger, Barbary 31
  Catherine 84
  Peter 31, 34, 81, 84
  Polly 58
  Reuben 84
  Sandy 81
  Susanna 34
  Wyney 55
Wood, James 35
Woodall, Bella 5
  James 3
  John 7, 20
  Mary 7
Wooddard, Hugh 10
Woodrum, John 2
Woods, Catherine 38
  Ellenore 10
  Jacob 68, 74, 76
  Samuel 42
Woody, Jane 67
Woolfinbarger, Jacob 23
  Sally 23
Woolsey, Stephen 79
Wright, Anny 14
  Isaac 89
  John 20
Wringler, James 73
Wrinkles, William 68
Wyer, Jacob 6
Wyett, Joseph 19
Wynne, Herman 20
Wyrick, Andrew 55
  Christian 40
  Eave 27
  Henry 28, 38, 40, 55,
    57
  John 24, 58, 68, 81
  Joseph 53
  Michel 38
  Peggy 55
  Peter 30, 54
  Philip 58
  Robert 65
  Samuel 55

Wyrick (cont.)
  Solomon 89
Wysnor, Henry 58
Yancey, Ambrose 1, 2,
    19
  Richard 10
  Robert 11, 68
  Robt. 6
  Sam'l 11, 15
Yarvis, Mary 54
  William 54
Yate, Milton 60
Yates, Benjamin 17
  Dacas 48
  Hiram 76
  James 45, 47, 52, 73
  John 50
  Julia Y. 76
  Meredith 52, 62
  Meredy 45
  Nancy 47
  Ruben 52
Yeaden, Anna 83
  Jacob 17
  Joseph 17
Yeadon, Sally 26
  William G. 26
  William P. 40
Yeats, Meredith 58
  Polley 17
Yerby, James 80
York, Clements 69
  Erick 26
  George 2
  John 34
  Pleasant 52
  Sarah 48
  Seamore 23
  Simon 35
Young, Betsey 35
  Elizabeth 5, 27
  Francis 21
  Frank 30
  Henry 55
  Mary 26, 80
  Rebecka 4
  Robert 21
  William 38
Youngblood, Alfred 63
Zachary, William 35
Zachery, James 10, 55
  William 55
Zackary, William 25
Zechery, Nancy 48

ADDITIONS

Farmer, Leurana 85
McAnally, Charles 41
McCocke, Sarah 47
McElhaney, Alexander 65

McElhaney, Mary 69
Russel, Wilburn 89
Taylor, Sarah 48
Trodgen, Abraham 68

Turley, Thos. 16
Tuttle, Elizabeth 55
Zachary, John 79